The
Facility Manager's
Field Guide

Cornel Rosario, CFM

Mark Sekula, CFM, LEED-AP, IFMA Fellow

With a Foreword by

Teena Shouse, CFM, IFMA Fellow

This book is available at a special discount when ordered in bulk quantities. For more information, Contact Us at: www.CorMarkPublishing.com.

The Facility Manager's Field Guide /

Cornel Rosario and Mark Sekula

Cover Photo: Two Park Plaza, Milwaukee, WI

Photo by: Cornel Rosario Photography

ISBN # 978-0-9825116-1-9

www.CorMarkPublishing.com

Dedications

To my wife, Donna, my inspiration and my strength.
To my mentor, the late Floyd Preslan: without his support and encouragement, I would have never made it in this profession.
And to IFMA, for providing the foundation upon which I was able to build a successful career.

Mark Sekula

To my loving, patient, and ever-supporting wife, Kathy.

Cornel Rosario

Introduction to *The Facility Manager's Field Guide*

The role of the facility management (FM) function, whether this consists of an individual, a small team, or an entire department, is to coordinate and oversee the safe, secure, and environmentally sound operations and maintenance of a company's facility assets in a cost-effective manner, aimed at the long-term preservation of these assets.

The Facility Manager's Field Guide is written for people who are responsible for FM services in small to medium-size companies (perhaps in the range of 5,000 to 50,000 square feet), as well as those who may not be experienced FM professionals. It could be that FM is your principal responsibility, or a part of your overall responsibilities. If you are responsible for FM services full-time, you may be the sole person in this position, or part of a team. In other cases, a position such as Human Resources Manager, Operations Manager, or Office Manager may be given FM responsibilities. Your FM duties may range from space planning to lease management to furniture procurement. The differences in FM responsibilities from one position to the next are as varied as there are different types and sizes of companies. In some cases, FM services might even be provided by a property management firm and included in the building lease. But there will always be FM-related issues to deal with, and those duties have to be assigned to someone in the company. That person – you – will need to have some knowledge of basic FM services.

The Facility Manager's Field Guide is a convenient, comprehensive, portable guide that covers the most common FM activities in a simple and descriptive manner. The topic chapters are organized alphabetically, written in short narrative form that allows you to grasp the subject matter quickly. In no time at all, you will understand the subject and be able to extrapolate from the text the information required to implement a desired FM activity.

In addition, our website (www.cormarkpublishing.com) includes appendices, bulleted lists, outlines, forms, and templates that will further enable you to fulfill your FM responsibilities quickly and efficiently without having to "reinvent the wheel." And, if you need more information, a list of references is provided at the end of each chapter.

FM services are integral to every company, regardless of size. We believe this book will help you, as well as others who may have FM as part of their overall responsibility, to provide these services to your company effectively and efficiently.

Cornel Rosario, CFM

Mark Sekula, CFM, LEED-AP, IFMA Fellow

Milwaukee, WI
June, 2011

iii

What Is Facility Management?

Facilities are typically a company's second-largest asset, right after its employees. This is a very important point because facilities play such an important role in supporting the employees. A well-designed, well-managed facility can help employees be more productive. When people are able to do their best work, they are more fulfilled and happier. This can help a company retain its best employees and attract new ones. Thus, a well-managed facility can have a positive impact on a company's bottom line.

Facility management is a profession that encompasses multiple disciplines to ensure functionality of the built environment by integrating people, place, process, and technology. Currently, eleven competencies define the practice arena of professional facility practitioners. They are:

- Emergency Preparedness and Business Continuity
- Operations and Maintenance
- Real Estate & Property Management
- Human and Environmental Factors
- Environmental Stewardship and Sustainability
- Planning and Project Management
- Leadership and Strategy
- Business and Finance
- Quality Assessment and Innovation
- Communication
- Technology

Within the competencies listed above, there are many duties the facility manager could perform at any given time.

Following are some examples of the things you could be involved with in each of the above competencies:

- Developing an emergency evacuation plan; conducting a fire drill.
- Responding to a roof leak; contracting a cleaning service.
- Negotiating a lease; coordinating the response to a maintenance issue with your property manager.
- Implementing an ergonomics program.
- Establishing a green purchasing policy for all maintenance supplies.
- Space planning; implementation of a workspace reconfiguration.
- Managing a facility management staff; developing a strategic facility plan.
- Developing operational and capital improvement budgets.
- Implementing a Balanced Scorecard for your department.
- Developing and implementing policies and procedures.
- Selecting a computer-aided facility management software system.

According to the International Facility Management Association (IFMA), the top ten things that building occupants complain about (and thus become the facility manager's problems) are:

1. It's too hot.
2. It's too cold.
3. There aren't enough conference rooms.
4. The office isn't clean.
5. There isn't enough filing or storage space.
6. I always have computer problems.
7. The office is too stuffy.
8. There's never enough parking.
9. I need more privacy in my workstation.
10. The smokers outside the building are offensive.

The level that a facility manager gets involved in the various competencies and specific activities depends on many factors, such as:

- The amount of space you're managing.
- The number of buildings you occupy.
- The type of building(s).
- Whether you lease or own your building.
- Your company's philosophy regarding performing facility management duties in-house versus outsourcing them.
- Your building's geographical location.
- The type of business your company is in.

Within smaller companies that lease space, there may not be enough facility management responsibilities to justify a full-time facility manager. The facility management function is often assigned to a non-facility manager such as the Office Manager or the Human Resources Manager as a part of their regular duties. Conversely, in larger companies, there will likely be a facility management department. The facility management department may also include other departments such as reprographics, mail services, shipping and delivery, and food services. In some cases, even departments like purchasing, corporate travel, health and safety, and security may fall under the facility manager's purview.

The facility management department could consist of one person, or in the case of a college campus or large museum, it could comprise hundreds of people. This is the beauty of the facility management profession. It can be so many things. It can start small and grow. It's never dull. A facility manager must be able to multi-task, have excellent communication skills, and not be afraid to jump in and perform hands-on work. Having a thick skin and a sense of humor helps, as well.

Acknowledgments

We are grateful to:

- John Schauble (of John N. Schauble Communications) for his technical assistance in laying out this book, as well as his tireless work in editing and proofreading the chapters.
- Jennifer Erdman (of Jennifer Creative) for her assistance with the book's layout.
- David Heide (of David Heide/Associates) for his marketing and PR assistance.
- IFMA for providing us the network and resources to succeed in our profession.
- The Southeastern Wisconsin Chapter of IFMA for its support and encouragement.
- Teena Shouse, for writing the Foreword to our book and for her encouragement, mentorship, and friendship.
- Ernie Allen (of Environmental Services, Inc.), Flint Bridge (of AVI Systems), Jeffrey Lubka, Steve Seer (of Johnson Controls, Inc.), Barbara Whitstone and Shawn Jeanquart (of CleanPower), and Stephen Ashkin (of The Ashkin Group) for their consultative assistance with various chapters.
- All the facility managers who so generously contributed their testimonials to the chapter, "What Makes My Facility So Special."
- The Ford and Carter administrations for providing the recession in the 1970s. If it wasn't for that, one of us would have found a job in architecture, as originally

planned, and would never have had the opportunity to accidentally fall into the profession of Facilities Management.

- Our Valued Sponsors, without whom this finished product would have been impossible. They are all listed in the Valued Sponsors section of this *Field Guide*. A big Thank You to all of them!!!

Foreword

I was recently interviewed by a Cornell University student who was interested in entering the world of Facility Management. His questions centered on why someone would enter this field, and how best to get educated about the profession. "How do facility managers learn all they need to know?" "What is a Balanced Scorecard?" "How can a facility manager not commit the mistakes of those who have gone before?"

The answers to these and more questions can be found in *The Facility Manager's Field Guide*. I explained that there is really nothing like hands-on experience to make this amazing profession come to life! However, you cannot always be exposed to everything you need to know within the first few years of your time on the job. That is where *The Facility Manager's Field Guide* comes in.

A facility manager's days are jam-packed, and very seldom does one have time to sit down and read an 'Everything you ever wanted to know about FM' book from cover to cover. So, wouldn't it be nice to have at your fingertips an easy reference to assist you in those times when you just need a little reassurance that you are on the right track around a subject/project/activity, or you really have little or no exposure to that particular task to be accomplished?

This *Guide* is meant to assist you with those situations. It is written by FM professionals who have 'been there and done that,' which makes all the difference in the world. Facility Management education is supporting a much more sophisticated profession than it was when I entered the field almost 25 years ago, but there is still nothing like practical experience to guide you along your way.

The *Guide's* well-designed format will make it an easy reach as you keep it handy on your desk for those quick references. The forms, templates, and outlines, available on the associated website [www.cormarkpublishing.com], will save you many hours of re-creating the wheel; so take advantage of them.

Bottom-line, we are all looking for a little help along the way, and I am convinced that *The Facility Manager's Field Guide* will not disappoint you. The next time a student asks me for references, I'll definitely refer him or her to this **Guide!**

Teena Shouse, CFM, IFMA Fellow
Kansas City, Kansas
June, 2011

Table of Contents

Table of Contents

Allergies in the Workplace

It's hard to say how common this issue might be in any given facility. It is well known that the air in an office may contain allergens emanating from several sources, including carpet, cubicle panel fabrics, live plants, office equipment, and even fragrances used by co-workers.

Workplace allergies account for up to 10% of all asthma cases reported in the U.S. And the symptoms are easy to diagnose: They appear when you are at work, worsen as the day progresses, and improve when you go home! (See the website: www.healthcentral.com/allergies.) It may be caused by something as simple as a co-worker's perfume or after-shave. If there is construction work taking place in the vicinity, the painting, sanding and staining can also set off an allergy attack. Sometimes an allergy may be triggered by poor air-circulation in the building.

The symptoms exhibited by employees who are affected by workplace allergens include: headaches, sore eyes, nausea, difficulty concentrating, muscle and joint pain, and shortness of breath.

Avoidance (staying at home) is the best remedy, but sometimes that's not possible. The next best option is to relocate the affected employee to an area removed from the offending source of the allergen. It may be difficult to mandate a fragrance-free workplace: In addition to perfumes worn by fellow employees, many soaps and cleaning agents also contain perfumes.

You may be surprised to learn that severe allergies fall under the ADA (Americans with Disabilities Act). (Please see our chapter, "Americans with Disabilities Act.") This may require employers to make reasonable accommodations for the affected workers to enable them to do their jobs. Encourage your company's Human Resources Department to develop an information campaign to educate employees about the effects of perfumes on allergy-prone fellow employees, and suggest that employees minimize the use of their favorite fragrance at work. FMFG

Additional Resources

- www.osha.gov
- www.ncchem.com/accommod.htm
- http://hr.blr.com/whitepapers/HR-Administration/Facilities/Your-Cologne-Is-Making-Me-Sick-Fragrances-Allergie/

Alternative Workplace Strategies

Alternative Workplace Strategies (AWS) are strategies to house workers in accommodations other than the traditional assigned cubicles and private offices. According to the International Facility Management Association (IFMA): "As technology made virtual working a more attainable reality, facility managers were tasked with creating and supporting off-site working environments. These technological advances coupled with companies looking to reduce their real estate portfolio, increase employees without adding more square footage or positively impacting the environment spurred the growth of (alternative) work strategies." Also, more and more work is done in collaboration with others, or in teams. Employees today are spending as much time working in different types of spaces throughout the day as they are in their personal workstations.

Alternative Workplace Strategies can be divided into two categories: on-site and off-site options.

On-site options involve providing unassigned spaces in the workplace, such as touch-down spaces, huddle rooms, hoteling workstations, kiosks or enclaves, war rooms and convergence areas. These spaces are often provided within the same-size footprint of a traditionally designed office, so that the assigned workstations become smaller. The operant logic is that, with the availability of unassigned spaces and the advent of collaboration and team work, employees will not spend as much time in their 'permanent' workstations, which consequently can be designed to be smaller. Technologies are available that enable you to monitor occupancy easily during the course of the day and determine which workstations are unoccupied most often and thus are available for sharing.

In some cases, companies provide shared workstations (unassigned) for employees in departments where people are using a variety of workstations. When they come to work, they reserve a workstation through an electronic reservation system or through a concierge or reservationist located in the office. The idea is that if there are sufficient shared or team spaces, such as conference rooms, team rooms, project rooms, formal and informal collaboration spaces, the work of mobile employees will dictate that they spend considerable time in those types of spaces, working in teams.

The most common **off-site** Alternative Workplace Strategy is telecommuting. When telecommuting became more prevalent a few years ago, it usually meant working from home. But now workers, especially younger ones, want to work anywhere, and advances in mobile communication and computing enable them to do just that.

More and more companies are implementing Alternative Workplace Strategies. Currently, 70% of U.S. companies offer some type of telecommuting opportunity to their employees, as do 84% of the Fortune Magazine 100 Best Places to Work. The benefits of telecommuting are: a potential reduction in real estate costs, the flexibility that workers desire, and its potential for creating a better balance between work and personal life.

If you choose to implement an AWS, you should first consider these points:

- Before you begin, make certain that you determine what's driving the Alternative Workplace Strategy.

- Get senior management's support.
- Understand your organization and its culture and how they might be resistant to the development of an Alternative Workplace Strategy.
- Understand your company's appetite for change.
- Analyze the nature of your work, how it might change in the future, and ways in which an Alternative Workplace Strategy might help support your employees in doing their best work.
- Engage employees in the process.
- Engage IT and Human Resources fully in the process.
- Don't make telecommuting a blanket policy -- give employees a choice. Some employees simply cannot work remotely, even if their job permits it.

AWS provides a flexible workspace solution, which, as research shows, is the preferred option for younger individuals entering the workforce. Providing an AWS could serve to help your company attract and retain the best new workers. FMFG

Americans with Disabilities Act

The Americans with Disabilities Act (ADA) is a wide-ranging civil right law that was enacted by the U.S. Congress in 1990. Its purpose is to establish a clear and comprehensive prohibition of discrimination on the basis of disability. Signed into law on July 26, 1990 by President George H. W. Bush, it was later amended with changes that took effect on January 1, 2009. The ADA is divided into five parts, or 'titles':

Employment (Title I)

Summary: This title covers all aspects of employment, and states that reasonable accommodations must be made to protect the rights of individuals with disabilities. This may include, but is not necessarily limited to, the application process, hiring practices, wages and benefits.

Examples of Accommodations: Restructuring jobs, altering the layout of the physical workplace, and modifying equipment.

Public Services (Title II)

Summary: Public entities cannot deny services to people with disabilities or bar them from participating in activities that are available to people without disabilities. Public services include state and local governmental instruments (e.g., department, agency, special-purpose district), The National Railroad Passenger Corporation, public transportation systems and other commuter authorities.

Examples of Accommodations: Making public transit buses accessible.

Public Accommodation (Title III)

Summary: This title has its primary impact on the physical workspace and is most pertinent to facility managers. All new non-residential construction must be made accessible to individuals with disabilities. Renovations and alterations made to existing non-residential buildings must make them accessible, if readily achievable. If an alteration affects or could affect the usability of or access to an area of a facility that contains a "primary function," an accessible path of travel must be provided to the altered area. In addition, restrooms, telephones and drinking fountains serving the altered area must also be made accessible to the extent that the cost is not "disproportionate" to the cost of the overall alteration. Disproportionality is defined as an amount not to exceed 20% of the cost to alter the primary function area.

Examples of Accommodations: Ramps, curb cuts, repositioning equipment and furniture, accessible door hardware, grab bars in bathrooms, higher toilets, and allowing 18 inches of wall space on the pull side of a door.

Telecommunications (Title IV)

Summary: Telecommunications companies offering telephone service to the general public must provide interstate and intrastate telecommunications relay services to the extent possible, and in the most efficient manner, to hearing- and speech-impaired individuals.

Examples of Accommodations: Telephones equipped with TDD (Telephone Device for the Deaf) to accommodate those with hearing disabilities.

Miscellaneous (Title V)

Summary: Title V clarifies that both States and Congress are covered by all provisions of the ADA and includes a provision for prohibiting either: (a) coercing or threatening, or (b) retaliating against the disabled or those attempting to aid people with disabilities in asserting their rights under the ADA.

As mentioned earlier, Title III, Public Accommodation, is the section that typically affects facility managers. According to the "ADA Compliance Guidebook" compiled by BOMA International, this title divides covered buildings and facilities into two categories, "Public Accommodations" and "Commercial Facilities." A commercial facility is one that is intended for non-residential use by a private entity and whose operations affect commerce. Examples include office buildings, warehouses, factories, and other buildings in which employment may occur. The responsibilities for providing auxiliary aids and for removal of barriers do not apply to commercial facilities. However, "reasonable accommodation" under Title I of the ADA must be made for employees with disabilities to enter and use the facility.

The basic process for complying with the ADA is to:

1. Learn about the program requirements of the ADA and how they apply to a facility or program. Architects, professional space planners and interior designers are required to design to ADA standards.
2. Conduct an ADA building survey to identify barriers.
3. Establish a list of potential modifications, including changes to policies and facilities.
4. Establish cost estimates for each modification.
5. Prioritize the modifications, and develop an implementation plan.

Many renovations and alterations typically require approval from the local building inspector, and in many cases the local building code is stricter than the ADA and therefore governs. However, be aware that while many alterations do not require approval of the building inspector, they do still need to meet ADA standards (e.g., replacing door hardware, relocating a door, relocating an electrical outlet, or replacing faucet controls).

When any renovation or alteration is proposed, you should confer with a professional to ensure compliance. FMFG

Additional Resources

- www.ada.gov
- "Americans with Disabilities Act Accessibility Guidelines (ADAAG), Checklist for Buildings and Facilities," www.access-board.gov/adaag/checklist/a16html
- "Americans with Disabilities Act, A Summary," www.dol.gov/odep/pubs/misc/summada.htm

Architectural and Engineering Services

If you are involved in a remodeling, renovation or new building project, you will likely need Architectural and Engineering Services, commonly referred to as AE or A/E Services. On most building projects, the architect is the lead person in the design process, with engineers working subordinate to the architect. Some architectural firms are designated A/E firms because they have both architects and engineers on staff. Other architectural firms do not have engineers on staff, but partner with outside engineering firms, bringing them into the project as needed.

The engineering disciplines typically needed on a remodeling, renovation or new building project are: mechanical engineers, who design heating, ventilating and air conditioning (HVAC) systems; electrical engineers, who design lighting and electrical power distribution systems; and plumbing engineers, who design plumbing systems. On larger building projects you may also need: a structural engineer, who designs building structural systems; a civil engineer, who designs roads, parking lots, walkways and other exterior site elements; and a landscape architect, who designs the exterior landscape and plantings. Others who may get involved include: information technology and telecommunications engineers, environmental engineers, soils engineers, construction materials engineers and other specialists.

Engineers typically hold a college degree in their chosen discipline. Architects, on the other hand, are schooled in all aspects of architecture and have earned a degree in architecture. Likewise, landscape architects have their degree in landscape architecture. Many architects and engineers choose to become registered and earn a license to practice in their profession. This usually involves passing an exam in the state where they do business. Some engineers and architects are licensed in multiple states. Many states have reciprocity agreements and do not require another full exam for licensing if the professional is already registered in his or her home base state. Each state differs somewhat in its requirements.

Some engineers and architects choose not to become licensed. This does not prevent them from practicing their profession, but it precludes them from stamping drawings. Most non-residential construction documents must be stamped by a licensed professional (engineer or architect) before a municipality, city or state will conduct a plan review. A plan review and approval is usually required for all buildings, but in the case of a non-residential building, these plans must first be stamped with the architect's or engineer's registration seal, which includes their license number. Once the plans are stamped, they are sent to and reviewed by the local and/or state building inspector for building code and life-safety compliance. The person or entity that stamps the plans is then liable for the integrity of the building design and accountable for any problems that may occur due to faulty design.

Most architects are capable of designing any type of building. However, they often choose to specialize in a particular building type – office buildings, office interiors, hospitals, schools, etc. Sometimes they become known as specialists in a certain building type by virtue of having concentrated on that building type over the course of time.

The architect's role is to understand the client's needs in terms of the function of the building, and then develop an appropriate design that is closely coordinated with the other design and engineering disciplines. The architect and each participating engineering discipline then design their respective portions of the project from a set of base plans that the architect provides. The architect coordinates their efforts so that all of the various systems work together with the overall building design, and result in a complete building.

The five phases of a typical building construction project are:

Schematic Design (SD)

In this phase, the project's scope is developed and the owner's specific requirements are determined. Conceptual design is established, and the basic building systems are determined, according to the function, type, size and location of the building. These systems include the structural system (steel, wood, concrete, etc.). One of the structural design's primary drivers is the spacing of the columns, commonly referred to as bay size. The further apart columns are spaced, the stronger the structural elements (the columns, beams, and joists) need to be. Quite often, the building function will drive the structural design. For example, in a theatre or concert hall, where unobstructed views are essential, columns must be spaced such that they do not impede the view of the stage. In an office, column spacing may be driven by the anticipated layout of the cubicles. You would not design a space with columns spaced 20 feet apart if your cubicles are 8 feet by 8 feet, or you will end up with columns in the middle of cubes.

The other building systems, such as HVAC, plumbing, and elevators, must be carefully considered as well. Bathrooms are typically stacked over each other in a multiple-story building, so that the plumbing piping serving them is efficiently concentrated in certain areas of the building. Typically, elevators are centrally located in a building and may require a pit, special structural considerations, and an elevator equipment room. These types of building elements must be fixed early in the design process: trying to relocate them later on could result in additional costs. Likewise for HVAC equipment. Sizing ductwork early in the design phase will drive clear height requirements, which in turn will have an impact on the building's structural design.

The resulting plans will include preliminary floor plans, building elevations showing basic materials and finishes, site plan, structural plan showing column sizes and spacing, and a mechanical, plumbing, and electrical plan showing main trunk lines and spaces allocated to associated fixtures and equipment. A preliminary budget is typically developed during this SD phase.

TIP: The vertical pipes that are tied to roof drains (also called roof conductors) and connect to the underground storm sewer typically run through the interior of the space. It is desirable to conceal these pipes in the finished space: hence roof drains are designed so that the pipes run alongside columns in the space. Where this occurs, the columns are often boxed out with studs and drywall to conceal the pipes. A 6-inch pipe, boxed out with studs and drywall, can increase a column size by 9 inches, which ultimately could conflict with the cubicle spacing.

Design Development (DD)

In this phase, the conceptual design undergoes further refinement. Size, shape and aesthetics of the building are set. The building systems are more fully detailed. Materials and finishes are selected and approved during this phase. The budget is also further refined as details of the building become better defined.

Construction Documents (CD)

Construction documents include the construction drawings, (sometimes referred to as working drawings) and the specifications. Construction documents are very detailed, and are used to bid the project. The contractor will use CDs to build the building. These are the plans that the architect and engineers will stamp, and that the building inspector will review for approval. The contractor will be awarded a building permit based on these plans.

Bidding and Negotiation (B & N)

During this phase, the construction documents are submitted to contractors interested in providing pricing to the owner. In the traditional design/bid/build process, the owner solicits bids from a general contractor, who then solicits individual bids from subcontractors on each section and subsection of the work (from boilers to door knobs). The general contractor will then mark up the subcontractor's pricing, add it all together, then tack on a charge for general conditions (including everything from construction fencing to project management) and profit. The total of these costs becomes the contractor's bid.

In some cases, the owner may choose to bid out the mechanical, electrical, and plumbing (MEP) separately. In this scenario, the general contractor does not hold the contracts with the MEP contractors and cannot mark up their prices. The owner holds the contracts. The owner may then choose to negotiate a fee with the general contractor to coordinate the work of the MEP contractors. Other methods may be employed in construction projects: these include design-build and fast-tracking.

Construction Administration (CA)

Construction starts once the plans are approved, bids are accepted, and contracts are in place. During construction administration, the architect oversees the construction of the project. This includes making regular inspection visits to the site to ensure that the project is being constructed according to the intent of the construction documents. This is an important point. The construction documents are not meant to describe construction means and methods. Instead, they are intended to show design intent. The contractor is responsible for meeting the design intent, as well as the means and methods used to accomplish it.

Other CA responsibilities of the architect are to answer questions about the design, review payment requests, issue construction bulletins, requests for information and change orders, and review shop drawings. During this phase, the architect will review the contractor's request for payments and ensure that the work for which the contractor is requesting payment has been completed, and that the materials have either been installed or are in the contractor's possession.

In large, complex projects, the owner may choose to hire a construction manager (CM) to manage the overall project. The architect will still be required to perform some of the CA duties described above, but the CM's responsibilities may take into account some of the architect's CA duties. It is important to delineate the responsibilities of each position so there is no duplication of duties and billing.

At the end of the project, and before making final payment to the contractor, the architect and the contractor will agree upon a date when substantial completion has been met. When that date arrives, the contractor will request final payment (less retainage, which is an agreed-to percentage of funds withheld from the contractor's monthly application for payment by the owner) and the architect will prepare a punch list. The punch list is a list of deficiencies that the contractor must remedy before final completion is established and before the local governmental building agency awards the final certificate of occupancy. Without a certificate of occupancy, the owner cannot move into the building. When the architect (and/or CM) deems the project complete, the building inspector conducts a final inspection and awards a certificate of occupancy. The contractor will then make the final request for payment, which typically equates to the remaining retainage that has been held throughout the project.

The most common methods for calculating the architect's and engineer's fees are a percentage of construction cost or a lump-sum fee. Typically on larger projects the fee will be a percentage of construction cost (usually in the range of 3% to 10%). Fees usually include the services associated with the five phases listed above. Pre-design services, such as programming, preparing presentation drawings, and presenting to building approval boards, are typically considered additional services and an additional fee is charged. Frequency of project meetings and site visits above and beyond what is considered typical is also an additional service, as are things like special design services, scale models, furniture planning and selection, and artwork selection.

Selecting an architect and engineer or an A/E firm should be both an objective and subjective process. The architect you select should have the skills, experience, and resources required to conclude your particular project successfully. The architect will be your partner and your representative during the design and construction phases, which can be complicated and cumbersome. As such, you should base your selection process in part on 'softer' criteria – teamwork, personality, and compatibility. Create a short list of potential architects and then interview each. A good source to find an architect suited to your project is the American Institute of Architects (AIA). Select your architect and/or engineer like you would any other professional. Although their fee is important, it should not be the only factor in selecting an A/E. FMFG

Additional Resources

- www.AIA.org
- For A&E Services selection criteria and an outline of an RFP, see www.cormarkpublishing.com/Resources.

Archives

A business archive is a collection of older documents pertaining to the business, arranged in a systematic fashion for purposes of storage and future retrieval, generally on an infrequent basis. It is also the term assigned to the location or facility where these documents are stored. Regulatory requirements from local, state and federal entities will dictate how long you should store documents listed under various categories. By their very nature, documents assigned to archival storage are not urgently needed or frequently accessed, so they may be stored away from the areas generally assigned to everyday work files.

Having an orderly system of cataloging and storing these records will facilitate subsequent retrieval. However, this issue may be confounded by the fact that very often archival storage is located off-premises. Your primary facility may lack the space for an on-premises storage system. Generally, the cost of storage space within a given facility is no different from that for accommodating your staff. The cost of off-premises storage, on the other hand, may turn out to be half the cost or less compared to space in your main facility.

Each archived document needs to be associated with a name and / or number (policy number, client number) and a Destroy Date. Start a spreadsheet that catalogs the following essential data elements: File Name, ID number, department / category, Destroy Date and box number (of the archives box in which the file is stored). Retain the spreadsheet for your reference, whether you choose to establish the archival records center within your facility or in an off-site storage facility.

It is best to file like documents together (within an archives box, for example) that share a common Destroy Date. Then, when the Destroy Date arrives, the entire contents of the box can be quickly disposed of, generally through a document-shredding process.

As stated earlier, archives boxes may reside at an off-site storage facility or within your own facility, generally in a basement or windowless storage area. Boxes can be stored on shelving that can go as high as the ceiling and sprinkler system permit. Within your facility, archives boxes can be numbered in any one of a number of ways, including consecutive numeral, or using x-y-z coordinates where x denotes the row number, y the section of shelving, and z the level above the floor. In addition, if there is depth-space on a shelf to file boxes front and back, the box in front may be given an A suffix (for Aisle) and the box in the back a B suffix.

In addition to storing paper files, archives boxes can be used to store medical records such as X-rays, and data media (e.g., back-up tapes, disks, cassettes).

When a file is needed, an archives clerk taking this request should be able to quickly access the database to determine the file's physical location. The box is located, and the file retrieved and delivered to the requestor. An out-of-file index card can be inserted in the box as a marker to denote that a file has been removed, and the exact location that it needs to be returned to.

Should you decide to use an off-premises archive facility, make sure that it is temperature- and humidity-controlled. This will ensure that the documents will not deteriorate from poor climate conditions. Generally, paper documents will do well in a facility where the temperature can be controlled within the 50 to 80 degrees F range, and the relative humidity maintained at or below 55%.

If you outsource the archives function to a firm specializing in this area, plan to visit and inspect their facility. Observe the condition of the building. Evidence of roof leaks may indicate a poorly maintained building. Depending on the critical nature of the archived materials, you may also require that the building have a fire sprinkler system. Check with your Legal department. Also, take a look at the off-site facility's standard procedures:

- How the archival records are stored – shelving, boxes, aisle widths, equipment used to access higher shelves.
- The climate controls.
- Days and hours of operation during which records may be accessed.
- Procedures used to store and retrieve archival records.

In addition, consider these archiving service concerns:

- Will the prospective storage vendor supply you with archival boxes and labels?
- Will the vendor deliver requested files to your facility? How quickly? Can they fax the files you need?
- Does the storage facility carry adequate insurance? How much coverage will you need to purchase?
- When a box of documents has met its Destroy Date criterion, does the vendor have the capability of mass-shredding the contents of each box earmarked for disposal?

In order to maintain control of your records as they flow through the archives system until final disposal, you will need to set up an Archives Policy and its associated procedures. The procedures should align with a corporate records retention timetable, which stipulates how many years each category of document needs to be retained prior to destruction, if ever. You may wish to set up a regular schedule – once every quarter or once every year – for reviewing your retention timetable to see which files (or boxes of files) have met their Destroy Date criterion. Circulate a list of these files, or boxes of files, for one final review by the respective department heads or designated reviewers, prior to making a final decision to have them shredded. FMFG

Artwork

Artwork can make a dramatic impact on any work environment, regardless of the size of the space. It enhances the ambiance and gives it a particular character, one that generally reflects the corporate culture. (Please see our chapter, "Image and Ambiance.")

The first choice to make is whether or not to have artwork. Some companies choose not to decorate their blank (available) wall space with artwork of any sort, opting instead to leave the space bare, or hang company-related posters showing products, services, and financial goals instead. Some office spaces, due to a preponderance of exterior window walls, have very little space available to hang wall art.

For companies that choose to install artwork, the options are endless. The choice of artwork genre selected, often in collaboration with an art consultant, generally reflects the corporate culture or the taste of its leader. Varieties can range from abstract art to impressionistic landscapes, from posters to original oil paintings. Art can also encompass framed art, fabric wall-hangings, and metal and ceramic sculptural pieces, as well. One possible compromise: within private offices, allow the occupant to have his or her choice of artwork from among a range of acceptable styles. Over time, this may lead to multiple changes in private-office artwork as the occupants of any given office change. In the common areas – hallways, conference rooms, cafeteria – the corporate standard would prevail, with final selections being made by your art consultant.

One affordable way to display artwork, and create a rotating exhibit as well, is to rent it from a local art gallery or museum. Certain galleries and art museums provide this service: it promotes their collections outside the confines of their traditional environment, and enables you and your visitors to enjoy a veritable "moving feast" of varied artwork. Some companies rotate artwork produced by local artists. You can also work with an artwork consultant, who typically has a large source of suppliers who can provide artwork that meets your budget. The consultant can also suggest placement of the art, recommend framing and matting, and even hang the artwork.

Artwork should enhance the space that it occupies and be sized appropriately to the space available. For any given expanse of wall, the choices may be one or more pieces in a horizontal (landscape) or vertical (portrait) format. You should also take care that the spot selected for a particular piece is well lit, either by an existing ceiling light fixture, wall sconce, dedicated spotlight, or natural light from a window or skylight.

One way to go about this phase of the project is to do a walk-through of the work space, floor plan in hand. Mark on the plan, with a V for vertical or H for horizontal, all the bare spots on the walls where you (or the consultant) would like to see artwork hung.

Next, you need to take into account the wall's color and other colors in the vicinity (cubicle panels, lateral files, etc.) when selecting the material (wood, metal, etc.) and color of the frame and mats (the material used to fill the space between the edge of the artwork and the inside edge of the frame).

A helpful rule of thumb: The center of the piece of art should be at comfortable viewing height, generally five feet above the floor. It is best to use two or more sturdy hooks to hang each piece of framed art, especially if it incorporates a heavy pane of glass.

When you are done, you will have changed the ambiance of your work space and brought it to life! FMFG

Asset Management

In the realm of facility management, assets are those tangible, physical things that companies need to run their business. Examples of physical assets are:

- Buildings and building equipment
- Mechanical equipment typically associated with the heating, ventilating & air conditioning (HVAC) system
- Electrical equipment such as emergency generators and uninterruptible power supplies (UPS)
- Furniture
- Office equipment such as copiers, printers, scanners, and fax machines
- Vehicles
- Computers and related equipment
- Telephone systems and audio/visual equipment

Physical assets are either owned or leased. Each company has its own strategy for owning or leasing its physical assets. The most common leased assets are buildings, office equipment and vehicles.

If an asset is owned, it may be depreciated over a certain number of years, as governed by U.S. tax laws. The depreciation period is typically the expected useful life of the asset. Since a company's physical assets are often its second-highest cost (behind employee costs), they should be tracked carefully. This responsibility often rests with the facility manager.

Asset Management Planning and Tracking

The purpose of having an asset management plan is to identify a company's physical assets and track some of their characteristics, such as:

- Type of asset
- Date of acquisition
- Age
- Expected life
- Original cost
- Current replacement cost
- Owned or leased status
- Building and equipment depreciation
- Building lease terms and extension / termination notices
- Maintenance record
- Disposal method

Tracking of real estate assets can become complex, especially when multiple sites are leased. You could conceivably be conducting several lease negotiations and site searches simultaneously. Without a good tracking methodology in place, your company could be forced into an unfavorable lease simply because you started negotiating a lease or seeking new space too late in the process.

If you lease space, you won't have to worry about tracking the actual building equipment – that's the landlord's responsibility. However, if your company owns the building, you will need to pay special attention to building equipment. A preventative maintenance plan can track the associated equipment and store the right information about each piece of equipment to ensure proper maintenance.

Tracking office equipment can help in move management as well. If you move people around in your space, you will likely be moving their desk-top printers, PCs, and office equipment, too. Properly tracking this type of equipment could speed up the move planning process. It also helps the vendor to prepare the machine for relocation.

Tracking desktop computer equipment typically includes identification of data ports and can save the IT department time in move planning. The IT team will not have to trace individual cables back to their source in order to make changes at the data ports.

Software is available to help you track assets. The most common is a Computer-Aided Facility Management (CAFM) software system. (Please see our chapter, "Computer-Aided Facility Management Systems (CAFM).") The software is typically based on electronic floor plans or CAD plans of your building or space. (Please see our chapter, "Computer-Aided Design and Drafting (CADD).") These floor plans must be inputted into the system, and each asset located on the floor plan. The software then generates a database of the desired information, which is dynamically "attached" to the asset on the floor plan. When a move takes place, you can move the assets on the floor plan, and any information that changes due to the move (location, occupant, etc.) automatically changes in the database. Move lists can then be created and handed out to the other support people involved in the move (Human Resources, IT, telephone and cabling vendors, etc.)

Asset management gets more complex in buildings like hospitals and manufacturing plants that have a large amount of equipment. Regardless of the type of building you manage, asset management is an important and necessary component that helps your company manage its business. FMFG

Audio Visual Systems

A well-designed and well-installed audio visual (A/V) system can provide the basis for effective and efficient meetings and presentations that enable your audience to hear and see everything that is presented. In addition, modern A/V systems create a high-tech look and feel for your organization that can help attract and retain employees.

At the simplest level, the mark of a good A/V system is to provide an image that everyone assembled in the room can properly see. You need to size the display appropriate to the room size and ceiling height. A useful rule of thumb is to set up the room such that the distance from the screen to the viewers seated farthest away is 4 times the screen height when spreadsheets are displayed, or up to 6 times screen height for a Power Point presentation. With the bottom of the screen located 4 feet off the floor, a 6-foot high screen would need, at minimum, a 10-foot high ceiling and a room no greater than about 36 feet deep (distance from screen to the back row of seats).

It is also important to display content that is suitable for presentation. In other words, don't clutter the screen with volumes of text, interminable columns of data or detailed city maps, all of which will cause viewers to squint!

A good A/V system can be a very effective training tool for your workforce. It can be implemented either in a dedicated training room or distributed throughout the organization using internet protocol (IP) technology.

Videoconferencing has improved significantly over the years, especially with the advent of high-definition (HD) technology. Pictures are crisp and clear, and motion artifacts are gone. Nearly all systems today can operate over your IP network, with PC images sent and viewed at full resolution. If your staff does a lot of traveling, videoconferencing can significantly cut travel expenses and reduce your carbon footprint. A videoconferencing system will work in just about any small to medium-sized room. But if you have the time to plan (and an adequate budget), you can enhance the space with the proper lighting, wall coloring, and acoustical treatments.

As with most facilities projects, planning is key in setting up a successful A/V system. Work with an A/V systems integrator or specialist, whether you are starting from scratch (setting up a new facility) or adding the A/V system to an existing space. This individual can help you avoid some potential pitfalls and minefields. Proper planning will result in a better outcome and help eliminate cost overruns. Here are some basic considerations:

- It is critical to keep ambient light off the screen. In order to do this you may need to have the front row of ceiling lights on a separate circuit so that they can be turned down during a presentation. If the room has windows, you may need to install window blinds to block out sunlight that could wash the screen.

- If you use a ceiling-mounted projector, install it as close to the ceiling as possible in order to gain the greatest screen height. Typically, the projector should line up with the top of the screen, so anything else that hangs below ceiling height – such as pendant light fixtures – would have an impact on the maximum screen height.

- Consider whether the room walls and ceiling can support the weight of an oversize screen.

- Do you have power outlets and voice and data jacks in the correct locations? Will you need to pull additional cabling under-floor or in the ceiling plenum?
- Where will the A/V systems equipment be housed? In a separate room or in the same room as the audience? Consider suitable cabinetry or millwork, and be sure to provide adequate cooling for the equipment housed inside it.
- Plan for the eventual switch from analog cabling and connections to the new (HDMI) digital world.
- Plan for an A/V floor box to allow you to connect and power up your tabletop equipment without running cables over the carpet to wall outlets and jacks.
- In a conference, training or board room, plan to use furniture that is A/V-compatible for greater efficiency, and in order to achieve a clean, uncluttered look.
- Plan for the locations of microphones and speakers. Be aware of ambient noise, either from a nearby highway or an adjacent high-traffic hallway.

If you have clearly set out goals and objectives for your A/V system in the initial planning phase of the project, you should measure how well you have succeeded when the project is completed. FMFG

Additional Resources

- www.avisystems.com

Balanced Scorecard

Some of the basic tenets of business are to plan, evaluate, and measure. How can anyone's performance be assessed without some sort of measurement and tracking process in place? In business, we evaluate and measure people, functions, and entire organizations. Measurement is crucial to a business' success.

There have been many business measurement processes throughout history. The Balanced Scorecard (BSC) has been around since the early 1990s and is now a recognized performance management system in many countries. Strategic planning, always a valuable management tool, is now more than ever before considered an essential activity for any business.

The BSC is based on the principle that a company's business strategy adheres to a vision, mission, and values that are non-negotiable. It wraps measurements and targets around four perspectives within which all activities can be captured. It starts at the top of the organization and cascades down through the company's divisions, departments, teams and individual employees. This cascading effect ensures that everything and everyone involved is measured against the same standards, principles, and values. It brings continuity to the performance management system. Once people are trained in the process and understand it, they see the BSC as a fair and equitable system and tend to readily accept it.

The BSC was introduced to the business world in the early 1990s by Robert Kaplan and David Norton with their book *The Balanced Scorecard: Translating Strategy into Action*. It is based on the premise that intangible or knowledge-based assets – employees, volunteers, information technology, image – are increasingly important to an organization's success. The BSC measures financial outcomes, and it balances the financial perspective with employee, business process, and customer perspectives. The International Facility Management Association (IFMA) uses the BSC extensively as its own organizational management tool. Many facility managers have begun to use it, as well.

According to IFMA, the BSC provides a method for aligning business activities to organizational strategy. An organization's vision and mission statements are translated into specific and calculable goals, and a set of performance measures is established to monitor the organization's success in achieving those goals. The process steps are:

- The vision is translated into operational goals.
- The vision is linked to departmental (and even to individual) performance.
- A plan for business processes is outlined.
- The strategy is modified based on feedback.

The BSC process involves viewing the organization from four perspectives, developing measurements to gauge performance, and analyzing data relative to each perspective:

- The stakeholder perspective – measures that have a direct impact on customers and customer satisfaction.
- The internal perspective – measures that reflect performance of key business processes.
- The learning and growth perspective – measures that reflect an organization's learning curve.

- The financial perspective – measures that reflect financial performance.

The four perspectives of the scorecard allow for a balance between:

- Short- and long-term objectives
- The outcomes desired and the performance drivers of those outcomes
- Objective and subjective measures

In a perfect planning cycle, the BSC is derived from the organization's strategic plan; the strategy map is derived from the BSC; and the operating budget stems from all three. Let's look at how this relates to the facility function.

The stakeholder perspective – The facility management function has many stakeholders. The Facilities Management (FM) employees, the internal customers (the occupants of the buildings), visitors, the company's external customers, and the community in which the buildings reside are all FM's stakeholders who can be affected by the facilities, either directly or indirectly and either positively or negatively. Take, for example, your internal customers. If you provide a well-designed workplace that makes people feel safe and comfortable and enables them to be highly productive and to do their best work, they will be happier employees and will feel more fulfilled. This can result in less stress, less absenteeism and lower healthcare costs. It can also help your company retain its best employees, which provides continuity to the business, and huge savings in recruiting and training costs. Happy employees will tell others and make attracting new employees easier, as well.

The internal business processes perspective – Processes are what make an organization tick. There is a process for everything, and FM is full of processes. For example, there are processes for requesting, tracking and completing maintenance work, planning and implementing moves, adds and changes, ordering office supplies, and issuing and processing purchase orders. The processes, owned by FM, must be intuitive for those who use them and assist people in their jobs, not hinder them or burden them with more bureaucracy.

The learning and growth perspective – When a business faces tough times, professional development, training and education budgets are often the first to be reduced or eliminated. Yet professional training or continual learning (as it is sometimes referred to) is so very important to the professional well-being of employees. This perspective focuses on the goals and measurements that are specific to the amount and type of training that employees are offered, and then tied back to measurable positive impacts that ongoing education can have.

Financial perspective – Although the FM function is considered overhead and not a profit center, it directly affects a company's bottom line. According to IFMA, a 4% reduction in operating costs can result in the "same profit" as a 25% increase in sales. Keeping FM costs in line is integral to the success of the company. The goals and metrics related to this perspective are solely financial, and measure things like energy cost savings, cost per work order, operating costs per square foot, and total cost of occupancy.

How the Balanced Scorecard works – The BSC is built upon the overall vision and mission of the organization. The FM Balanced Scorecard is based upon the goals that the FM organization must meet to help the company meet its overall objectives. Those goals are grouped under the appropriate perspective, and each goal is assigned a measurement and a key performance indicator (KPI): a measurement and a target. For example, under the financial perspective one of the company's overall goals may be to increase profit by 10%.

The FM organization's goal could be to reduce operating costs by 5%. A KPI might be energy costs, and the measurement would be of energy cost reduction. A measured result exceeding 20% in energy cost reduction is excellent, 10% to 19% acceptable, and less than 10% unacceptable. In larger companies, with large FM teams, these measurements can be numerous, and may require a "dashboard" to track them on a weekly or daily basis.

A Balanced Scorecard for each individual employee can be developed that cascades from the FM organization's BSC. The employee BSC then becomes the tool on which individual performance evaluations are based. FMFG

Additional Resources

- For an example of the Balanced Scorecard, please see our website at www.cormarkpublishing.com/Resources.

Benchmarking

According to www.fmpedia.com, benchmarking is "a process for comparison with a best-practice peer group, where the primary aim is not to copy but to emulate inputs, process, etc., with a view towards increasing output performance and hence value to the organization." The benefits of benchmarking are: to measure the performance of your facility management organization or function in comparison to others like yours; measure the performance of FM outsource providers; demonstrate FM cost savings to your company's management; help support budgeting; and help gain approval for FM projects.

Typical areas to benchmark are:

- Square feet per occupant
- Sustainable operations and maintenance practices
- Janitorial costs, practices
- Maintenance costs and practices
- Utility costs and consumption
- Environmental costs
- Life and safety costs
- Space planning costs
- Security costs
- Project costs
- Emergency and disaster planning costs
- Churn rate
- Costs for moves/adds/changes
- FM information and technology costs
- Employee amenity cost
- Cost of operations
- Occupancy cost
- Total annual facility cost

FM operations vary a great deal depending on the size and number of buildings, building type, industry, and function. When benchmarking, make sure that you are comparing entities that have enough similarities to allow a useful comparison. You must understand the underlying assumptions, formulas, and definitions that make up a benchmarking statistic. Feel free to benchmark metrics other than costs: It is just as important to compare what you do, and how you do it, as it is to compare facility-related costs.

There are different ways to benchmark. You can benchmark to industry standards such as those published in the Benchmark Reports that the International Facility Management Association (IFMA) produces. You can also form a consortium with fellow facility managers who manage like buildings, in your geographical area, and who agree to share their FM data with you. FMFG

Additional Resources

- www.IFMA.org
- www.APPA.org
- www.BOMA.org
- www.rsmeans.com/consulting/benchmark.asp

Bird Mitigation

It is not uncommon to find birds making their homes – at least temporarily – on your facility building, or around the grounds. While birds may be a joy to behold, and their songs and chirps uplifting, they can also, at times, be a nuisance.

Canada (or Canadian) geese are one of the most common such offenders. Their droppings (as much as a pound a day from one bird) can pollute streams and ponds and mar the aesthetics of lawns, sidewalks, and driveways. In addition, they can exhibit aggressive behavior towards humans, especially when defending their nests and goslings.

Geese love manicured lawns that are rich in nutrients and have proximity to water (such as retention ponds). They also prefer unobstructed views so they can keep an eye out for predators. In order to combat these pests, you need to upset their balance, usually through a multi-pronged approach.

Here are a few low-cost solutions:

- Post "Do not feed the geese" signs in public areas. Feeding geese simply encourages them to congregate on your property.
- Create a six-foot-wide buffer of un-mowed native grasses (20 inches to 30 inches high) around the perimeter of ponds. This blocks their view of potential predators and makes your facility's grounds less attractive to them.
- When establishing a new lawn, consider fescues over the more-traditional Kentucky blue grass.

Other solutions include:

- Create barriers around the shoreline using string, fishing line, chicken wire, mylar tape or chain link.

- Dogs, such as border collies, can be trained to chase away geese without harming them, and have been used successfully on golf courses, parks, and athletic fields. This technique requires a trained dog and its handler. Dogs may be purchased, or the services of a dog and handler may be rented from a firm specializing in this service, which can be expensive and labor-intensive.

- Certain chemical repellants can be sprayed on the lawn, rendering the grass tasteless to geese and causing them to move away. This can cost over $100 per acre.

- Try scaring the geese away by a combination of devices such as plastic flags, inflatable plastic owls or hawks, and recorded distress calls. These tend to work – until the geese become accustomed to the tactics, or your neighbors start to complain about the noise!

- There are also specialized products available for purchase, such as a thin wire system used in areas like along roof edges, where birds tend to perch. These systems produce a low-level electrical current that will not harm the creatures, but effectively keeps them from congregating on your roof.

Another widespread bird problem involves their collision into windows. It is estimated that each year over 100 million birds fly into windows because they simply do not recognize glass as a barrier. (See: www.bcnbirds.org/window.) They are confused by the reflections of trees and sky, and at night by the bright lights of buildings, especially in cloudy, rainy, or foggy weather. Half of all birds that strike windows will be killed by the collision.

Some solutions:

- Especially during the migration season, turning off lights and closing blinds can reduce bird-deaths by 80%.
- Put a decorative film, decal, or other covering on the outside of the window to alter its appearance. FMFG

Additional Resources

- www.oakgov.com/water/assets

Budgeting

Developing and adhering to a budget is an essential component in the life of a facility manager. An old adage states: If you can't measure it, how can you manage it? The budget is the common language of an organization. The annual FM budget reflects the day-to-day operations of the facilities department, including projects, and is a measure of these activities in dollars and cents.

Correctly formatted, the budget permits the tracking of progress from one year to the next. It is also a benchmark against which your performance can be judged. You are the steward of your company's funds as they relate to the facility, and through proper monitoring of your departmental budget, you can track expenses and compare them to the budget figures as the year progresses.

The characteristics of a good budget are:

- It contains those categories that you and your company's senior management agree need to be managed.
- It is work plan-driven, reflecting projects being managed during the budget cycle.
- It is structured the way you operate, tying together resource management and responsibility.
- It provides management information on total costs, comparative costs, and easy-to-compute unit costs.
- It identifies the responsibilities of the subunits (Shipping, Print Shop, Groundskeeping, etc.).

Budgets may be developed by modifying a prior year's budget, by applying an inflationary increase percentage multiplier, or by starting from scratch with a blank spreadsheet (zero-based budgeting).

If you do any facility planning, it needs to be reflected in the facility budget. If you plan to add or cut back on staff, add or replace equipment, or add a project or program, include the associated costs into your budget.

In broad terms, we may consider the facilities budget to break down into three distinct categories: operations, administration, and capital budgets.

The **operational budget** covers funds that the company provides to permit you to carry out the FM mission. Operations include, but are not limited to: lease payments, utilities, maintenance, design, janitorial, and remodeling and moving expenses. You need to work out the level of budget detail with your company's Finance Department. A detailed budget is favored since each item needs to be estimated anyway. Each line in the detailed budget can be further divided into materials and labor components. In the final analysis, if you are frequently asked about a certain line item, it makes sense to include it in the budget detail.

The **administrative budget** refers to those overhead items that your department shares with other departments. Administration includes: salaries, benefits, travel, training, and office supplies expenses. Very often, the rules governing the budget relate not only to the cost of personnel, but the numbers and categories as well. This may make it difficult to substitute staff from one category with another. In addition, you may be precluded from transferring funds from one budget category (such as Office Supplies) to another (such as Training).

The **capital budget** addresses your company's long-lived assets such as buildings, equipment, and furniture, and typically includes assets with a useful life greater than one year. The capital budget is generally part of the company's strategic plan, and may be a multi-year exercise. Many capital projects have implications that affect the operations budget. For example, the construction of a new building may eliminate a corresponding lease cost and temporarily reduce alteration costs. Administrative costs, utilities, and maintenance costs may also be affected. Consult with your Finance Department regarding the types and threshold costs of items that would typically fall into the capital budget category.

Capital costs are carried on a company's books in a different manner than operational costs. Capital costs are calculated for the expected useful life of the asset, and are reduced each year as the asset ages (as specified by the IRS in the U.S. tax laws). This is called depreciation. The depreciation cost of a capital asset, once identified, is then carried in the operations budget.

Charge backs are one way to try and control your expenses. The reasoning behind this method is that, if a particular department needs some special product or service, it will be more judicious in its request if it is required to pay for it out of its own departmental budget. However, charge backs involve a lot of work, and sometimes become associated with internal favoritism and double standards, when two departments are not treated the same way. In one variation of charge backs, a department may be charged only the difference in cost between a standard product or service and the requested upgrade.

Budgets generally increase from one year to the next because of program growth and inflation. Typically, the financial forecast is a combination of historical data extrapolated to the budget year in question, adjusted for increases or decreases caused by new requirements in the plans, and adjusted for inflation. As part of the budgeting process, be sure to include notes in your spreadsheets that explain how you developed each budget figure, the assumptions used, and your justifications.

Listed below are techniques for reducing costs, and potential areas for savings when developing budget items:

- Market conditions play into the timing of favorable lease negotiations -- new, renewal, or modification, and the various business terms that are a part of the lease. (Please see our chapter, "Leasing a Facility.")
- In space planning, avoid wasted unused space. Lease as little space as you can; build in an option clause to allow you to expand into either contiguous or non-adjacent vacant space at a later date, when you need it. You will be aided by more-accurate staff projections and business forecasts.
- The timing of the acquisition or disposal of property can help you financially. Also, does your company absolutely require Class A space, or will Class B space (at a lower cost per square foot) suffice?
- Good project management when performing adds, moves, and changes will help to minimize the following: remodeling costs; disruptions to the staff affected by these changes; and hours wasted during these projects.
- Good preventive maintenance of the equipment in your building can help lower or eliminate the cost of maintenance and repairs.

When you have completed compiling your annual budget, review it with the heads of those departments that will feel the effects of your budget, to make sure that you have properly included budget items that relate to those departments. Compare next year's budget with previous years' budgets to make sure that nothing is out of line, and that any item whose cost appears too high or too low can be explained by changes in program growth, planned projects, or inflation.

> **TIP:** Use unit costs ($ / sq. ft.) or ratios (sq. ft. / employee) as they relate to your particular facility to reassure yourself that your budget is in line.

Once the budget has been approved, it needs to be implemented. This should become second nature to you. Out-of-the-ordinary requests for products or services should send up red flags. When in doubt, check to make sure that the cost of the requested item has been included in your budget.

Finally, at regular intervals – monthly, quarterly, annually – you may need to perform a year-to-date budget analysis to compare actual to budget. As you do this analysis, be sure to include reasonable explanations for any variances. FMFG

Additional Resources

• www.todaysfacilitymanager.com, and search on "Budgets"

Building Automation Systems

Building Automation Systems (BAS) help to improve the comfort level for building occupants, lower energy consumption, and provide for system monitoring and control over the Internet. They use computer-based monitoring to optimize building subsystems such as lighting, security, and life and safety systems. They also help optimize the start-up and performance of heating, ventilating, and air conditioning (HVAC) equipment, and integrate various building and alarm systems so as to greatly increase their efficiency.

A BAS may represent a considerable investment for a small-to medium-sized company. However, if your company should fall into this category, and you are a tenant in a larger office building, there is a good probability that the building owner has invested in a BAS, or may do so in the future.

HVAC and Lighting Controls

Historically, BAS were mostly used in commercial buildings to control HVAC systems and energy management system applications. With HVAC and lighting systems together accounting for nearly 70% of a building's total energy load, it's clear that even small increases in equipment efficiency will result in large cost savings.

Systems Integration

Systems integration revolves around orchestrating the operation of multiple building subsystems so that the equipment involved works together, saves energy, and improves occupant comfort. It is quite common to have individual control systems that are *not* centrally monitored and coordinated, that are prone to work *against* each other, thereby reducing occupant comfort, wasting considerable energy, and causing premature failure. With seamless integration, systems run smoothly at a high performance level, without expensive duplication of cost and effort.

Web-Based Graphical Operation

Simplifying the operation of, and integrating the data from, various systems is best accomplished with a point-and-click graphical user interface (GUI). Moreover, providing end-user monitoring and control of building systems over the Internet enables facility managers to manage their building assets from anywhere and at any time.

Direct Digital Controls

With today's open-protocol smart devices, equipment integration is easier, less costly, and more reliable, and it provides more sophisticated monitoring and control schemes than ever before. Traditionally, HVAC system design has been sized to handle the building load under *worst-case* conditions. Most conventional controls are set up to meet these design criteria at all times. With building automation, control set-points and strategies can now be adjusted to meet only the *actual* load, thus eliminating unnecessary waste.

Energy Conservation

The objective of energy conservation, of course, is to use less energy. This should be an inherent part of the entire life cycle of the building. It should be considered during initial design, through building construction, and during operation and maintenance.

Conception and Design: Architectural choices can increase or decrease the energy consumption of a building significantly. For example, you need to be aware that large, un-shaded windows that face the afternoon sun can greatly increase the cooling load during warm weather.

Construction: The best possible design will not produce the desired results if the installation and commissioning are not properly executed. If windows and doors are not properly sealed, if insulation is installed unevenly, and if mechanical systems are not fully calibrated and functionally tested, energy efficiency and occupant comfort will be compromised.

Operation: If the facility staff members do not know how a system is supposed to work, it is highly likely that they will operate it in a less-than-optimal manner. Continuous commissioning ensures that building systems operate at their peak efficiency.

Maintenance: With only limited maintenance, even the best equipment is susceptible to failure within a short period of time. Controls can fall out of calibration; linkages may wear out; damper seals can lose their flexibility; cooling equipment can lose its ability to transfer heat. The list of preventive tasks is long, but taking the proper preventive steps is critical for maintaining energy-efficient building performance.

Three Ways to Save Energy

The common mantra in energy savings is: Turn it off. Turn it down. Turn it in.

- **Turn it off:** The simplest route to energy savings is to turn off the unit or system. If a load is not required, turn it off. Reducing run-time will reduce energy use.
- **Turn it down:** Turning it down means reducing the amount of heating, cooling, or other process, while still providing an acceptable level of service. Most HVAC systems are designed to combat the most extreme of regional conditions. The rest of the time the system does not have to run at full capacity. It is possible to reset

system parameters to reduce energy use without affecting occupant comfort.

- **Turn it in:** Turning it in means replacing the piece of equipment. This may be your toughest energy savings decision. But when one considers full life cycle cost including energy savings and reduced operating and maintenance costs, it may turn out to be less expensive to replace that older, less-efficient model. You should also investigate whether any incentive credits are available for the purchase of a new piece of equipment.

Basic BAS Capabilities

Across manufacturers, basic system functionality is universal.

Scheduling

In today's systems, building automation supports time-of-day scheduling not only for on/off control of equipment, but also set-point adjustment for temperature control. The goal of scheduling is to shut equipment off when it is not needed and reduce demand for heating and cooling when spaces are not occupied.

- Make sure zone HVAC schedules are consistent with lighting control.
- Sweep schedules, which turn off lights at scheduled times, should be set so that they work for tenants as well as the cleaning staff, so as to minimize both lighting on-time and nuisance overrides.
- Daily schedules provide multiple start/stop periods for each day of the week. Customize these schedules to fit the needs of the occupants.
- Calendar schedules can override regular daily schedules so as to automatically turn off equipment during pre-defined holidays.
- Special event schedules can be used if there is an exception to the regular schedule (e.g., half day, or longer

hours than normal). This feature allows you to program an exception for that day only (rather than change the regular schedule). Once the exception period has passed, the program returns to the original schedule.

- Systems automatically adjust for daylight savings time.

Set-Point Control

Set-point is the target value for which you are controlling. Some set-points are defined by the operator and can be changed regularly, while other set-points are calculated by the system (e.g., as outside air temperature falls, the hot water supply temperature automatically increases).

Space temperature set-point: Controlling space temperature may be the single most time-consuming and problematic task a building operator deals with. The balancing act between maintaining occupant comfort and identifying ways to reduce energy consumption is a continuous challenge. Rather than controlling for a building-wide space temperature set-point, multi-zone buildings provide opportunities for energy savings. For each zone, consider the following:

- Time of day.
- Number and fluctuation of occupants in a zone.
- Size and location of zone.
- Zone exposure (perimeter or core, south or north).
- Impact on reheat or simultaneous heating and cooling.
- Equipment in the zone (computers, copiers, laboratory equipment).

Safeties

Safeties are sequences that respond automatically in order to protect equipment, property, or life (freeze-stats, high pressure limits, and smoke detectors). Safeties should not rely on software or programming functions to work – they should be hard-wired.

Lockouts

Lockouts are used to ensure that equipment does not come on when it is not needed. For example, the boiler can be locked out when the outside air temperature is above a preset limit. Similarly, the chiller and its associated pumps can be locked out below a certain outside air temperature.

Lighting Control

The main energy saving strategy with lighting is scheduled on/off control.

- A 'sweep' strategy turns all lights off at a given time. Individual override switches can be provided to turn lights on for a specific zone.

- Occupancy sensors may be used to turn lights on in a specific zone when occupants are present.

- In perimeter zones with sufficient windows, lighting can be dimmed to maintain a minimum light level.

- Zone lighting control can save energy by allowing only occupied zones to be lit (as opposed to the entire floor).

Demand Limiting

The goal of demand limiting is to reduce whole-building electrical demand, rather than individual pieces of equipment. Reducing demand at peak times contributes to lower demand charges from the electric utility.

- Exercise caution when implementing demand strategies. Most of the time, demand is highest when maximum cooling is needed. It may be difficult to reduce demand without sacrificing comfort.

- Load shedding is the process of shutting equipment off and/or globally increasing space temperature set-points in an effort to hold off further increases in demand (or to reduce overall demand).

- Another strategy is to start equipment sequentially (introduce delays between successive equipment starts) to eliminate demand spikes.

Access Control

Security is of premium importance to most building owners, and magnetic card key systems are a standard form of access control. Their minimum function is that of a lock and key. However, there is an increasing opportunity to integrate security systems with other building systems, such as HVAC and lighting.

When HVAC and lighting systems are integrated with the security system, card key readers can act as a form of occupancy sensor to augment zone control. As such, access control produces not only security benefits, but energy savings as well.

Alarms

Registering and recording off-normal occurrences are a critical part of any BAS. In addition to basic alarming, modern automation systems allow you to configure how alarms are monitored, routed, reported, and managed.

In addition to alarms, which may be reported as the result of a system failure, alerts are often generated to bring operator attention to pending service or off-peak performance.

Alarm routing is a feature that provides flexibility in reporting alarms and alerts. Once categorized, alarms and alerts can be routed to different recipients (at different times) for appropriate and timely response. In addition, alarm escalation can be used to elevate the importance of an alarm that is not being acted on.

Nuisance alarms: If alarms are poorly defined and too easily set off, the operator may acknowledge them without follow-up. This could lead to real problems being ignored, resulting in equipment failure or personal injury. It is advisable to review alarm logs regularly to improve alarm rules and limits.

Monitoring and Trending

In addition to controlling equipment, building automation systems can monitor and record operational parameters. The term *trending* refers to periodic recording (in a trend log) of system data for virtually any point in the system. BAS trends are used to verify equipment operation, performance, and energy conservation results. Trend data can be rendered (printed or displayed) in a table or in various graphical formats.

Immediate Benefits of Building Automation

Lower operating costs: On average, building automation systems save about 10 percent on overall annual building energy consumption.

Increased comfort: A more comfortable building means fewer complaints from occupants. This means less time spent resolving complaints, happier occupants, and a more productive business environment.

Simplified building operation: Computerized controls and real-time graphical displays let you see exactly what is happening with the equipment in the building without having to go up on the roof or poke your head up into the ceiling plenum. With all of the computational power and data-trending capability of systems today, you could find yourself drowning in data. Bringing that data out in ways that are meaningful, and presented in an executive summary form, supports sound strategic decision-making.

Lower maintenance costs: Running the equipment less, and controlling it better, not only reduces energy use, but also reduces wear and tear, and keeps maintenance costs under control. Statistics show that properly maintained systems can save you 5 to 10 percent in annual energy costs, not to mention 15 to 25 percent in annual repair costs.

Avoid business interruptions: Unexpected equipment breakdowns can trigger very costly business interruptions. The cost of employees and/or processes in a building can easily be 50 to 100 times the facility operating cost on a square-foot basis. The impact is even greater when your customers are directly affected. Advanced fault detection can detect manual overrides, failed components, and deteriorating or off-peak performance conditions ahead of full failure. FMFG

Additional Resources

- www.thinkESI.com

Building Codes

Building codes are rules that architects, engineers, interior designers, space planners, contractors, and facility managers must follow when designing, building, and managing a facility. Building codes exist to protect the life and safety of building occupants and users. Some of the main categories covered in most building codes are:

- Fire protection, such as fire-rated materials and assemblies, fire exits, emergency egress, alarms, strobes, etc.
- Building occupancy classifications
- Structural design
- Aisles, hallways, ramps, railings, etc.
- Minimum bathroom wheel chair access requirements
- Minimum bathroom fixture requirements based on expected occupancy
- Minimum ventilation requirements
- Energy-efficient controls
- Minimum sizes of conveyance materials like piping and conduit
- Electrical system safety
- Accommodations for people with disabilities

There are many different types of codes, such as: municipal codes, state codes, and national codes. Most of these codes are accessible on-line. Each municipality varies in terms of which code takes precedence. Most often the national or international building code is the dominant one. The different types of codes are:

- Building/dwelling codes
- Structural codes
- Plumbing codes
- Heating, ventilating, and air-conditioning (HVAC) codes
- Electrical codes
- Fire/life safety codes
- Accessibility codes
- Energy codes
- Elevator codes
- Boiler codes

The organizations that publish and administer these codes are:

- Each state, city, and municipality may have building codes specific to its region
- National Fire Protection Association (NFPA), which publishes both the National Electrical Code (NEC) and the national fire and life safety code
- International Plumbing Code, published by the International Code Council
- International Mechanical Code, published by the International Code Council
- International Building Code, published by the International Code Council
- Standard Building Code (SBC), published by the Southern Building Code Congress International (SBCCI)
- Uniform Building Code (UBC), published by the International Conference of Building Officials (ICBO)
- BOCA National Building Code (BOCA/NBC), published by the Building Officials Code Administrators International (BOCA)
- Occupational Safety and Health Administration (OSHA)

Who Needs to Know These Codes?

Architects, engineers, interior designers, and space planners must know these building codes and follow them in order to get municipal or state approval of their plans before a building permit can be issued. Without a building permit, a building cannot be legally constructed. Contractors must know building codes as well as construction safety codes. Facility managers typically do not have to be as knowledgeable about building codes as architects and engineers, but should have a basic knowledge, especially if they have space planners and/or maintenance workers on staff. Many seminars are offered that provide the basic knowledge needed by a facility manager to manage a building.

Code enforcement is usually the responsibility of the local or state building inspectors, fire chiefs, and OSHA inspectors. If you are found to be non-compliant with a particular aspect of a code, you will be required to correct the violation as soon as possible, and may be fined depending on the nature of the offense. FMFG

Additional Resources

- www.icc.org
- www.osha.org
- www.standard-building-code.com/sbcci-codes.shtml
- http://construction.com/ResourceCenter/BuildingCodes.asp

Building Information Modeling (BIM)

Many technologies are available to help you manage your facility more effectively. One of these technologies is called Building Information Modeling (BIM). BIM is a digital repository of three-dimensional building information, linked to a database of project information. Currently, it is used mostly in the design and construction process to produce three-dimensional views of buildings, building systems, and building components. Architects often use BIM to produce presentation drawings, and contractors find it helpful in clash management. Clash management is the process of identifying those areas of construction where two or more building components interfere with each other – such as a plumbing pipe following a path perpendicular to a heating duct – resulting in a field conflict. BIM can identify "clashes" before the components are installed. This technology can reduce costly change orders in the field after the installation has already started.

Although BIM has been around for many years, it is still in its development phase. BIM has great potential value when used to manage a building, after the building has been designed and constructed. The cost of design and construction of a building is a fraction of the total cost of ownership over the life of the building. If the correct information is inputted during the design and construction process, the facility manager will have a powerful tool going forward. As an FM you need to be familiar with BIM. If you are involved in a large construction project, you should meet with your architect and contractors early in the process, and develop expectations about how BIM can be used from the very start, and ultimately become a valuable facility management tool for you. FMFG

Additional Resources

- www.buildingsmartalliance.org/index.php/nbims/

Building Operations and Maintenance

One of the most time-consuming activities in managing a building is operating and maintaining it. According to the International Facility Management Association (IFMA), operations and maintenance (O&M) is the source of 95 to 97% of the problems faced by the facility manager. Clogged plumbing, leaking pipes, broken chairs, and complaints from building occupants who say they are either too hot or too cold are everyday occurrences. In fact, IFMA conducts a regular annual survey of the most common complaints by building occupants, and each year the top complaint alternates between too-hot and too-cold calls.

Maintenance is the work necessary to maintain the original, anticipated useful life of a fixed asset such as property and equipment. Typical maintenance activities may include inspection and assessment, lubrication, adjustments, parts replacement, minor repairs, and painting.

Operations is the work required to keep the facility performing the function for which it is intended, and includes things like providing utilities, heating, cooling, ventilating, and life safety.

The facility manager's O&M responsibilities will vary according to the size of the building, the skill sets of the maintenance staff, and whether the building is owned by the company occupying it, or if the occupant is leasing the space.

O&M can be broken down into three major components and the related subcomponents for each. They are:

Roads and Grounds
- Roadways, sidewalks, and parking lots
- Parking structures
- Landscaping
- Site utilities

Building Structural and Exterior Systems
- Structural systems
- Roofs
- Building exterior systems

Building Interior Systems
- Interior finishes
- Furniture, fixtures and equipment
- Heating, ventilating, and air-conditioning systems (HVAC)
- Electrical and plumbing systems
- Elevators
- Fire and life safety systems
- Security systems

In multiple-building settings, such as a large medical center or a college campus, there is a fourth category of O&M that would need to be considered, called Utilities and Site Systems. However, given the scope of this book, this category will not be considered here.

In those cases where the company owns the building it occupies, the facility manager will likely be involved in all of the above O&M components. For example, some of your day-to-day O&M responsibilities may include:

- Janitorial services
- Window washing
- Carpet cleaning

- Landscape maintenance
- Snow removal
- Repairs and renovations
- Fire alarm testing
- Routine HVAC, electrical, and plumbing maintenance and trouble calls
- Roof leaks
- Physical security, including both systems and personnel (security guards)
- Damage to the building due to weather or vandalism
- Preventive maintenance
- Capital improvements, such as roof replacement, parking lot paving, and large and small remodeling projects.

In smaller owned buildings, where an in-house maintenance staff is not warranted, the facility manager will be responsible for responding to occupants' needs and to maintain the various building systems. However, the actual work will typically be done by outside contractors with whom you will have established service agreements. These outside contractors will have to respond to trouble calls and make the necessary repairs. They will also perform preventive maintenance on various building systems as listed above.

In the case where the company leases a space within a building, most of the O&M work will be the responsibility of the building owner or the building owner's property manager. However, depending on the terms of the lease, you may still be responsible for paying for utilities, and contracting for services such as cleaning and security.

Whether you lease space within a building or own the building, you will need to have a process in place that allows occupants to request routine maintenance. If you own the building and are responsible for all maintenance, the requests will be directed to you or your maintenance staff. If you lease your space, the requests may come to you and then be forwarded to the landlord or property manager. Or your landlord may have a system that allows all maintenance requests to be sent directly to him. In most cases, today's maintenance request systems are automated. (Please see our chapters, "Computer-Aided Facility Management Systems (CAFM)" and "Computerized Maintenance Management Systems (CMMS).")

Whether the space is leased or owned, you will be responsible for relocations and move management.

In a lease situation, you will act as the liaison between the occupants and the property manager. This role may include interfacing with the property manager's computerized work order request system. It typically involves submitting an order for a maintenance activity via the computer, in lieu of calling the maintenance department. You can usually circumvent this system in case of an emergency, such as a water leak.

If your company owns your building, you will typically perform maintenance in one of three ways:

- With in-house staff capable of performing most maintenance activities
- By contracting with outside service providers to perform all maintenance
- Using a combination of in-house staff and outside contractors

If you contract with outside contractors to do some or all of the maintenance work, you will need to write performance specifications and service level agreements spelling out the work you want them to provide, how often, anticipated response times, and at what cost. (Please see our chapters, "Contracts and Proposals" and "Service Level Agreements.") If you bid out the work, the contractors will be bidding on the same things, and you should be able to compare "apples-to-apples" when evaluating their bids.

You may want to consider service contractors who can offer complementary services under one contract. For example, it is not uncommon for landscape maintenance contractors to perform snow removal as well. Another example is a contractor that has the ability to perform electrical, plumbing, and HVAC maintenance. Consider submitting your RFP to both single-service contractors and multiple-service contractors. In the latter case, make sure that you specify that the vendor provides a separate cost for each service, so that you are comparing "apples-to-apples" when evaluating the bids of a single-service and a multiple-service provider.

Whether you own or lease, you will need to prepare a budget. With regard to operations and maintenance, budgeting falls into two categories: operational or expense budgets and capital budgets. (Please see our chapters, "Budgeting" and "Leasing a Facility.") These budgets will be part of your company's overall operational and capital budgets and will likely constitute a significant part of those budgets. Therefore, it is imperative that whether you lease or own, and regardless of building size, you need to be familiar with the costs of operating and maintaining your building.

Responsiveness to maintenance issues is a major component of the customer service you provide to building occupants. If your company owns the building, make sure that you have established expectations with your contractors and service providers and that your customers know how to request maintenance work. If you lease your space, you should be perfectly clear regarding the maintenance services that the property manager or landlord is providing, how those services are requested, and what the expected response time is for various types of maintenance requests. FMFG

64

Building Owners and Managers Association (BOMA)

The Building Owners and Managers Association (BOMA), founded in 1907, is a professional organization whose membership includes building owners, managers, facility managers, and commercial real estate professionals, among others. BOMA International's office is located in Washington, DC. The organization currently has 17,500 members in 91 chapters. It publishes the BOMA Magazine. Its professional designations – RPA, FMA, and SMA – are awarded through BOMI International.

Since 1915, BOMA has been noted for its floor area measurement standard, specifically rentable floor area, in new and existing commercial real estate properties. BOMA's measurement definitions and techniques are recognized as an industry standard, making it possible to compare real estate values and rents based on an accepted method of measurement. It applies to any type of construction or architectural design. The BOMA measurement includes, within rentable space, areas such as lobbies, service rooms, and mechanical areas. BOMA issued its most recent Office Measurement Standard in 2010. Some terms and definitions:

Rentable Area: The building's Rentable Area remains constant for the life of the building, regardless of changes in corridor dimensions or floor configurations. It provides a measure of the income-generating capacity of a building, the pro-rata portion of any floor occupied by each tenant, and the corresponding rent-escalation amount for each tenant. It is computed by measuring the floor area to the inside finished surface of the dominant portions of the permanent outer building walls, excluding any major vertical penetrations of the floor. (Many terms used here are defined below.) No deductions are made for columns or projections necessary to the building.

Usable Area: This is a measure of the area on a given floor or within an office suite that a tenant can occupy and use to conduct its business. The amount of Usable Area on a floor can vary over time as corridor dimensions or floor configurations change. Usable Area is measured from the finished surface side of the office side of corridor and other permanent walls to the center of the partitions that separate the office from adjoining Usable Areas, and to the inside finished surface of the dominant portions of the permanent outer building walls. No deductions are made for columns or projections necessary to the building. The Usable Area of an entire floor is the sum of all the individual Usable Areas on that floor.

Load Factor: Also known as the Loss Factor or the Common Area Factor, it is the percentage of space on a floor that is not usable, expressed as a percent of Usable Area.

Finished surface is a ceiling, wall (including glass), or floor surface, prepared for tenant use, excluding the thickness of any special surfacing materials such as paneling and carpet.

Dominant portion is that portion of the inside finished surface of the permanent outer building wall that is 50% or more of the vertical floor-to-ceiling dimension measured at the dominant portions. If there is no dominant portion, or if the dominant portion is not vertical, the measurement for area shall be to the inside finished surface of the permanent outer building wall where it intersects the finished floor.

Major Vertical Penetrations are stairs, elevator shafts, vertical ducts, pipe shafts and similar elements, along with their enclosing walls, which serve more than one floor of the building, but shall not include stairs, dumb-waiters, and similar elements, which exclusively serve a tenant occupying offices on more than one floor.

Besides its expertise in building area measurement standards, BOMA is actively involved in monitoring and responding to legislative, regulatory, and codes and standards initiatives to advocate the interests of property owners and managers.

Take time to familiarize yourself with the BOMA website (www.boma.org). It is a wealth of information for property owners and facility managers, including money-saving tips on energy conservation. Some examples: Calibrate thermostats; encourage tenants to turn off equipment when not in use; convert T12 lamps to T8 and T5; install occupancy sensors, especially in rooms that are used infrequently; switch to high-efficiency LED exit signs.

A BOMA-related website (www.boma-atlanta.org) is loaded with ideas, including the following for water conservation: detect and repair leaks; install aerators for bathroom faucets; insert water-displacement devices to reduce water usage in large toilet tanks; implement "dry" cleaning methods.

In North America, BOMA's member companies control or manage over 9 billion square feet of commercial properties and facilities. FMFG

Additional Resources

- www.officespace.com/boma

Cabling

L ow-voltage cabling is the spaghetti wiring that runs out of sight above, below, and all around the typical work space linking phones and computers to the parent equipment located in an out-of-the-way cable closet, computer room or server room. Cabling is generally not apparent to the casual observer because it runs under raised floors, in ceiling plenums, behind walls, and inside columns, power poles, and the bases or top caps of cubicle panels.

Even as companies explore the option of "going wireless" for their telephone and computer systems, many still pull cable as an insurance policy against wireless system failure. Over time, we may see a decrease in the amount of cabling strung throughout offices. Until then, we will generally find two types of cabling in use: Category 5e for phones, and Category 5e or 6 for computer use. In some high-density applications, you may also require the installation of a fiber optic spine.

In a typical office, after the space plan is completed, a cable drawing is prepared that shows all the voice and data jack locations. Work with a vendor who has at least one member on its staff with the RCDD (Registered Communications Distribution Designer) designation, obtained through BICSI, the professional association that supports the information technology systems industry. IT systems cover the spectrum of data, voice, audio and video technologies and electronic safety and security. After the cable layout has been designed, it should be bid out to at least three qualified cabling vendors.

Cable runs are made from a cable closet or server room to each location that needs a voice or data cable. You may wish to think strategically, and pull two voice and two data cables to each wired location. Some companies economize up-front and pull one cable of each type, only to discover how expensive it can be to add more cable later on. Server rooms are best located centrally within the space to be wired, and no farther than 295 feet from the farthest wired location (including up-and-down traversing of the cable run between floor and ceiling plenum). The room should be adequately cooled and ventilated, making allowance for all the equipment that might someday be installed there. All metal components (racks, panels, etc.) in the room should be grounded and bonded.

In many air-handling systems, return air is carried in the space (plenum) above the ceiling tiles. In this type of system the cables must be plenum-rated. Plenum-rated cabling is more expensive than non-plenum-rated cable.

In the server room or cable closet, cables should terminate on patch panels. This simplifies the swapping of cables any time an employee moves from one work space location to another within the building, without having to change that person's telephone extension number. Terminating jacks at both ends of each cable run should be numbered. Above a drop-ceiling, cable runs should be supported off the ceiling tiles by J-hooks, cable trays, or conduits.

At the end of the project, the cabling contractor should provide you as-built documentation. In addition, the new cabling should be tested and certified by the cabling contractor to be 100% correct and functional. FMFG

Additional Resources

- www.bicsi.org
- www.panduit.com

Carpeting

As the facility manager you will frequently get involved with carpeting. In a remodeling project you may need to decide which spaces should be carpeted, and which get resilient (hard-surface) floors. As part of your maintenance program, you may need to have the carpet cleaned. Carpeting is a common floor covering that hides defects in floors, is comfortable underfoot, and has the ability to dampen sounds in the areas where it is installed. When it comes to carpeting, there are as many options as there are shades in the color palate and textures in nature.

When specifying new carpet for a remodeling project, you will generally work with a representative from the carpet manufacturer (the carpet rep) to try and narrow the choices to a few, from which a final selection can be made. Here are the three common types of commercial-grade carpeting:

- **Low-density loop pile** carpet may not have the soft feel of plush carpet, but it is ideal for high-traffic environments because the short pile resists crushing and matting better than any other carpet type. In addition, because the surface is relatively smooth, it facilitates the use of rolling traffic such as wheel chairs and supply carts.

- **Tufted** carpeting is also popular in office settings. Here, multiple rows of yarn are used to create the tufts, which are stitched rather than woven. A backing is then added which helps to give stability to the tufts for practical long-term use. Tufted carpeting is higher than pile carpeting, but it is still good for high-traffic commercial use.

- **Woven** carpeting is produced on a loom, and in terms of height is somewhere between the pile and tufted carpets. It can easily last ten years in high traffic, and is popular for offices and conference rooms.

Commercial carpet is generally manufactured from synthetic fibers. The fibers are sturdy, color-fast (even in direct sunlight), resist staining, repel dirt, and are not easily matted down in heavy traffic. They can be maintained with routine vacuuming and occasional professional cleaning (steam-cleaning and dry-powder cleaning are the most typical types of carpet cleaning methods) and stain removal.

Commercial carpeting is available in a few widths of broadloom, or as carpet squares (tiles). Carpet squares have the advantage of being quickly installed. This choice also works well when a few squares are damaged or stained: they are easily replaced with attic stock, without having to replace a large area with broadloom. Carpet tiles can be conveniently installed in cubicle areas without having to dismantle and move the furniture. (See: www.carpetexpress.com.)

Work with the carpet contractor regarding whether you will need a carpet pad under the carpet you have selected. Finally, do your research to make sure that your carpet installer specializes in this work and uses qualified labor, as well as specified tools and accessories. A poor installation can lead to bumps and ridges forming in the carpet, which detract from the appearance, and could pose a tripping hazard.

The life of your carpet can be extended by proper and consistent maintenance. This will also sustain the carpet's appearance and performance level, and contribute to a healthy indoor environment in your facility. The Carpet and Rug Institute (CRI) encourages facility managers to develop and implement a complete carpet maintenance program for their facilities. Some of the benefits of such a program are:

- It maintains the value of your property.
- It has a direct impact on worker comfort and productivity.
- It improves the appearance of the facility.

Carpets today are very durable and long-lasting. Commercial carpet will often "ugly out" before it wears out. FMFG

Additional Resources

- www.carpet-rug.org

Closing a Facility

Closing a facility may be viewed as the extreme case of downsizing the facility. It may be triggered by one or more of many business or other conditions that have rendered the facility unnecessary.

If this is a leased facility, how close are you to the end of the lease? In any case, you may be liable for all rent payments through the end of the lease term. Discuss the situation with your leasing agent or landlord. If he has need for your space, you may be able to negotiate an early termination without paying too high a penalty. Alternatively, he may give you approval to sublet some or all of the space, thereby reducing your lease expenses through the end of the lease term. Review your lease to determine whether there are any clauses that prevent you from subleasing.

In many ways, closing a facility is the reverse of everything that was involved in establishing the facility in the first place. (Please see our chapter, "Establishing a New Facility.") Furniture systems have to be dismantled and removed, either to be sold, stored, or moved into another facility. The same goes for the equipment, phone system, the computer network, security system, artwork on the walls, filing cabinets, shelving, supplies, and the building and suite signs. The list goes on.

All your suppliers and service providers (janitorial, telephone, vending, shredding, plant care, etc.) will need to be notified –

by letter, phone call, e-mail -- that the facility is closing, the effective date of the closing, and the new contact information going forward. Cancel or reroute newspaper and magazine subscriptions. Coordinate utility services – electricity, water, and gas – with the landlord. Deliveries – including mail and packages – have to be stopped or redirected to a new address. Employees and customers have to be notified as well.

Once all your company's assets have been removed from the space, you may be responsible for cleaning the space prior to a walk-through with the landlord or leasing agent, to confirm that everything is in order according to the lease terms. Depending on the lease language, you may have to remove all data cabling from the vacated space, as well. Some leases even require tenants to return the space to its original condition. Finally, return all keys to the landlord. FMFG

Commissioning

Commissioning is the testing of the operating systems of a building to verify that they are operating within the parameters of their intended design and installation. In its most basic form, commissioning is the process of ensuring that the building systems are operating in accordance with the design intent and the owner's requirements. It defines building system performance criteria, provides a baseline for building performance, and provides a means of tracking performance over time. According to Facility Engineering Associates (a national facility management, sustainability, and engineering consulting firm), commissioning:

- Defines the building systems' performance criteria,
- Provides a validated baseline for building performance, and
- Provides a means of tracking and evaluating building performance over time.

In addition, commissioning can help identify unexplained rises in energy use, identify any unexplained increase in thermal comfort complaints, and help the building obtain LEED (Leadership in Energy and Environmental Design) certification. (Please see our chapter, "Sustainability.") Statistics show that proper commissioning of a building can decrease energy costs by anywhere from 15% to 30%. A study performed by Lawrence Berkeley National Laboratory in December 2004 found that commissioning in new buildings found 3,305 deficiencies (28 per building, with 34 projects reporting). The study found that heating, ventilating, and air-conditioning (HVAC) systems presented the most problems, particularly within air-distribution systems. The most common correctional measures focused on operations and control. According to the study, the median payback time for commissioning new buildings was 4.8 years, and when non-energy impacts were factored in, those payback periods were considerably reduced. In existing buildings, the results are much more dramatic, with typical payback periods ranging from 6 to 18 months.

Commissioning is conducted on new buildings at the completion of a building project, and prior to occupancy. Typically an outside party – independent of the original architects, engineers, and contractors who designed and built the building – is engaged to perform the commissioning. Operating systems include HVAC systems, electrical systems (such as transformers, switchgear, and lighting controls), plumbing systems and components, and life safety equipment (such as fire alarms and smoke detectors).

Commissioning services can be provided for existing buildings, as well. By reviewing the original design criteria and current system performance, commissioning can be a way for you to benchmark the performance of existing systems, recognize system problems, correct problems that may reduce the useful life of equipment, and identify opportunities for energy savings.

Don't ever assume that just because the building has been built, or a renovation has been completed, everything has been installed properly. Even in small projects, there are a large number of contractors involved in the project. Their work is interrelated and must be carefully coordinated. If it isn't, problems will occur. Examples of things that are found during the process of commissioning are:

- Ductwork disconnected from diffusers, sending conditioned air into the above-ceiling space instead of the space to be conditioned.
- Reheat valves in air supply boxes that are stuck open, causing overheating in the building.
- Lighting controls that are programmed incorrectly, causing lights to stay on longer than necessary.
- Cross-connected HVAC sensors, causing systems to overheat and overcool.
- Improperly installed condensate drainage systems, resulting in water pooling on the roof, and creating the potential for roof damage.
- Non-working duct smoke detectors, emergency lights, and exit lights.
- System controls that are out of calibration.

Commissioning should be performed by a commissioning agent or an engineering firm experienced in all building systems. The fee for commissioning is often based on a cost per square foot. It is wise to get competitive proposals. Base your final selection of vendor not only on price, but on the contractor's experience, as well.

Re-commissioning is the commissioning of a building some time after it has been originally commissioned. Some building owners choose to re-commission every few years in order to verify that the building is still operating at its intended design parameters. If not, they can then make repairs or adjustments to bring the building systems back in to spec.

Retro-commissioning is the commissioning of an existing building that was never originally commissioned. This type of commissioning can be more expensive than either re-commissioning or commissioning because it usually requires research into what the original design parameters were. Accurate drawings of the building may not be available and there may not be proper documentation of what equipment exists and what the original design specifications were. In some cases, equipment may be obsolete and relevant information no longer available.

Re-commissioning and retro-commissioning are often some of the first steps taken when a building is going to go through the LEED process, as administered by the United States Green Building Council.

Re-commissioning and retro-commissioning are often part of the due diligence process in real estate transactions. FMFG

Additional Resources

• United States Green Building Council (www.usgbc.org)

Communication and Interpersonal Skills

There are two aspects to almost every job: the technical and the "people" aspects. Most people spend a lot of time improving their technical skills. Unfortunately, the "people" skills, those needed to work successfully with other people, and commonly referred to as "soft skills," are taken for granted. However, the "soft skills" are critical. Mastering them will help you work better with your manager, peers, colleagues, and the people who report to you. What are these "soft skills"? They are primarily communication and interpersonal skills.

Communication

Good communication is integral to all jobs. If you manage people, you have probably run into situations where someone could not explain a problem or issue without delivering a one-hour treatise on the subject. Sure, that person knew what he or she was talking about, but could not summarize the problem and present a concise solution. Developing a reputation as a good communicator can build your credibility with senior management; a lack of good communication skills can ruin it.

Let's look at the competencies one must have to be a good communicator.

1. Effective communication strategies:
   a) Know your audience. If you are talking to a technical person, he or she may need a more technical

explanation of the issue. If it is your boss, she may want an executive summary and a clear presentation of alternatives and recommendations. If your boss is the Chief Financial Officer, she will want a payback analysis. If you report to the Vice President of Human Resources, she may want to know how the recommendation, proposal, or action will improve the work environment or affect the company culture.

b) Identify all the people who need the information you are preparing to share, why they need it, and what they plan to do with it.

c) Understand the urgency of the need to communicate the information or the urgency of the information itself. Something that's important to you may not be important to the next person. Know how to structure the information in order to maximize its impact and obtain productive feedback.

d) Use the appropriate delivery method. Use face-to-face communication whenever possible, and then follow up with a written or electronic summary for the record, if necessary.

e) Communicating bad news may be just as important as communicating good news.

2. Give good directions. Make certain that expectations are clear. Identify time frames. Show how the directions fit into the overall strategy. Verify understanding of your directions.

3. Clarify interpretations, and confirm understanding.

a) As an FM you deal with many diverse issues and you will encounter a great deal of information. You must be able to analyze this information, interpret it, and understand its purpose and value.

b) You must quickly determine the importance, urgency, and completeness of the information you receive, and whether any action is required.

4. Make oral presentations.
   a) As an FM you are constantly selling ideas. You must be able to get people to understand issues, policies, procedures, etc. and persuade people to adhere to them. Give people information in a form they can use. Tailor your presentation to your audience and the situation at hand.
   b) There is an ongoing need for you to be visible and approachable. Create a comfortable atmosphere that encourages employees to come and talk to you. Their input is critical, so solicit it.
   c) Follow up, especially if you promise to do so.
   d) Have a sense of humor. If you don't have one, get one! It is the great diffuser.
5. Listen. Listening demonstrates interest. You cannot get information from someone without listening. Listening saves time. Learn how to listen and think at the same time.
6. Write well. Learn to write succinctly and to the point. State your conclusions or recommendations clearly. Develop a reputation for good written communications.
7. Conduct effective meetings. This is one of the best ways to communicate information to a group of people. Here are some tips for running a successful meeting:
   a) Invite only those who have a stake in the topic.
   b) Prepare an agenda. Get input from others, if appropriate.
   c) Summarize conclusions, points, recommendations, actions, etc.
   d) Document and distribute the results.
   e) Follow-up: assign actions.
   f) Structure the meeting (formal or informal).
   g) Be on time and stay on schedule.
   h) Beware of personal agendas.

i)   Make it productive. Clearly identify the purpose and intended result of the meeting. This will make every meeting worthwhile for you and the attendees.

Remember: Good communication enables, while bad communication disables.

Interpersonal Skills

Webster defines "interpersonal" as: "...being, relating to, or involving relations between persons." We have interactions with all kinds of people every day. How we interrelate with them dictates how healthy these relationships will be. Another definition might be: "The ability to communicate with people in a manner that encourages, promotes, and creates an atmosphere for response and interaction."

One of the best ways to engage a person in a discussion, formal or informal, is to listen and be genuinely interested in what the other person is saying. Don't be thinking about what to say next, while the other person is talking. Instead, listen to what the person is saying and respond to it naturally and honestly. Understand the person's viewpoint. Treat the conversation as a partnership of ideas and opinions between two (or more) people. Listen, understand and learn. Quoting Stephen Covey: "Seek first to understand, then to be understood."

Most of the time, more can be accomplished by a few people than by just one. People often achieve their best results by working with other people. In order to get the benefit of, and be a benefit to, another person, you must first and foremost be sensitive to their needs. You must understand their perspectives.

Some people use information as power. They share as little information as possible, thinking that they will always be of value because they have more information than the next person. They expect that other people will have to come to them for information. How long do you think people will keep coming back to them for information before they just figure it out on their own? Or get the information by combining their efforts with someone they enjoy engaging in conversation and solving problems with, someone who listens in order to understand? Yes, someone with interpersonal skills.

Here are some things you can do to improve your interpersonal skills and enhance your relationships with the people you interact with every day:

- If you're working with someone on a project, and a problem arises that affects the work of the other person, show support for the person and a willingness to work on a solution together.

- Avoid being defensive. If someone tells you that you have a problem, don't respond defensively. Rather, ask for more detail and clarification. Find out the scope and potential impact of the problem. Ask what that person thinks should be done, and ask for help in solving the problem.

- Be pleasant. Everybody has a bad day now and then, so don't take it out on others. Develop a reputation as someone who will listen to the problems of others.

- Disclose personal information occasionally. Everyone likes to know a little about what makes others tick. It will help people understand you better, and people may tend to open up to you more. It will benefit you by giving others a view on your perspective.

- Admit mistakes and then remedy them proactively. If your mistake affects others, get their input as to how to remedy the situation. No one wants to hear excuses.

- Solicit the opinions of others. Get their feedback and input. If a person is reluctant to offer a viewpoint, try and draw it out by asking questions. Create an atmosphere for people to want to contribute their thoughts and ideas.

- Be flexible. Be willing to compromise and meld others' ideas with your own, to create even better ideas.

Summary

Possessing people skills in combination with your technical expertise will help you stand above the rest. There's a good chance you know someone who is a good communicator, is better organized, and has better interpersonal skills than the average person. They get along better with people, enabling them to sell their ideas more easily and complete projects successfully. They communicate clearly and make sure they understand and are understood. When working in groups, everyone tends to look to them to be the team leader. Their thoughts are organized, and they give clear directions. These are people who appreciate the importance of having good soft skills, and they consciously work to improve and apply them. By doing so they are helping themselves and enriching their own lives and careers, and those that they come in contact with. Getting things accomplished with the willing help of others can be very fulfilling.

Most of us have to work for a living. Practicing soft skills can make your work just a little bit easier, and you might even have some fun along the way. FMFG

Company Culture

Company culture manifests itself in the common, shared values, beliefs and practices of the management and employees of your company. It is something that develops over time and may change gradually as new employees bring in their own values, or a new CEO takes the reins. The culture may also evolve as the company grows and matures. Your company's culture may also be affected by environmental changes such as changes in laws, the economy and industry regulations.

To understand a company's culture, you only need look around you. What are some of the visible cues when you step into the lobby, general office, or plant? Is the workplace as quiet as a cemetery, or bustling with activity and conversation? How are employees dressed – casual, business-casual or formal? Is there even a dress code? How much freedom of expression do employees have in the way they decorate their individual workstations? How do they behave towards each other, with customers, stakeholders, and the general public? Culture is about "how things get done around here." (See: Humanresources.about.com/od.)

Company culture permeates everything you do. It is analogous to an individual's personality, and everything that goes into making it what it is – upbringing, habits, values, assumptions, and beliefs. Look at your company's website, company-related message boards, promotional literature, press releases, etc. Your company's culture should be reflected in its mission statement, if you have one.

Is employee input encouraged in the creation of company policies and procedures? Is the individual's productivity and output stressed, or is the emphasis placed more on team or group collaboration (or competition)? Do employees provide suggestions to help improve productivity? Or are these dictated by upper management? Each is reflective of the company's management style.

Company traditions are generally developed over a long period of time. They may include rituals such as an annual company picnic (sometimes with employees' families included) or an end-of-year holiday party, or a bonus. Are employees' birthdays and anniversaries celebrated? Are the individual's or team's accomplishments announced to the rest of the organization? Does the company observe "casual-day" or half-day Fridays? A company's culture has a lot to do with the values and style of its founder, as well as its upper management, their vision for the company, and their management style.

A company's culture is very evident when interviewing candidates for a job. The interviewer is judging – consciously or otherwise – how well the applicant will fit into the company's culture. This cuts both ways, as the applicant gauges how well he may fit into the organization, based on a phone interview or during the course of a face-to-face interview. Applicants may do well to try and set up an interview outside the interviewer's comfort zone, such as at a restaurant, over lunch. Applicants should research the philosophy and leadership style of the company's leader, as his or her beliefs will very likely be reflected in the company's culture.

While culture in and of itself is neither good nor bad, many of the aspects (customer service, accountability, communication style) that go into its make-up can lead to failure or success depending on how they are defined and implemented. Culture is learned from the company's reward system for certain preferred behaviors and performance. It is also picked up by new employees as they watch and learn through interactions with fellow employees. In addition, employees may find rewards, and have their most important needs met, within departments and project teams, where subcultures may develop and flourish.

A company's culture is often manifested in its physical space. The level of interior finish may indicate what type of culture exists. A space with many private offices along the window walls and cubicles located away from windows may indicate one type of culture.

Before you even think of changing any aspect of your company culture, you should evaluate what you currently have in place.

- How clear is your mission statement (if your company has one)?
- How effective is company leadership?
- How committed are your employees to company values and leadership?
- Do you have empowered, customer-focused employees?
- How would you evaluate your company's rewards and compensation systems?
- Does your company promote lifelong learning and employee skill development?
- How well do you communicate?
- Are you able to recruit and retain quality employees?

Next, you need to determine where it is you want the company to go for the long term, and what its culture should resemble.

If there is a gap between where you are and where you need to be in your company's strategic vision, you need to take the next step and develop action plans to correct the situation.

Embrace the good that you currently have. Brainstorm ways to improve policies and procedures. Agree on a new set of values you wish to adopt, and which behaviors need to be changed. Then, communicate the changes up and down your organization. FMFG

Additional Resources

- www.management.about.com

Computer-Aided Design and Drafting (CADD)

Few architectural and construction drawings are drawn by hand any more. Today, space planners use Computer-Aided Design and Drafting (CADD or CAD) software because it is more efficient, consistent, and automated. If you intend to do your own space planning or are going to employ a computer-aided facility management system (CAFM), it is to your benefit to take a class in CAD. (Please see our chapter, "Computer-Aided Facility Management Systems (CAFM).") Most colleges and universities that provide interior design, architecture, facility management, or engineering curriculum will likely have a CAD class available through their extension program. If you do not have CADD skills yourself, you may find that your furniture dealer or other consultants, such as architects and interior designers, can provide CADD expertise that you can turn to.

Before you invest in a CADD system at your company, think about what you'll use it for and how much you will use it. If it will be only for occasional space planning, leave the drafting to your furniture dealer! FMFG

Computer-Aided Facility Management Systems (CAFM)

Technology plays an important role in facility management today. One technology tool most often used in facility management is the Computer-Aided Facility Management (CAFM) software system. Essentially CAFM is a software-based asset management system. A CAFM system can help you manage:

- Floor plans
- Space planning
- Move planning and implementation
- Charge backs
- Building and property information
- Building and office equipment leases
- Conference room reservations and set-up requests
- Space characteristics and usage
- Employee and occupancy data
- Workplace assets (furniture and equipment)
- Business continuity and safety information
- Data and telecom information
- Site assets and characteristics
- Facility maintenance activities
- Facility budgets

CAFM systems are typically based on electronic floor plans of a company's existing space. (Please see our chapter,

"Computer-Aided Design and Drafting (CADD).") For example, a CAD plan will include the basic fixed components of a space such as walls, doors, windows, columns, stairs, elevators, built-in counters and cabinets, ceilings and light fixtures, ventilation supply and return grilles, and any other components that may need to interface with a space plan. Then, movable objects like office furniture, cubicle panels and components, office equipment, and floor-mounted electrical and data boxes are overlaid onto the base plan. The next layer will include the names of the occupants of each office and cubicle. Attached to each name is information about the occupant that is required when planning a move, such as data jack number, telephone extension, employee number, etc. All of this information is inputted into a dynamic database so that when assets are moved on the plans, the information attached to each asset is automatically updated in the database. The CAFM system can also generate move documents that can be distributed to the various move team members, such as the IT and telecommunications staffs, to assist them in accomplishing their tasks.

You can track any asset you want by including it on the CAD plan and in the database. You can then attach any information you wish to know about that asset. For example, if you want to track a copy machine, you could attach lease and service information about the machine and set up reminders when it requires routine maintenance, or a reminder that its lease is about to expire. This can be done with buildings and building equipment, as well. For example, if you are responsible for building maintenance, you could include a rooftop air-handling unit as an asset, and attach information on the routine maintenance that it requires. So, if filters need to be replaced on a quarterly basis, you can create a report that automatically alerts your maintenance staff to schedule this work.

The maintenance module of a CAFM system can also include a work order system. This is an automated process for users to request maintenance work. For example, someone in the Marketing Department with a broken chair could use the CAFM system to send a request to you or your maintenance department to get the chair fixed. A work order would then be generated, and the CAFM system would track the work order from initial request to completion. You could then run monthly reports to see how many requests were made, their categories, the average time to complete them, and the number of open requests. (Please see our chapter, "Computerized Maintenance Management Systems (CMMS).")

If you lease multiple office spaces, you can set up the CAFM system to alert you that the lease for a particular building is going to expire in one year. This would let you know well in advance that it's time to start negotiating with your landlord to extend the lease, or to start looking for new space.

Many different CAFM systems are available on the market. They range from the very simple, single-license systems to expensive, multiple-license systems. There are also web-based systems. Most CAFM systems are modular in design, with individual modules for space planning, real estate management, maintenance management, financial analysis, etc. With some systems you must purchase the base CAFM software package and then pay extra for each module. With other systems, all of the modules come with the base package.

Just as with any other software system, a CAFM system is only as good as the information inputted into it. When analyzing the purchase of a CAFM system you must factor in the time it will take to input the information that you wish to track. For example, if you have up-to-date CAD plans you will be able to input them into the CAFM system. However if you only have hardcopy plans, you must first convert them to

CAD plans and make sure they are up to date. This will take considerably more time. If you need an architect or space planner to convert the hardcopy plans to CAD, you will need to add the cost of their time. If you have a well-functioning, but paper-based, work order request system, it may be quite simple to automate that process within the CAFM system. However if your maintenance request system is unorganized, it may be a nightmare to automate.

Once you've set up your CAFM system, you must keep the data up-to-date. If you do not keep the data current, you may wind up with an expensive but useless tool.

The basic steps in selecting, purchasing, and implementing a CAFM system are:

1. Understand your requirements. Why do you want to purchase a CAFM system? What will you use it for? What assets will you track? What kind of reports do you need in order to manage your facility? What kind of reports would help you demonstrate progress to your boss?

TIP: Before you talk to CAFM vendors, make sure you fully understand what your requirements are. Then select a CAFM system that meets those requirements rather than letting a particular system's requirements dictate how you must use it.

---

2. Develop a plan. How will you use it initially? How will you use it in the future? How many people will use it? Who will input the initial information? Who will maintain and manage the system? In what time frame will this happen?

TIP: Don't try to do everything at once. Start with the basics. What is the first thing you want to use the system for? Space planning? Move management? Maintenance management? One of the most common reasons that CAFM systems fail is that the facility manager wants to do too much from the start. Start small and build on the system over time.

3. Develop a budget that is based on your plan. Factor in the cost of the CAFM software, the time and cost to input the initial data, the time and cost of implementation, the cost to expand the system gradually, the annual maintenance fees, licensing fees, and cost of future upgraded versions from the manufacturer. If you don't have up-to-date floor plans, you must factor in the cost of hiring an architect to survey your space, and prepare "as-is" plans. If your floor plans are not in electronic format, you'll also have to factor in the cost of digitizing them.

4. Conduct thorough and methodical research as to what systems are available that meet your requirements and budget.

TIP: Trade shows are often good places to see and compare multiple systems in action.

5. After you have narrowed down the field to about three to five CAFM systems, compare them side by side on a spreadsheet displaying your requirements and the attributes of each manufacturer's system.

> **TIP:** Ask your IT colleagues to take part in the analysis. They may have insights that you haven't thought about.

If it is selected for the right reason, and implemented methodically, your CAFM system can prove to be a very powerful tool that makes managing your facility more effective and efficient. FMFG

Computerized Maintenance Management Systems (CMMS)

Whether you own your building and are responsible for its maintenance, or you lease your space and your landlord is responsible for maintaining it, the occupants of your building will have periodic maintenance requests. (Please see our chapter, "Building Operations and Maintenance.") You will need a process to manage those requests.

A common way to manage maintenance work order requests is to implement a Computerized Maintenance Management System (CMMS). A CMMS is a software system that allows users to make their maintenance requests via e-mail or through some other automated method. Typically, the party making the request accesses a request form on the automated system. The form lists typical maintenance requests, and the person checks the appropriate one (e.g., light burned out, broken chair, special cleaning issue). The request then goes to the maintenance department or the facility manager, who then processes the request and assigns it to a maintenance technician to assess the problem and complete the work.

In the case where the landlord is responsible for maintenance, the request is forwarded to the landlord by the facility manager or it may be sent directly by the requestor to the property manager. In this case the CMMS system is owned by the property manager, whose responsibility is to complete the maintenance requests. The requestor may get an e-mail that confirms the request was received, and possibly an estimated completion time. After the item is completed, typically another e-mail is sent to the requestor indicating that the request has been fulfilled. It may even include a short survey inquiring whether the request was completed to the requestor's satisfaction and in a timely manner.

If the property manager has responsibility for multiple buildings, whether locally or nationally, the automated maintenance system may be web-based and the tenants in all of the buildings under management may use the same work order system. Maintenance requests are made in one of two ways:

1. The requestor sends an e-mail to the maintenance department describing the issue. The maintenance manager then assesses the request, inputs the data into the CMMS system, generates the work order and assigns it to a maintenance technician. Or
2. The requestor inputs the data directly into the central CMMS system.

In the latter case, a limit is often placed on the number of requestors. Each department may have one person designated as the administrator of the CMMS system, and is specially trained to input into the CMMS system. Depending on the cost of individual CMMS software licenses, limiting the number of requestors can save the property management company money. It also reduces the amount of time required to train users.

CMMS systems can be purchased as stand-alone packages or as part of a larger Computer-Aided Facility Management System. (Please see our chapter, "Computer-Aided Facility Management Systems (CAFM).")

The basic steps in selecting, purchasing, and implementing a CMMS system are as follows:

1. Understand your requirements. Why do you want to purchase a CMMS system? How will you use it? How simple or sophisticated should the system be? What kind of reports do you need in order to manage your maintenance function? Should you purchase a stand-alone CMMS system or one that is part of a CAFM System?

> **TIP:** Before you talk to CMMS vendors, make sure you fully understand what your requirements are, and select a CMMS system that meets those requirements rather than letting a particular system's requirements dictate how you must use it.

2. Develop a plan for how will you use CMMS initially. How will you use it in the future? How many people will use it? Who will input the initial information? Who will maintain and manage the system? In what time frame will this happen?
3. Develop a budget that is based on your plan. Factor in the cost of the CMMS software, the time and cost to input the initial data, the time and cost of implementation, the cost to expand the system over time, the cost of annual maintenance and licensing fees, and the cost of future upgraded versions from the manufacturer.
4. Conduct thorough and methodical research as to what systems are available that meet your requirements and budget.

> **TIP:** Trade shows are often good places to see multiple systems in action and to compare them side by side.

5. After you have narrowed the field to three to five appropriate CMMS systems, compare them side by side on a spreadsheet, and evaluate them according to the attributes of each system and how they meet your requirements.

TIP: Ask your IT colleagues to participate in the analysis. They may have insights that you haven't thought about.

If selected for the right reasons, and implemented slowly but surely, your CMMS system can be a very powerful tool that makes managing your facility maintenance function both efficient and effective. FMFG

Construction and Renovation

The success of any construction or renovation project hinges on detailed planning and a team-based approach. The end result needs to be delivered on schedule and within the approved budget. You may find that your construction or renovation project has to be timed so that it can be done in conjunction with other related pre-approved work, such as the upgrade of a building system, a furniture upgrade, introduction of new space standards, or a carpet replacement.

You may have to decide whether to perform these projects one at a time in a phased (department by department) approach, or all at the same time (within the scope of a single project). The latter may be a practical approach if the space under consideration is currently unoccupied, so that you will not be disrupting any staff. However, if the area is occupied by employees in their work spaces, you will have to organize the construction work in such a way as to minimize any distractions. Safety is also a consideration, as is sealing off the construction area from occupants to prevent dust and noise from permeating the adjacent spaces. In some cases, you may have no option but to relocate workers to other areas, so that construction/renovation work can proceed in the space they now occupy. With careful planning and team work, you will survive the process and have a successful project.

Construction and renovation projects may range from a small office renovation, to the build-out of a retail store, to the construction of a superstore or large office project from the ground up. We will look at a global process to achieve a successful project:

- Prepare your stakeholders for the upcoming change: This involves establishing goals, communicating them, and listening for feedback and reaction. Whether you are adding on to existing space, starting with raw space, or renovating an existing space, you need to communicate – with your staff, management, investors, and focus groups – your goals (what you are doing) and why. Listen to their feedback, even complaints and objections.

- Build your team and use it: Define your team, give each member specific responsibilities, share in the success, and always keep an eye on the big picture. Based on the nature of the work to be performed, your team may consist of any combination of the following: unit or department heads (who will be affected by the project), architect, space planner, studs and drywall installers, painters, and individual crews handling demolition and removal, HVAC, electrical, plumbing, ceiling and lighting, sprinkler system, floor coverings, security, phones, millwork, cabling, cleaning, moving, and project management.

- The team approach is critical: Responsibility should rest with everyone to make the project a success, not just the architect and construction manager. The coordinating or project team should meet weekly at a minimum. Whenever there are issues, they should be brought to light, and resolved prior to the next team meeting. Some key decisions may need to be made between team meetings: all team members should be empowered to make decisions without having to run them up the proverbial flagpole. Delays can lead to cost overruns. Keep the final goal and big picture in mind, and don't be distracted by little issues that will crop up along the way: handle them off-line so that you are not wasting everyone's time and slowing the project down.

- Assess the impact of the construction and prioritize what gets done: Balance the work that needs to get done with those who may be disrupted by the work in progress around them.
- Crisis management: Expect the unexpected and know when to let go. There's no question that you will face delivery snafus, design changes, furniture backorders, bad weather, elevator outages and issues that are out of your control. For each setback, your team will need to bounce back with resilience and devise an alternative plan to get you back on track again.
- Use all of the talent available: Use your staff resources to the maximum extent possible. Know when you might need to call for outside help, in the form of consultants, in order to get the project completed successfully.
- Communicate to make a difference: Communicate progress of the project to all stakeholders on a regular basis. You may wish to under-promise and over-deliver!
- Maintain good records and as-built drawings.

Changes, especially last-minute changes, requested by owner or tenant can be very expensive and may cause delays in the project's completion.

Renovation costs are generally lower than the cost of new construction. However, this must be balanced against the distraction to employees working in the space, not to mention the noise and dust from the renovation work in progress, and the potential need for temporary moves. FMFG

Contracts and Proposals

In the course of carrying out your facility management responsibilities, you will at times purchase products and services. For example, you may purchase products such as paper supplies, office supplies, restroom paper products, furniture, coffee, cups, maintenance supplies, and office equipment. You may also purchase services such as architectural services and janitorial services. (For a broader discussion on purchasing products and services, please see our chapter, "Purchasing." This chapter deals with the purchasing of services.)

Request for Proposal

In the realm of facility management, services can be broken down into two categories: professional services and maintenance services. Professional services can include the folowing:

- Architectural
- Engineering
- Space planning
- Facility planning consulting
- Management consulting
- Real estate brokerage
- Property and building development
- Construction

These services are contracted for in different ways. For example, construction services may be bid, while certain specialized consulting services may be more easily secured through negotiating a not-to-exceed fee. Architectural and engineering services are more likely to be based on the size of the construction project being designed and is generally calculated as a percentage of the total construction cost.

Maintenance services are typically obtained via a maintenance contract. It might be an annual contract with conditions for renewal, or it could be a multi-year contract. Typical maintenance services that facility managers contract for are:

- Janitorial
- Snow removal
- Grounds maintenance
- Heating, ventilating, and air conditioning
- Electrical
- Plumbing
- Window washing
- Elevator maintenance

There are several ways to request a proposal for professional or maintenance services. The first way is to prepare a Request for Proposal (RFP). RFPs are typically issued early in a procurement process. The purpose of issuing an RFP is to solicit proposals from providers for a particular ongoing service such as landscape maintenance or for a particular project such as a building remodeling. In the private sector, RFPs can be issued to select providers. In the public sector, RFPs typically have to be advertised publicly, allowing any provider to respond with a proposal. The RFP process brings structure to the procurement decision and allows the risks and benefits to be clearly identified up-front.

The RFP may dictate to varying degrees the exact structure and format of the provider's response. The creativity and innovation that providers build into their proposals may be used to judge the proposals against each other, at the risk of failing to capture consistent information between bidders and thus hampering the decision-making process. Effective RFPs typically reflect the strategy and short- or long-term business objectives, providing detailed insight upon which suppliers will be able to offer a matching response.

A typical RFP for *professional services* will include the following:

1. Description of the Project
This is a general description of the project, its phases (if applicable), the start date and completion date, and a general description of the services to be provided.

2. Scope of Work
This is a description of the specific work to be performed by the professional services provider. If you know in detail what you expect of the provider, this description may be very specific. It would include what deliverables are expected and in what time frame. It should also include any special conditions of the project that might affect the pricing of the services. For example, in a construction project that is to occur adjacent to an occupied space, the work may have to be completed on second shift, or special temporary walls may have to be built to reduce noise. Another example might be that you expect the consultant to attend weekly progress meetings or to provide a project website, both of which have costs associated with them.

3. Qualifications of the Proposer (often referred to as the Offeror)
Here you may request a description of the Offeror's experience in like projects. You may ask the Offeror to describe in some detail how the project was similar to yours and how the provider successfully completed the project.

4. Project Team, Organizational Structure, and Résumés
This includes who the Offeror will assign to the project, how the team will be organized, how you will expect to interface with the team, and a brief résumé of each team member.

5. Project Approach

Depending on the scope of work, you may request the Offeror to describe the steps that will be taken to meet the scope of work. This is more of a subjective question, and it provides the Offeror an opportunity to differentiate himself from other Offerors.

6. Description of the Offeror's Company

Here you may ask specific questions about the firm (e.g., number of professional and administrative employees on staff, services offered, office locations, annual revenue, a list of their top clients). You may also opt to let the Offeror decide which format to use in providing the information. In this way, as in the project approach, it provides an Offeror an opportunity to differentiate himself from other Offerors.

7. References

Ask specifically for the names of clients the Offeror has worked with, including complete contact information.

8. Pricing

You may ask for pricing in several different ways depending on the project. One way is a lump sum, which is the amount you will pay the provider upon successful completion of the project. Another is a lump sum with a not-to-exceed amount. You may also ask for hourly rates of each person that the Offeror expects to have work on the project. You may also go so far as to require a detailed work plan with estimated hours to complete each task and deliverable. Reimbursable expenses such as long-distance telephone calls, travel and entertainment, office supplies, printing, and copying should be provided separately from the professional fee. It will typically be an estimate and is often based on a percentage of the total fee. An estimate of 10% of the professional fee for reimbursable expenses is common. You should require the Offeror to state what their mark-up (if any) would be on reimbursable expenses. You may also specifically require that the Offeror *not* mark-up reimbursable expenses.

9. Selection Criteria

Ultimately you will have to select from among several Offerors. It's best to develop specific criteria for selecting the successful Offeror and weight each of them. Selection criteria might include things like: experience in similar projects, the experience of the proposed project team, project approach, local versus out-of-town, disadvantaged business, pricing, and whatever else you deem to be important. Including these criteria in the RFP will give the Offeror a clue as to where it might rank in terms of their capabilities relative to the project, and then to emphasize their strengths. Conversely, it will also give them a good idea about where they may lag in their capabilities. They can then develop a strategy to demonstrate how they would overcome those weaknesses, such as by partnering with a sub-consultant.

10. Selection Process and Schedule

Describe the selection process. For example, you may have a selection committee and a specific review process. If you have five or more Offerors, you may first wish to create a short-list and then ask those Offerors to make an in-person presentation to your committee. Specify the final selection time frame and call out important milestones.

11. Terms and Conditions

Describe the general terms and conditions you expect the successful Offeror to abide by, such as payment terms, insurance requirements, termination procedures, warranties, general provisions, and confidentiality agreements. If you require that the successful Offeror enter into a contract that is standard to your company, you should state that in the RFP and attach a copy of the contract.

If the scope of work is unclear or undetermined, you may want to start with a Request for Qualifications (RFQ). In this type of document you will ask for much of the same information as in the RFP except for scope of work and pricing. In this case it will be important to describe the project and then ask Offerors to describe what services they think they should provide and why.

A typical RFP for **maintenance services** will include the following:

1. Description of the Work or Service Level Agreement (SLA)

This is a description of the maintenance work being requested. It will specify the nature of the work, the frequency it occurs, specific times of the day or week that the work will be performed, supervision, communication methods, contractor liaison, and any conditions that may affect the contractor's pricing.

2. Qualifications of the Proposer (often referred to as the Bidder)

Here you may ask for a description of the Bidder's experience in providing the maintenance services.

3. Project Approach

Based on the SLA you may request the Bidder to describe what steps it would take to meet the scope of work, including number of people required. This is more of a subjective question and it provides the Bidder an opportunity to differentiate itself from other Bidders. It should specifically describe how the contractor will meet the requirements of the SLA.

4. Description of the Bidder's Company

Here you may ask specific questions about the firm (years in business, services offered, locations, annual revenue, a list of top clients, etc.). Or you may leave it up to the Bidder to provide you this information in a format of its choice. In this way, as with the project approach, it provides the Bidder an opportunity to differentiate itself from other bidders.

5. References

Request a list of clients that the Bidder has worked with, including complete contact information.

6. Pricing

Since most maintenance agreements are based on annual services, the bidder should provide you with an annual fee for his or her services. If it is a multi-year agreement, the bidder should include annual escalation. If it is renewable every year, the requirements for renewal should be specified. Also, labor rates and costs for typical products and parts should be itemized. If emergency service is required, the bidder should specify overtime rates.

7. Selection Criteria

Ultimately, you will have to select from several Bidders. It's best to develop specific criteria for selecting the successful Bidder and weight each of them. Selection criteria might include things like the Bidder's experience, the experience of the proposed supervisor, approach as to how the Bidder will provide the maintenance service, disadvantaged business, pricing, and whatever else you deem to be important.

8. Selection Process and Schedule

Describe the selection process. Specify your final selection time frame and call out important milestones.

9. Measurables

Describe how you will measure the contractor's performance. Make those measurements as objective as possible and establish specific times during which you will formally evaluate the contractor's performance.

10.   Terms and Conditions

Describe the general terms and conditions you expect of the successful Bidder, such as payment terms, insurance requirements, termination procedures, warranties, general provisions, and confidentiality agreements. If you require that the successful Bidder enter into a contract that is standard to your company, you should state that in the RFP and attach a copy of the contract.

> **TIP:** The most important thing to remember when contracting services is to establish clear expectations. For example, when writing an RFP for cleaning services, stating that the contractor will vacuum three times a week is insufficient information. Do you mean vacuum all floors or just carpeted areas? Do you mean just traffic areas or under desks and tables as well? Specifying clear and concise expectations will ensure that you are getting comparative bids that can be used to measure the provider's performance going forward.

Contracts

Once a professional services provider or maintenance services provider is selected, you should enter into a contract. The contract may be originated by you or it may be the contractor/consultant's agreement. In lieu of a formal contract you could issue a standard purchase order. This is typically dictated by your company's purchasing department, so check before you issue an RFP to see what the requirements are. In any case, the agreement should make reference to the original RFP as well as the Bidder's or Offeror's proposal. If you are entering into an agreement supplied by the provider, you should have your Legal Department review and approve it.

Purchasing professional and maintenance services are common business activities. If the bidding and selection process is fair, and the expectations are clear, you should be confident that you will be procuring the best services available for the best price. FMFG

A Day in the Life
of a Facility Manager

A typical day in the life of a facility manager has been described as a series of interruptions interrupted by interruptions. Some observers may envy your ability to be away from your workspace when you're most needed. And you've been known to wander around a lot, both inside your facility and outdoors.

What are you pondering while you wander? Perhaps your next major relocation or remodeling project? Working with real estate brokers, architects and contractors? Developing floor plans, making changes to your workplace? Or maybe you're just trying to stay calm.

You need to analyze a new product. Compare it against alternatives. Will it solve your problem? You have to keep abreast of new technology, look for a better deal.

Then there are other responsibilities: checking circuit breakers, calibrating thermostats, making sure that a flickering fluorescent light gets replaced. Accepting a delivery, poring over blueprints and floor plans. In the middle of a churn, you need to play field marshal over a team of subcontractors, including cabling technicians, furniture installers, electricians, and your in-house staff.

There's the unceasing daily stream of requests and questions. Can I have a new chair? Why is the cafeteria fridge such a mess? And what's that smell? I need another file cabinet for all my folders. We need more paper for the copier, for the fax machine, in the bathroom....

Here and there, you run into some near-emergencies. You sense the adrenaline flow as a situation is addressed, a crisis avoided. Your confidence level is high. You know how to resolve a host of problems, from the sublime to the ridiculous.

There are slow times, too. Sometimes. Time to write reports, catch up on phone calls and e-mails. Maybe handle some complaints, return a defective product, attend interminable meetings, reassign the staff when someone is ill. Or slog through the paperwork, and review procedures.

Time to make sure that the parking lot and sidewalks are free of ice and snow after the last storm. Does it feel too warm in this conference room? No, too cold!

Time for another major move. How tall should the cubicle panels be? Can I have a cube by the window? Subcontractors everywhere, drills buzzing, mallets pounding. Cubicles spring up, carpet is replaced, the floor vacuumed.

Check that the lawn, bushes, and trees are trimmed, the flags raised, and the lobby spotless. Did the mail get out on time, did the files get pulled (and filed back)?

And new projects and requests keep pouring in: new signs to be installed, write a new fleet administration policy. Start working on site selection for a regional office. Work on reducing postage expenses.

How does it all feel? Like a circus? Walking a tightrope. Balancing the budget. Wearing several hats. Juggling tasks and schedules. It's time to shed your cloak of invisibility, take your turn in the spotlight and hear the applause. You've earned it! You're the Facility Manager. FMFG

Downsizing a Facility

There are several reasons why a business might make the decision to downsize a facility. They could include market or economic conditions that have led to a downturn in business volume, and suddenly the company has too much space relative to its now-reduced revenues. Maybe the staff has been moved to another facility and the original facility is now too large for its needs. A decision to reduce the size of private offices and cubicles, or a rearrangement of workspaces, may also result in surplus space. In any case, you are left with too much space – space that you are paying for and that you no longer need to run your business.

Before you can gauge how much space you need to give up, you have to calculate how much space you really *need* to conduct your ongoing business operations. And, how much longer do you plan to stay in the current facility? Based on that time frame, project your needs to the future date.

If you are currently leasing space, approach your landlord or leasing agent to discuss the situation. Under the right conditions, he or she may be willing to take back your surplus space and lease it to another tenant. S/he would then construct a demising wall and amend your lease accordingly. Alternatively, if the terms of your lease permit it, you may receive approval to sublet the surplus space to a new tenant.

You need to lay out the surviving space for your future needs, and make plans to build a demising wall separating your space from the space you have given up. Generally speaking, the lease terms for a sublet space do not allow for much remodeling. You'll have to negotiate who – you or the new tenant – will pay for any remodeling needed.

In many ways, downsizing a space is the reverse process of expanding it. (Please see our chapter, "Expanding a Facility.") In the downsized space, cubicles may need to be reconfigured, along with any power, voice, and data cabling associated with them. Surplus furniture and equipment will need to be repurposed or disposed of.

TIP: One option will result in a win-win situation: offer your now-surplus furniture to the new tenant, which eliminates the need to move it from the space. You might build into your sublease agreement a nominal monthly rental fee for use of this furniture.

The downsizing process is complicated by the fact that you have to accomplish it while the surviving staff is at work inside the premises that you are busily downsizing. Clearly, you need to work with a team, and perform the transformation creatively and in a timely fashion. The team will consist of representatives from affected departments, space planner, various construction trades, the cabling company, and the furniture installer. A key decision that will need to be made is whether to perform the downsizing in a phased approach (over a period of time) or all at once.

Downsizing a facility can be stressful for all parties involved. Help reduce the stress level by communicating with the staff affected by the changes, before, during, and after the changes have been implemented. Work with your Human Resources department to craft these communications. And communicate the changes to all parties affected, including service providers such as the cleaning crew, equipment technicians, etc. FMFG

Elevators

Elevators are an essential component of any modern multi-story building, and it is critical to the day-to-day operation of the facility that they be kept in first-class operating condition. You need to make sure that your building elevators are well-maintained – through preventive servicing, repairs, and updating – for your building occupants' comfort and safety.

Your challenge will be to institute a maintenance package that suits your building's needs and is within your facility budget. (See the website: www.elevatorsource.com.) Elevator maintenance companies offer several levels of service contracts to match a diverse range of building-owner needs. In increasing complexity and price, they range as follows:

A **Survey and Report Contract** is a basic plan that will cover the periodic (quarterly, semi-annual or annual) inspection of the major elevator components and provide a report to you if any repairs are needed. It does not include any maintenance, dismantling of the equipment, or repair work. With this type of contract, the building owner will find it very difficult to avoid liability, should an accident occur.

An **Examination and Lubrication Contract** will include periodic inspections, lubrication of moving parts, and minor adjustments. It does not include the cost of repairs and parts. The cost of the contract is low, but overall annual costs can be high if repairs or parts are involved.

A **Parts, Oil, and Grease Contract** will include a list of the parts covered and those specifically excluded. The frequency of scheduled visits and trouble calls is included in the contract.

A **Full Maintenance Contract** makes the elevator maintenance company fully responsible for the proper functioning of the elevators covered under the contract. The vendor will determine how many service calls it needs to make on an annual basis to keep the elevators functioning safely. That makes it easier for you to budget for the annual costs under this type of contract, and it reduces your company's liability in case of an accident. The Full Maintenance Contract tends to be the most expensive: the servicing company bears the risk should your elevator need significant repair work. The service provider should also update you on the latest elevator codes, and make recommendations regarding upgrades and improvements to the elevators under contract.

Elevator maintenance can be provided by independent certified contractors or by manufacturers. If your elevator runs on proprietary software, you may have no recourse but to seek out the company that manufactured the elevator to service it, too. You may pay a premium for this service, but you can be assured that you will reduce your elevator downtime because the servicing company will have ready access to needed parts, and should be thoroughly familiar with the elevator's operating systems.

Sometimes manufacturers of elevators other than yours may seek to service your elevator. If the prospective vendor is located in your geographic area, and is familiar with the operations of your particular make of elevator, you may find that it can provide service at a lower cost.

Independent elevator servicing companies maintain many different makes of elevator and are conveniently located all around the country. Their maintenance contracts are generally less expensive. However, you may wish to investigate the service company's level of expertise and its access to spare parts before signing a service agreement.

> **TIP:** Consider paying your elevator-servicing company for a technician to be on call when you have a project during which the use of the elevator(s) would be critical, such as during a major move.

If you lease space in a building, it is the responsibility of the landlord to maintain the elevators. However, if you need the elevators for a move or some other type of temporary use, check with the landlord first: You may be restricted to using the elevators only during off-hours. FMFG

Additional Resources

- www.facilitiesnet.com/elevators
- www.buildings.com

Emergency Preparedness

An emergency that involves your building and its occupants can occur at any time, so you need to be as prepared as possible.

The facility manager is usually tasked with the responsibility for emergency preparedness. According to Jim Whittaker, Adjunct Professor in Facilities Management at George Mason University and President of Facility Engineering Associates in Fairfax, VA, an emergency (from a facilities standpoint) can be defined as follows:

An emergency is an unplanned event that can cause death or injury to the building occupants, or that can disrupt operations, cause physical or environmental damage, and threaten the facility's financial standing or public image.

In order to understand how to develop an emergency preparedness plan you must first know what types of emergencies could occur. Some of them are:

- Fires and explosions
- Flooding
- Environmental contaminants
- Violence in the workplace
- Terrorism
- Major equipment failure
- Power outages
- Wind storms, tornados, and hurricanes
- Earthquakes

- Medical emergencies

Emergencies can be internal or external. For example, flooding could be externally caused by a breach in a sea wall, similar to what happened to buildings located in downtown Chicago in 1992. The flooding impacted scores of basements and ground floors in buildings along the Chicago River. Or a flood could be caused by an internal problem such as a broken water main inside your building.

Environmental contamination emergencies can be internal or external, such as a chemical spill inside a building, or the nearby derailment of a train transporting chemicals. Although both emergencies are caused by a chemical spill, you may have to deal with them differently. In the former case, you will likely need to vacate your building. In the latter, you may just need to shut down your building's fresh air intakes.

Fire is another example. A fire inside a building will require the building to be evacuated while the fire department responds and extinguishes the fire. In the case of a large fire in an adjacent building, you may only need to close your building's air intakes. However, if the fire department feels the fire is threatening surrounding buildings, they may order you to evacuate your building, as well.

Power outages can be either internal or external. When we think of power outages we often assume the cause is a problem at the electrical utility involving a downed power line or the proverbial squirrel shorting out a transformer. But if a piece of switchgear or other device within your building's internal electrical power system were to fail, it's your responsibility to find and fix the problem. If the air-conditioning system that cools your server room goes down, you will have an emergency. Even though people may not be put at risk by such a failure, your business could be.

Weather-related emergencies typically occur in specific geographic areas. So, although you may not have to worry about hurricanes if you're located in Wisconsin, you have tornados to deal with, which can be just as devastating. Hurricanes take time to build up and can be tracked for days before they strike, giving you time to prepare. But tornados can appear quickly, and sometimes with very little warning.

How you deal with emergencies will vary, depending on whether you own your building, or lease your space. In the former case, if the emergency is caused by an equipment failure, or has resulted in damage to the building, you will need to address the safety of the occupants as well as repair the equipment or the building once the emergency situation has been resolved.

If you lease space in a multi-tenant building, the expeditious repair or replacement of failed equipment, or repair of the damaged building, is the property manager's responsibility. However, if you are a tenant, you are at the mercy of the building owner in terms of how long it takes to make the necessary repairs. If you can still occupy the building after the emergency has occurred, but are temporarily impaired for some reason, you'll want the problem rectified as soon as possible. That would be the case, for instance, when a major piece of air-conditioning equipment has failed, and your computer room is in danger of overheating. If the emergency has forced you to relocate temporarily to another space, your business could be disrupted. In a lease situation, you should make sure there is language in the lease that protects you financially if you are forced to relocate temporarily. You should also make sure that the owner and/or property manager has an emergency preparedness plan in place for the entire building. Your emergency preparedness plan should dovetail with that of the building owner.

The steps involved in emergency preparedness are:

- Planning
- Business continuity
- Mitigation
- Preparation
- Response.
- Assessment and Restoration

Planning

The different kinds of emergencies that are possible, and the various people who should be involved at different stages of the emergency or disaster, make preparing an emergency plan a multi-faceted effort. An emergency plan cannot be created in a vacuum. You must understand who the stakeholders and constituents are, and involve them in the process. Following are the steps to developing an emergency preparedness plan:

Step 1 – Form an emergency planning team. The team should include representatives from the following departments: Human Resources, Finance, Legal, Purchasing, IT, Security, Safety, Risk Management, Public Relations, as well as representatives from senior management and production or manufacturing operations (if the latter occupy space in your building).

The involvement of the various team members in an emergency response will vary. IT and Public Relations may be involved from the moment the emergency arises, whereas Purchasing may not be involved at all until restoration begins. Each of these team members should provide input into the creation of the plan.

One of the critical activities in an emergency is communication: who needs to be communicated with, what do they need to know, and when do they need to know it? This should be discussed thoroughly by the emergency planning team. An emergency communications plan should address internal communications to employees, department heads, and management, and external communications to the media and the general public. You need to have a clear plan regarding what gets communicated during various phases of the emergency.

Step 2 – Identify who will be directly involved in an emergency. The two most important things that need to be addressed in any emergency are:

- The safety of the building occupants
- The protection of the building and its contents

Employees and facilities are typically a company's two most important and valuable assets. Since the facility manager is responsible for the building and its contents, and the facility houses the employees, the facility manager is the person most often looked upon to take charge in an emergency.

You will typically organize a first-response team (FRT) made up of employees, either hand-picked or volunteers. They will need to be trained in first aid, CPR, operation of AEDs (automated external defibrillator), and proper use of a fire extinguisher. Very often the FRT will include an employee with experience as a volunteer on a community fire department. The FRT should also include a representative and an alternate from each department or building floor. This person will be responsible for verifying that everyone in his or her respective group has been accounted for after an evacuation. They may also be responsible for knowing where any disabled employees are located within the building, and for helping to evacuate them or get them to an interim safe haven within the building, such as a fire stairwell.

Step 3 – Identify the types of emergencies that you could expect to encounter. Then identify the most critical areas in your building, and how they might be affected in each type of emergency. These areas might include the computer room, server closet, and records storage.

Step 4 – Two Emergency Response Plans (ERPs) should be written. The Employee ERP should document what is expected of employees in case of an emergency. It should be short and succinct, describing the various emergencies that could occur and the few basic steps to follow. Emergencies that require employees to take similar action steps should be grouped together. For example, in case of a fire, explosion, earthquake, chemical spill, internal flood, or a terrorist act, either the fire alarm would sound and employees would evacuate the premises, or there would be some type of audible notification, such as an announcement over the paging system. In the case of a tornado, the building would not be evacuated; instead, an announcement would direct employees to proceed to the building's interior storm shelters or safe havens. The instructions should address the safe evacuation of guests, as well.

The employee emergency plan should include: building maps showing evacuation routes; the location of emergency equipment such as first aid kits, AEDs, and fire extinguishers; interior and exterior emergency assembly areas; and safe havens. These maps should be posted around the building as well. Common places to post them are in non-assigned spaces like conference rooms, training rooms, the cafeteria, etc., as well as elevator lobbies, and adjacent to fire alarm pull-stations.

The FRT Emergency Plan will be more detailed, with instructions that are more specific to each type of emergency. It should delve into more detail in terms of steps to protect the company's critical assets as identified in Step 3. The FRT should meet at least every quarter and review the plan and the members' various responsibilities.

Business Continuity

In the event that your building or space is rendered partially or totally uninhabitable following a disaster, you must have a plan in place that allows your company to continue critical operations to keep the business running. A business continuity plan is one in which critical operations are identified, and arrangements have been made in advance to accommodate these operations elsewhere. For example, you may have a contract with a remote server site that you can be quickly switched over to. There may be groups of employees who must continue to perform their jobs to maintain business continuity. You will need to relocate them temporarily to another space. This could be in a space that is totally pre-outfitted for your needs in either another company building or a short-term rented facility. Or it could be a satellite office in which you need to quickly set up workspaces and cabling to minimize the business disruption. Whatever your company decides to do from a business continuity standpoint must be incorporated into the response portion of the overall emergency preparedness plan.

In the event of a wide-area disaster such as a tornado, it is likely that other buildings in the area will also have been damaged. As a result, local contractors will probably be inundated with requests for repairs and restoration. You may want to make arrangements with local contractors in advance of a disaster so that they would put you at the top of their list in the event of an emergency.

Mitigation

Mitigation is the reduction of potential emergency situations so as to avoid hazardous circumstances and reduce risks in the first place. To this end:

- Conduct building inspections to verify code compliance and eliminate obvious fire or other hazardous situations

(extension cords, a water stain on a ceiling tile next to a light fixture, overloaded electrical receptacles, etc.)

- Establish controls on the locations, types and amounts of stored hazardous materials (example: Cleaning solutions).
- Label hazardous containers and storage rooms properly.
- Have neutralizers on hand.
- Inform emergency agencies and the public of on-site hazardous materials.

Preparation

The most important things to consider in emergency preparedness are to have a plan in place, to document it, communicate it, and practice it often.

Ongoing training of FRT members in the use of AEDs, basic first aid, CPR, and the steps to take in each type of emergency should occur at least annually and preferably twice a year or more often. Your local fire and police departments are usually happy to assist in the training.

You should also conduct a general evacuation drill at least twice a year. It could be preannounced or unannounced. There are advantages and disadvantages to both, so discuss the options first with your company's management. Having either your local fire or police department in attendance at an evacuation drill will help communicate to participants the importance of such drills.

An overview of the emergency plan should be included in the company's on-boarding process so that new employees are indoctrinated in the details of the plan on their first day at work.

Response

In the event of an emergency, the following things should happen:

1. Identify the emergency

2. Take charge
3. Implement the appropriate plan
4. Protect the people
5. Save the assets
6. Communicate

Assessment and Restoration

Once the emergency has subsided, an assessment must be made. The steps included in disaster assessment are:

1. Assess the extent of damage.
2. Determine how much of the building or the leased space cannot be occupied.
3. Calculate what it will take to fix or repair the damage.

Once the assessment has been made, you'll need to make arrangements to restore the space.

1. What internal and external resources will be needed? (IT, Purchasing, Legal, architects, engineers, contractors, etc.)
2. Determine the time it will take to implement the restoration.
3. Determine the restoration cost.
4. Can the restoration be completed in phases?
5. Once you've determined the extent of the damage and the necessary repair steps, your business continuity plan should kick in.

In summary, when considering emergency preparedness:

1. Expect the unexpected.
2. Disasters affect different buildings in different ways.
3. Understand what it takes to keep your company operating.
4. The emergency preparedness plan is more than a static plan. It is a dynamic, living document that needs to be revisited and practiced regularly. FMFG

Environmental Health and Safety

In larger companies, environmental health and safety (EH&S) is a separate responsibility, generally of an EH&S department. However, in many organizations EH&S falls under the purview of the facility manager. Having a good EH&S program in place can be a great benefit to your company. Having a healthy and safe workplace can boost employees' morale and productivity. It can also help create a positive image of your company in the community, as well as help avoid costly fines for noncompliance.

In a commercial office setting, EH&S typically addresses indoor air quality, general life safety, and ergonomics. Indoor air quality is specifically related to temperature and humidity (thermal comfort) and ensuring the air being supplied to the building is a blend of conditioned and fresh air, and free of hazardous materials or particles, as well as noxious gases from building materials and office equipment. The best way to maintain optimum indoor air quality is to maintain your heating, ventilating and air-conditioning (HVAC) system. To ensure this happens, you (or your property manager) should have a preventive maintenance plan in place. (Please see our chapter, "Building Operations and Maintenance.") Preventive maintenance will involve regular inspections and maintenance, such as changing filters on HVAC equipment. According to the International Facility Management

Association (IFMA), other things you can do to improve and maintain indoor air quality are:

- Don't block air vents and grilles.
- Implement a no-smoking policy.
- Water and maintain indoor plants properly.
- Dispose of garbage promptly and properly.
- Handle and store cleaning compounds and other hazardous products properly.
- Position office furniture and equipment with air circulation in mind.
- Note any processes that take place in your space that may result in air pollution (e.g., printing).
- Seal off areas that are being renovated and make sure the HVAC system is not transferring dust from the construction area to occupied areas.
- Run the HVAC system at full force in newly-constructed areas for at least a week before moving people in. This will eliminate noxious out-gassing from new materials and adhesives.

Life safety is providing protection against fire and accidents. (Please see our chapter, "Life Safety.") Make sure that your fire sprinkler and fire warning systems are regularly tested. All paths of egress should be free of any materials that could hinder occupant evacuation in case of an emergency. And finally, an ergonomics program should be established. (Please see our chapter, "Ergonomics.")

The Environmental Protection Agency (EPA) and National Institute for Occupational Safety and Health (NIOSH) are good resources to learn more about what you can do to provide a good EH&S program in your building. FMFG

Ergonomics

The United Nation's International Labor Organization defines ergonomics as follows:

"The application of the human biological sciences in conjunction with the engineering sciences to the worker and his working environment, so as to obtain maximum satisfaction for the worker which at the same time enhances productivity."

More simply stated, it is the science of designing the job, equipment and workplace to fit the worker. Poor ergonomics can lead to illness or injuries, some of them long-term. The most common are called muscular skeletal disorders (MSDs) and can affect the body's muscles, joints, tendons, ligaments and nerves. Common symptoms of poor ergonomics are: back pain, neck pain, headaches, sore eyes and body stiffness. Most work-related MSDs develop over time and are caused either by the work itself or by the employees' working environment. Long-term disabilities can be expensive for companies. MSDs of any type have a negative impact on employees because of the decrease in productivity and job satisfaction that can result. Ergonomics is both the responsibility of the employer in terms of the work environment provided, as well as the employee. It is important, therefore, to have in place an ergonomics program that, at the very least, educates employees as to how to work more ergonomically.

Establishing an Ergonomics Program

The first step in developing an ergonomics program is to assess your current workplace. Conduct a walk-through of your workplace and look for signs of ergonomic problems. Examples might be:

- A desktop monitor set on top of a phone book.
- A pillow resting on a chair back or chair seat.
- A piece of cardboard taped to an overhead air vent.
- A sheet of easel paper taped to a window in the early morning or late afternoon.
- A space heater under a desk.

Look for obvious window glare, poor furniture configuration, and equipment placement. Consider not only the age of the chairs in your workplace but their functionality and adjustability.

You should also observe employees, as well. Do those who spend most of their time on the phone, have headsets? Are people who spend most of their day doing heads-down work at their computers, taking time occasionally to stand up and walk around? How long does the person in the copy room stand in front of the copy machine? What kind of floor surface is he or she standing on? Such a person may be young, and feel invincible now, but standing in front of the copy machine on a hard tile floor for hours on end could result in back problems 10 or 20 years in the future.

Talk to department heads, as well. They may provide insights into employee complaints, or those who take an unusual amount of time off, which could signal ergonomics issues.

Once you've done the assessment, develop potential solutions and prioritize them. Short-term solutions might be:

- Foot stools
- Glare screens

- Repositioning of equipment
- Configuration of workstation components
- Task lighting; individual chair adjustments or replacement

Longer-term solutions might include:

- Large-scale chair replacement
- Larger computer monitors; keyboard trays
- Window blinds
- Workstation reconfiguration

Once you've prioritized your ergonomic issues, you need to develop an implementation plan. Make recommendations of what you will do in the short term, in the long term, and why. Then create a budget for fixtures, furniture and equipment, labor, and any design or consulting that you might need. Next, develop an implementation schedule, which should include time frames for workstation design and price-bidding, if necessary.

It is important to educate your company's employees about ergonomics and to communicate the purpose of the ergonomics program to them. You could go to the local university and see if there are any ergonomists on staff that would come in and make a presentation for free or for a nominal fee. At the same time, develop an employee ergonomics pamphlet or card, which should include ergonomic tips, illustrations of correct ergonomic posture, and a process to report and rectify ergonomics problems. FMFG

Additional Resources

- Occupational Safety and Health Administration (www.OSHA.gov)
- American Physical Therapy Association (www.APTA.org)

Establishing a New Facility

S etting up a new facility for your company may very well be the most complex FM project you will ever undertake.

Real Estate Issues

Site Search: Once a decision has been made to open a new leased space, or to move from an existing leased office to a different location, you should retain the services of a real estate professional with comprehensive knowledge of the available spaces in the market that you are considering.

It is recommended that you interview three or four real estate brokers to determine which one is most familiar with the real estate market you are considering. Other important criteria before selecting a broker would include: the broker's current and prior client list; his ability to negotiate favorable leases on the client's behalf; his ability to develop a good mutual working relationship. Get a list of some of the brokers' current and past clients, and talk to them.

Once you have a broker on board, you will need to provide a list of the significant criteria pertaining to the space you are seeking. The list would include such criteria as: preferred location, proximity to downtown or the freeway system, approximate price range (cost per sq. ft.), size of space desired (sq. ft.), projected (maximum) count of the staff that would occupy the space over a 3, 5, or 10-year time-frame, the number of parking spaces needed, your preference for a single- (or multi-) story building, and proximity to other similar buildings, as well as restaurants, hotels, shopping, etc. Establishing specific criteria will allow your real estate broker to hone in on specific properties that meet your needs rather than hauling you off to inspect every empty space in the area that you're looking. This will result in a more efficient, effective and productive site search.

Ask your real estate broker to present for your consideration several possible office sites that match your criteria, along with floor plans of these buildings, their location on a city map, lease rates, amenities provided, etc. You should conduct a survey of these sites along with the broker, with a view to reducing the number of contenders to possibly two or three finalists that meet all of your requirements. A presentation could then be made to the Site Selection Committee (which would typically consist of upper management), at which point a single "winner" would emerge.

Lease Negotiation (Please see our chapter, "Leasing a Facility."): Once you have zeroed in on a specific space, request a lease document from the target building's leasing agent. In reviewing this document, it is desirable to secure agreement with the lessor on the business terms of the deal, before turning the document over to your attorneys for their review. If agreement cannot be reached on the business terms, it would be pointless to incur unnecessary legal expense.

The business terms contained in the lease document would relate to items such as: size of space being leased, lease rate, rent escalators, term of lease, number of parking spaces, build-out (tenant improvement) allowance, right of first offer on adjacent space, renewal rights, etc.

Construction: The final floor plan and lease terms will determine whether major construction work will be needed at the site, or only minor remodeling, before occupancy can take place. Sometimes you get lucky and find a space that you can move into as-is. That is rare, and even if you do find an as-is ready space, you may want to consider upgrading wall and floor finishes as well as possibly replacing lighting with more energy-efficient fixtures that distribute light more ergonomically. (Please see our chapters, "Ergonomics" and "Lighting.") The extent of any construction will be spelled out in a Construction Work Letter and in the final blueprints.

The terms of the lease will dictate whether the landlord will award the project to a construction company of his choosing without the benefit of a bidding process, or whether the project will be bid out to two or three qualified competing construction companies. If the landlord awards the project immediately, work can commence without further delay. If the job is bid out, make allowances for the receipt and evaluation of the bids before making a final selection. (Please see our chapter, "Contracts and Proposals.")

Construction drawings will need to be produced covering the general construction, electrical, HVAC, plumbing, lighting, sprinklers, etc. The general contractor (GC) will have to obtain permits from the local authority and/or your state building plan approval office, allowing him to move forward with construction. A general kick-off meeting should be scheduled, attended by representatives of the GC, all the subcontractors, landlord and tenant, so that everyone gets to meet each other, and establish ground rules and deadlines. The location and schedule of future meetings (to monitor construction progress) can also be set up at that time. A Planning Schedule can be prepared, which would cover the scope of the project through completion.

When the work has been completed (or substantially so), conduct a walk-through with representatives of the landlord and the general contractor. Keep notes of all incomplete and unsatisfactory work that would need to be completed in a timely manner, generally before occupancy. Generate a "punch list" of open items: as they are completed, they can be crossed off the list. The local building inspector will also do a walk-through, and if everything is satisfactory, will issue an Occupancy Permit, allowing you to move forward with plans to occupy the new space.

Remodeling: If the space being leased is taken as-is, or with only minor changes, a remodeling project can be undertaken that is not as extensive or time-consuming as the construction work detailed in the section above. Typical changes may involve re-carpeting some or all of the space, wall-painting or installation of wallpaper, and some minor changes to the floor plan. This level of work can usually be completed in a period of days or weeks, with only minor supervision, and no need for several scheduled weekly progress meetings.

As in the section on Construction described above, a punch list of all open items is generated, that would need to be completed in a timely manner.

Space Planning

The Space Planning process begins with the business plan for the facility. (Please see our chapter, "Space Planning and Programming.") The business plan will determine the projected staff needs over a 3- to 5-year horizon. If your company has corporate space standards, staff needs are then further subdivided into the number of individuals who will be located in private offices (at X sq. ft. each) and those who will be assigned cubicle space (at Y sq. ft. each).

Armed with the above information, as well as square-foot data on other rooms required to be constructed in the new facility (conference rooms, lobby, phone/server room, cafeteria, supply room, etc.), it is possible to develop an estimate of the square foot requirements for the entire facility. The next step is to introduce the preferred adjacencies that will help the office operate efficiently. Examples: Recruiting staff located adjacent to the lobby; account executives located close to each other, etc.

The next step is to develop a floor plan that will incorporate all of the above offices, cubicles and rooms into a cohesive whole that fits comfortably within the outline of the space proposed for leasing. In most cases, landlords will provide prospective tenants with this space planning service at no charge. Generally, this service stops short of a detailed furniture layout for offices and cubicles. Fortunately, this service can be obtained from a furniture dealer, whether or not the furniture order is eventually placed with them. (Please see our chapter, "Furniture.")

In the case of office moves, expansions, or reconfigurations, new and existing furniture need to be incorporated together to make a synergistic whole, while minimizing expenses.

Once an initial floor plan has been developed, upper management needs to approve it. When this approval has been obtained, you can proceed to develop additional detailed drawings, including lighting plans, installation drawings, etc.

The next step is to select colors and finishes for case goods (free-standing furniture such as desks and credenzas), panel fabric for the systems furniture, trim colors, chair fabric, metal cabinets, etc. Try to limit colors to within a palette of approved colors, generally established at a corporate level, in the interest of standardization.

In a typical office, a wide variety of furniture has to be selected and specified for the various rooms and spaces within the office. This may include: case goods for private offices; systems panels and components for cubicles; lobby, conference room and interview room tables and chairs; cabinets, work tables, etc.

When the entire furniture list has been developed, you can bid it out, or if a qualified vendor has been identified with whom you have already placed orders in the past, request a quote (including freight and installation) and place the furniture order. Don't forget to request a firm delivery date. Provide the furniture vendor with details of the ship-to address, whether a loading dock is available, hours when the freight elevator may be used, landlord's name and phone number, and any other relevant information that will expedite the delivery process.

For situations where cubicles are being installed, the work schedule of the furniture installation crew needs to be coordinated with that of the cable installers and the building electrician (who will hard-wire the panel system). If there is packaging material to be disposed of, you may need to make special arrangements with the building's property manager for a dumpster.

Equipment Issues

Cabling (Please see our chapter, "Cabling."): Once an initial floor plan has been developed, it is possible to obtain competitive quotes for the installation of phone (voice) and computer (data) cabling. Cabling needs to be strung between the phone/server room panel and each individual location (office, cubicle, or conference room, etc.) that needs to be wired for voice and data. Cabling standards may require that Type 5e cable be used for voice, and category 5e or 6 cable for data. Each cable will terminate in a numbered voice or data jack. Provide the cabling vendor with a final floor plan showing the locations of all voice and data jacks.

Data Network: The company's Information Technology (IT) department may be responsible for the data network at each facility. They may also be responsible for re-connecting and testing all the network computer equipment prior to occupancy.

137

Computer Equipment: For each new facility, purchase and install desktop and laptop PCs for each employee who will be located in that facility. Other equipment includes servers (and associated racks), as well as networked and dedicated printers. In the case of an office relocation, existing computer equipment will need to be labeled and scheduled for moving.

General Office Equipment (Please see our chapter, "Office Equipment."): Included in this category are copiers, fax machines, mailroom equipment (scale, letter opener, mailing machine, and meter), cafeteria equipment (microwave oven, refrigerator, vending machines, and water cooler), and audio-visual equipment for training and conference rooms. All of the above can be identified in the planning stage, and can generally be ordered about 30 days before the office is scheduled to open. Take care to specify an adequate number of electrical outlets in the areas where the equipment is to be located, as well as phone jacks for any fax machines, and data-jacks for network printers.

Security (Please see our chapter, "Security."): You may choose to install an electronic security system in your facility. Many multi-tenant buildings provide card-key access to their tenants. These access systems allow employees to gain entry into the main doors of the buildings, and may also extend to the individual suites. In addition, you may choose to specify card-key access to your confidential-records room, server room, etc.

Storage (Please see our chapter, "Storage."): Give some consideration to the space and cabinets needed for the storage of active and inactive files, supplies and forms, as well as surplus equipment and furniture. In a smaller facility, storage space may be limited to a few lateral files for paperwork and a storage cabinet for office supplies. Generally there is no need to inventory surplus equipment and furniture. For a larger office, it is usually necessary to have a supply room (which may share space with the mailroom equipment and copier). Sometimes it is possible to negotiate for storage space in the basement of a building where one may store surplus equipment and furniture as well as archives storage boxes.

Budgets (Please see our chapter, "Budgeting.")

The cost of a new-facility project is developed through a budget. In the very early stages of the project, an Estimated Budget is developed. When the project is completed, a Final Budget can be prepared.

Estimated Budget: This budget is typically prepared once you have received sufficient direction to proceed with the project. At this stage, it is possible to obtain from vendors "for budget purposes" figures for all the major expense items involved in the project. Compile an estimated budget and present it to upper management for approval (and sometimes course-correction).

The major budget items that will make up a significant portion of the total budget include: rent (from the lease document), construction, furniture (both cubicles and case goods), computer equipment, office equipment, cabling, phone switch and voice mail system, moving expense, and stationery.

Final Budget: Once the project and the estimated budget have been approved, you should obtain competitive quotes for all the major items: furniture, phone system, and cabling. During the course of the project it is very likely that changes will be made to various categories of products and services purchased. For example, you may need to install additional data lines, add a couple of chairs, etc. These costs should be tracked. When the project has been completed, prepare a Final Budget that captures all the final costs associated with the project. This can be forwarded to the general manager and the controller.

Insurance (Please see our chapter, "Insurance.")

The Insurance clause of a typical facility lease agreement will generally spell out the types of coverage and limits of insurance in a policy that your company would need to purchase. Work with your insurance agent to satisfy this requirement.

Miscellaneous

Mailing and Shipping (Please see our chapter, "Office Services."): A mailroom is recommended for any facility with a staff count greater than ten. The mailroom may share space with other functions such as supplies, storage, copier, and fax machine. A mailroom will typically have the following equipment: letter opener, postage scale, and mailing machine. For a new facility, these items can be ordered about a month prior to the opening. Be sure to notify the local post office and package-delivery service whenever you open or move a facility. In a larger multi-tenant building, a mail station is usually available in the lower level of the building. Mail would have to be picked up from, and delivered to, this area on a daily basis.

Asset-tagging (Please see our chapter, "Asset Management."): All property (furniture and equipment) over a specified threshold value may need to be asset-tagged and entered into your fixed assets database. In a new office, perform this task when new furniture and equipment are brought into the space. If assets are transferred from one office to another, it is important to complete an asset-tracking form showing the asset numbers and the offices between which the transfer has taken place.

Sometimes, assets that are no longer needed may be disposed by sale to employees or other building tenants. In such situations, keep a record of the items being disposed, their asset-tag numbers, and the sale price. Use this information to update the fixed assets database, and share it with the Accounting Department, which can use the figures to reduce the corporate personal property tax obligations.

Signage (Please see our chapter, "Signage."): There are several types of building signage, depending on the building you are occupying and the terms of the lease. Some buildings may permit a sign on the face of the building, or provide a parking lot monument sign. In most leases, the Landlord will provide lobby signage showing your company's name and suite number. In addition, signage may be provided on or beside the main suite entrance door. You may also wish to install a company sign in the reception area within your suite.

Stationery/Letterhead items: With every new facility or relocation, you will need to reprint your company stationery (letterhead paper, envelopes, business cards, brochures, etc.) to show the new address and telephone numbers. This may require a one-month lead-time.

Keys: If you are moving into a renovated suite previously occupied by another tenant, it is best to change the locks of all suite-entry doors. Once the floor plan has been finalized, you should determine which, if any, of the private office doors need to be lockable, and issue keys accordingly. In many facilities, a card-key access system may be specified. One advantage of such a system is that the employees generally do not need to carry keys. A further advantage is that whenever there is staff turnover, the departing employee's card key may be either retrieved or disabled.

Vending: You may choose to contract for coffee, soda, and bottled water service when you establish a new facility. The coffee vendor will generally provide one or more coffee-brewers. You can typically lease vending machines for soda and juices from the same vendor. The bottled water service will generally include a unit to chill or heat the water being dispensed.

Communications: In anticipation of a move to a new facility, be sure to notify your clients, business partners, vendors, and others (post office, package delivery service, etc.) about the opening of the new facility or the relocation of the facility to a new address. This is generally orchestrated by your company's communications manager about one to two weeks prior to the move. FMFG

Event Planning

Whether you are organizing a 2-hour or a 3-day business event, many of the significant components that make for a successful event are common to both.

Brief Business Event: Let's first tackle a short 2-hour business meeting. You'll need to know the date, and the start and end times. You may have a range of selections for the location: company conference room or cafeteria, nearby hotel, or a local restaurant meeting room. For each option, your invitees may need a map and directions. Is parking readily available at the meeting venue, and will there be a charge? Or should attendees be prepared for street parking?

It is usually advisable to work within a budget. Budget items would include: cost of renting the facility, refreshments, and sundry items that may be consumed or rented.

Will you or someone else create the agenda for the event? The program may include time for registration, networking and introductions, followed by the main event – speaker(s) and topic(s). If there is time for refreshments, either before or after, this can be listed on the program, as well.

The registration process may include having attendees pick up their preprinted name badges, paying a fee, and picking up an agenda and any handouts related to the event.

Prior to the event, the critical pieces that need to be confirmed early in the planning process are the venue, the date, and times. Once this has been achieved, a program document such as a brochure – either paper or electronic – can be created, and invitees notified. The program should list the name of the event, the location, date and times, and the name(s) of the speaker(s) and the topic(s).

You will need to determine, in advance of the event, whether any speaker will be making a presentation that will require more than a stage and podium. Any audio-visual presentation may require some combination of microphone, laptop, projector, and projection screen.

TIP: Always try to bring a company-owned laptop and video-projector to the event: renting them can be quite expensive.

Whether the meeting is held on premises or off-site, signage that directs attendees to the room where the event is taking place will prove very helpful.

Seating arrangements may also play a major part in the event planning. If attendees will need to take notes, it may be best to have a classroom arrangement with tables and chairs. Otherwise, a theater-style seating arrangement -- simply rows of chairs -- will work fine. If the talk is arranged around a meal, seating attendees at round tables for the meal portion of the program will work; after the meal, chairs can be turned around so that all attendees are facing the speaker.

If you obtain the speaker's bio and a topic synopsis, you will be able to provide this information to the master of ceremonies (MC) to use for the purpose of introducing the speaker. The MC's duties may also include welcoming the attendees, making sure that the program is running on time, and thanking the speaker and attendees at the end of the presentation.

If attendees are allowed to pre-register for the event, preferably via an online registration system or service, the organizer will be able to collect any applicable fees, as well as the data necessary to get a count of attendees for seating and refreshments, and to have printed name badges ready.

Extended Business Event: An extended event, one day or longer in duration, generally requires a much longer planning timeframe. You may need additional help, so establish a small planning team; at some point in the process you can start to distribute tasks among its members.

The number of venues capable of accommodating a longer event may be limited. You may need to contact several facilities in order to determine which of them are available on the date(s) of your choice. Make plans for your committee to visit the top contenders to get a first-hand feel for the facilities and their meal arrangements. Your final decision will be based on a winning combination of the facility's ability to meet your key requirements, and at an acceptable price.

For a longer-duration event, you will be working with a correspondingly larger budget. In addition to all the key elements listed for the Brief Event, you will be dealing with multiple speakers (including possibly opening and closing keynote speakers), multiple topics, a longer agenda, meals and breaks, overnight accommodations, sponsors, give-aways, and door prizes.

Your committee may have to work on several aspects simultaneously. While you are scouting a suitable location, you will also need to identify and confirm your speakers and topics. Good opening and closing keynote speakers are more difficult to come by, so it is best to locate and confirm them as soon as possible. Some speakers will require fees, and you will have contracts to distribute and sign.

Once the speakers are confirmed, request their bios and topic synopses. These can be used in the program, for marketing communications, and by the moderators on the day of the event to introduce the speakers. Ask speakers for: their preference of morning or afternoon session, Day 1 or Day 2, whether they will need any audio-visual equipment for their presentations, whether they plan to stay for lunch or spend the entire day at the event, etc. Will they need overnight accommodations, rides to and from the airport, etc.?

The subjects of registration and seating arrangements have already been covered in the section on Brief Business Event, and are equally applicable here.

You will have to make detailed arrangements for several meals (as well as breaks) when planning a longer event. You may wish to assign a committee member to work with the venue's catering manager, and then make recommendations to the committee on menu selections and prices. (In your event budget, remember to add tax and gratuity to the meal costs.) The catering contract may require you to call in the final attendee counts for each of the meals a few days before the actual event.

You may wish to assign a moderator for each speaking session, whose duties would include: introducing the speaker, watching the clock and providing appropriate cues so that the speaker concludes on time, thanking the speaker at the end of the session, making any gift or monetary presentation, and announcing the next session scheduled in that room.

You will need to spend a lot of time, before, during, and after the event, communicating with all the parties who are critical to its success. This includes: invitees, attendees, speakers, the venue staff, committee members, and your upper management.

You may choose to broaden the scope of the event by incorporating a trade show, product or service demonstration, or a facility tour during the course of the event. If you do, that would need to become part of the program, and arrangements would need to be made for them.

Event sponsors may help defray some of the event expenses. In exchange for picking up the tab for a breakfast, lunch, or speaker fee, they may be able to make a sales pitch during the event, or have their company name featured on a sponsor board or on the event program.

It's a nice, practical touch to provide a pad of writing paper and a pen for each attendee. Some venues provide a pitcher of ice water and glasses at each table. In a large facility, provide attendees a facility map. At each room entrance, provide signage showing the speaker's name and topic title.

You may wish to budget for give-aways and door prizes for attendees, as well as some sort of remuneration (or gift cards) for the speakers.

If attendees wish to stay overnight, provide information in the registration packet on available hotels in the venue area. Let attendees make their own hotel room reservations.

You may choose to budget time after the business meeting for a social gathering and continued networking opportunities. This could be at the event venue or at a nearby restaurant or bar for the convenience of attendees.

Have attendees complete and turn in an evaluation survey before they leave at the event's conclusion. This will give you a good indication of how they felt about the facility, food, speakers, topics, etc. Moderators can provide gentle reminders to attendees to have surveys completed as the event progresses. FMFG

Expanding a Facility

Favorable market conditions, a booming business projection, or a recent or planned acquisition may give rise to a need for additional space within your facility.

You will have to project how much additional space you will need in order to accommodate your company's expansion plans. This projection will have to be over a future timeframe of about three to five years.

If you are currently leasing space, approach your landlord or leasing agent to discuss the situation. If your current lease includes a clause regarding rights to additional space – whether contiguous or not – within your current building, he may be able to offer you a few options. He may need to take down or modify your present demising wall in order to effect the expansion. Your lease will need to be amended to take into account the additional space and all the other relevant factors, such as the total new space under lease, new monthly rent, new lease termination date, etc.

If the landlord does not have vacant space within your current building, he may offer you additional space in another building that he controls. He may also have to consider whether to relocate another existing tenant in order to make space for your expansion within your present building.

In a more radical alternative, the landlord may offer you all the space you need – to meet your current and projected needs – in a totally different building (also under his control). In this scenario, should you decide to accept it, you would need to plan for a move of your entire facility. It may require a major remodeling of the proposed space, as well. You may want to ask for price concessions when negotiating a new lease. (Please see our chapter, "Leasing a Facility.")

Once you have established where your expansion space will be, it will need to be laid out for your future needs. You'll have to negotiate with the landlord regarding the cost of any needed build-out, although he will probably give you an allowance within which he would expect you to retrofit the space to meet your needs.

In the newly expanded space that you now control, cubicles may need to be reconfigured, along with any power, voice, and data cabling associated with them. Additional furniture and equipment will need to be ordered.

The expansion/construction process is complicated by the fact that you have to accomplish it while your staff is working in close proximity to the area where the expansion work will be progressing. Clearly, you need to work with a team, and perform the transformation creatively so as to minimize disruptions. The team would consist of representatives from departments affected by the expansion, as well as space planners, various construction trades, the cabling company, and the furniture installer.

If your expansion has been achieved through a relocation to a new facility, you will need to communicate the move to several groups of stakeholders, including employees and customers. Your suppliers and service providers need to be notified – by letter, phone call, e-mail – that your facility is relocating, and the effective date of the move. Utility services – electricity, water, gas, telephone – have to be initiated. Finally, deliveries – including mail and packages – would have to be redirected to the new address. FMFG

Facility Handbook

The purpose of a facility handbook is to communicate the policies, procedures and processes that relate to the physical workplace.

Policies: These are the defined courses of action in areas that are administered by the facility management organization for the sake of expediency and consistency.

Processes: These are the services that facility management provides to building occupants and the means by which they are provided.

Procedures: These are the specific instructions related to how employees can access the various services provided by facility management.

Subject headings that are typically found in a facility handbook may include, but are certainly not limited to:

- Archives
- Artwork
- Conference rooms:
    - Reservation policies and procedures
    - Room set-up requests
    - Room clean-up
    - Policies for food in conference rooms
    - Equipment requests and operation
- Projectors, whiteboards, etc.
- Cafeteria service
- Coffee and beverage service
- Central filing

- Contacts within the facility management organization
- Emergency response plan (the employee handbook could include this, or it could be referenced and published separately in a "Quick-glance" brochure.)
- Ergonomics
- Furniture:
  - Typical furniture in workstations
  - How to request additional furniture or workstation accessories
  - How to get furniture repaired or replaced
- Fitness center:
  - Hours of operation
  - Employee use of
  - Locker policy
  - Towel policy
  - Safety
- Janitorial:
  - Expectations of what the cleaning staff does
  - Duties of the day porter (if there is one)
  - Reporting spills and other cleaning-related accidents
  - Special requests
  - Clean desk policy
- Life safety
- Mail service:
  - Access to mail (delivered to desk, mail slots, etc.)
  - Incoming
  - Outgoing
  - Postage
  - Mailing supplies
- Maintenance requests
- Moves/adds/changes
- Office protocols:
  - Speaker phones

- Conference rooms
- Food
- Eating at your desk
- Privacy
- Coffee service
- Dirty dishes
- Kitchen policing
- Personalizing offices and workstations
- Housekeeping
- Music and radios
- E-mail (may be governed by HR or management)
- Internet use (may be governed by IT, HR, or management)
- Inter-cubicle conversations
- Meetings (designated meeting rooms, etiquette)
- Cell phones
- Office supplies:
  - What the company provides
  - How to request items
- Parking:
  - General parking
  - Reserved parking policy (None, executive, employee of the month, car or van pool, hybrid vehicles, etc.)
  - Handicap parking
  - Visitor parking
  - Drop-off areas
- Indoor plants
- Purchasing (if it's FM's responsibility)
- Records management
- Recycling (what and how)
- Security policy:
  - On-site security staff
  - Parking lot security (stickers or dashboard permits)

- After-hours security
- Security badges
- Replacement badges
- How to request a badge
- Is there a fee?
- Visitors/guests:
  - How to sign them in
  - Escort policy
- Card readers and building access:
  - Normal hours
  - After-hours
  - Strangers in the building
  - What to do if you see a security issue
- Shipping and package handling:
  - Outside services: (UPS, Fed Ex, etc.)
  - Drop-off locations and times
  - Packaging and mailing supplies
- Workspaces:
  - Who gets an office and who gets a cubicle
  - Office and cubicle sizes.
- Personal items (radios, fans, space heaters, etc.)
- Decorations (calendars, sports memorabilia, plants, etc.)

The facility handbook should enable employees to find answers to their questions quickly. The format of the handbook should make topics easy to find, with content organized in short paragraphs or bullets. Busy employees will not read long narratives, and if they can't obtain their answer quickly, they will call or e-mail you, thereby negating the purpose of the handbook.

The facility handbook should be introduced to employees and reviewed with them at their new employee orientation. The handbook can be distributed to each employee in hardcopy format, or via the company's intranet. FMFG

Facility Planning

Facilities support the work of your company's employees. The employees are responsible for doing the things that help the company meet its strategic objectives and be successful. According to the International Facility Management Association's 2007 Forecast Report titled, "Exploring the Current Trends and Future Outlook for Facility Management Professionals," the top trend is to link facility management to strategy. The report goes on to say: "Since IFMA's formation and early research into the roles of facilities and facility management professionals began, it has been clear that a critical facet of successful facility management is the ability to link the role of facilities to an organization's core business strategies. In the coming years, we believe this will be of even greater importance. Physical facilities can have a large role in determining productivity, supporting innovation, efficiency, employee satisfaction and public perception of an organization. Every dollar invested in improving and maintaining facilities must be analyzed for return on investment (ROI)." To that extent, as the facility manager, you will be required to participate in, and/or initiate, various planning initiatives.

Facility planning is a general planning discipline that incorporates different types of planning processes that cascade down from the overall business strategy of the company. The progression of these processes is as follows:

- Strategic Facility Planning
- Master Facility Planning and Master Facility Management Organizational Planning
- Tactical Planning

(Please see our chapters, "Strategic Facility Planning," "Master Planning," "Tactical Planning," and "Space Planning and Programming.")

One of the core competencies of the facility management profession is planning and project management (Please see "What Is Facility Management?" and our chapter, "Project Management.") There are two parts to the planning process: Development of the plan, and its execution. It is in the execution where most plans fail. Plans must be constantly revisited and adjusted, based on both external conditions (e.g. economic downturns) and internal ones (e.g., new management team). Without incorporating flexibility into the planning process, success will be difficult to achieve. FMFG

Finance

When justifying projects to senior management, it is necessary to prioritize them based on criteria that are rational, objective, and meaningful, and conveyed in a language your managers understand. Finance is the language of business. Following are some financial definitions and examples to help you along in the process:

Average Rate of Return

The Average Rate of Return (%) = Average Net Income x 100/Average Investment

The average investment is the average of the initial cost of the investment and its salvage value. In the table below, you would select Investment B, with the higher average rate of return.

	Investment A	Investment B
Cost	$5,000	$7,000
Salvage value	$1,000	$1,000
Average investment	$3,000	$4,000
Average net income	$500	$700
Average rate of return	16.7%	**17.5%**

Average Payback Period:

Average Payback Period (years) = Net Investment/Average Annual Cash Inflow

In the example shown below, you would select the project or investment with the shorter average payback period, namely Investment A.

	Investment A	Investment B
Net investment	$3,000	$8,000
Avg. annual cash inflow	$1,000	$2,000
Average payback period	**3 years**	4 years

Actual Payback Period:

Actual Payback Period (years) = Investment/Annual net cash flow

This method uses the same data as the average payback period analysis, but calculates an actual payback time. Select the investment with the shorter payback period.

Net Present Value (NPV):

This method determines the dollar value, at time zero, of a series of future cash flows, discounted at the company's cost of capital. It measures the future expected benefits (cash flows) against the initial investment. It recognizes the time value of money. All cash flows over the life of the investment are converted to present-value (PV) dollars. In comparing investments, you would choose the one with the higher NPV.

Net Present Value (NPV) = Present value of future cash flows – Net investment

	Investment A	Investment B
Net investment	$9,000	$10,000
Savings each year	$2,500	$3,600
No. of years with savings	4	4
Discount rate	10%	10%
PV of future cash flows	$7,925	$11,412
NPV	($1,175)	$1,412
Preferred investment		**Investment B**

Some factors that can complicate your calculations are Salvage Value and Depreciation. Salvage value should be considered a cash inflow and converted to present value. Depreciation is not a cash expense; however, it does tend to reduce tax owed. Hence, depreciation times the tax rate should be converted to present value for each year that depreciation is taken.

Internal Rate of Return (IRR):

Internal Rate of Return is the discount rate assuming an NPV equal to zero. In order to use this method, you need the initial investment, future cash flows, and your company's cost of capital. Next, the IRR is calculated for all competing projects, and the one that has an IRR greater than the company's cost of capital is selected.

Benefit-Cost Ratio (BCR):

Benefit-Cost Ratio = Value of benefits of the project/Costs of the project.

Both costs and benefits are stated in same-year dollars. This presumes that dollar values can be assigned to all benefits. A project may be selected if the ratio exceeds a certain predetermined value, but seldom if it is less than 1.

For a more detailed analysis of cost justification tools, see *The Facility Management Handbook* by David Cotts and Michael Lee. FMFG

First Aid

In any workplace, accidents will invariably happen. The best that you can do is to be prepared to provide timely aid to the injured party until help, in the form of emergency medical service (EMS) workers, arrives.

The essential components of a good workplace first aid program consist of:

- Buy-in from management.
- Involvement of employees.
- A safety analysis of the workplace.
- Control and prevention of hazards.
- First-aid training for your staff.

You should be able to identify and assess the risks at your particular workplace that could lead to injury or illness to fellow workers. Next, design and implement a first-aid program with a goal to minimize the outcome of injuries, provide a stock of suitable first aid supplies and equipment, and in quantities appropriate to the size of your workplace, and train workers as first aid providers as needed, as well as arrange for ongoing refresher courses. Prompt and properly administered first aid can stabilize the sick or injured person, and can mean the difference between a rapid recovery and a prolonged one, or possible permanent disability or even death. (See: www.osha.gov.)

It is important that you consult with your local EMS provider as you design your program. Ask them what their typical response time is to reach your facility.

OSHA standards may require that you provide CPR training to select staff: this may help keep the victim alive until professional help arrives.

Develop a list of items for your facility's first aid kit based on the types of injuries that are most likely to occur. Consider upgrading your first aid kits if your workplace has unique or changing first aid needs.

Because of the risk of Sudden Cardiac Arrest (SCA), many workplaces have chosen to invest in Automated External Defibrillators (AEDs). These devices, now widely available, are a safe, portable and effective means of delivering an electric shock to the fibrillating heart of an SCA patient, and help it return to normal. Before setting up an AED program, however: assess your workplace need for such a device; consult with a physician; coordinate your program with the local EMS; be sure to follow applicable local, state, and federal regulations; set up a quality assurance program; and establish a schedule of periodic reviews.

Workplace first aid training programs are offered by the American Red Cross and the American Heart Association, among others. Attend a program that is tailored to your facility's needs.

A workplace training program should ideally be based on the latest scientific evidence. Trainees should be able to practice skills through working with live partners and with mannequins. Have adequate first aid supplies and equipment available. Emphasize the need for quick response in emergency situations.

As you prepare to respond to a health emergency, prevention is an important strategy in reducing injuries, illnesses, and deaths. Learn the importance of personal protective devices – masks, protective glasses, gloves, and the proper disposal of contaminated articles. Work in conjunction with your local

EMS. Keep a list handy with contact information of the nearest clinic and hospital, in case of an emergency.

Training should include handling of non-life-threatening emergencies (wounds, burns, insect stings, eye injuries, and broken bones) as well as life-threatening situations (treating an unconscious victim, rescue breathing, use of CPR and AED, and controlling bleeding).

In order to retain the critical skills that have been learned in the first aid arena, it may be necessary to have follow-up training in AED and CPR every six months. Re-training for non-life-threatening emergencies should take place periodically; for life-threatening emergencies, at least once a year.

Finally, it is important to put your first aid program in writing and disseminate it to all employees so they understand that if they get sick or injured, help will be forthcoming. FMFG

Additional Resources

- Please see our chapter, "Emergency Preparedness."
- www.redcross.org

Fitness Centers

The "wellness" trend has been around the corporate world for several decades now. The daunting challenge for the company that has the best of intentions for its employees' health and well-being has been the expense of establishing a physical fitness center on the premises, equipping the center, and then maintaining it.

Office buildings and companies see the on-site fitness center as a way of attracting and retaining valuable employees, while at the same time making it possible for them to conveniently work out and relieve stresses accumulated during the day, and provide an environment outside the workplace to get together. A corporate fitness center is perceived as a valued amenity. (See: www.wbdg.org.)

Such an on-site facility may consist of one or more rooms with associated toilet, shower, and locker-room facilities. The typical indoor fitness program can be divided into four categories: warm-up/cool-down, free-weight, circuit training, and cardiovascular. Each category will dictate its needs for special flooring, sound-absorption, and HVAC requirements.

Many of the activities may require cushioned training surfaces, impact-resistant walls, and mirror-walls. Since this area may get a lot of use, finishes should be durable and easy to maintain. In the weight areas, you may need to provide sound absorption or baffles, especially if they are adjacent to another tenant's space. You may also wish to employ measures that reduce moisture and the migration of odors: fitness centers are usually maintained at a negative air pressure relative to the rest of the building. Also check with your local building authority to determine whether you may need to install a monitored closed-circuit TV for your fitness center, and have an Automated External Defibrillator (AED) on the premises.

Fitness equipment may be purchased or rented. The equipment may consist of gym equipment and weights; in addition you may opt for an open space for group floor exercises. The hope, from the employer's point of view, is that employees working out will experience fewer sick days and lower health insurance costs, resulting in happier employees and higher morale. Since employees spend so much time at the workplace, time spent at the on-site fitness center would be a natural and convenient extension of the work day, and eliminate the necessity of commuting to an off-site fitness center at the end of the work day. Today, while many companies may pay for their employees' partial or full membership in a local fitness center as part of their fringe benefit package, only a small percentage include corporate gyms. FMFG

Additional Resources

- www.the-invisible-gym.com

Fleet Management

Fleet management refers to the management of your company's vehicular fleet. The fleet may consist of cars, vans, and trucks. It is most economical and effective to set up a single pool of fleet vehicles, rather than individual fleets for each department, branch office, etc. The number of vehicles in the fleet would be the determinant as to how sophisticated a management system you might choose to employ.

Typically, fleet management includes vehicle acquisition, financing, registration, maintenance, insurance and scheduling, through eventual disposal. (Please see our chapter, "Insurance.") It also includes driver, fuel, and safety management. If your company's core business is unrelated to vehicular fleets, you may not need vehicle tracking systems and their associated software, and it may be worth your while to investigate using a fleet management company to manage your fleet needs. (See: www.mikealbert.com.)

For a small fleet of vehicles, you may choose to manage the process internally. Company policy should dictate who is eligible to use a "company car." This group might consist of top executives as well as the sales team. Each of these positions could be provided a fleet vehicle on a long-term basis. If there are other individuals who may have occasional need to travel on company business, it may be worthwhile to provide them the temporary use of a "pool car" for a period of a few hours up to a few days for this purpose, rather than rent a car from an agency. Company policy may establish the size or class of vehicle, or a monthly dollar limit, for each position level.

TIP: In your selection of vehicles, you may wish to consult industry standards or other reports that list low-maintenance (high-predicted-reliability) vehicles, so as to reduce maintenance headaches down the road.

You will be responsible for acquiring vehicles, registering them, and assigning them to all the staff scheduled to receive them. Pool-car use would need to be set up on a scheduling system of your choice, which would show which vehicle was charged out to which employee and for what time period. You would also need to manage scheduled maintenance, as well as take care of cleaning and repairs (when needed). At the appointed time, you would be responsible for the disposal of the used vehicle. As an aid to drivers, you may wish to create a simplified list of fleet policies, accident-reporting procedures, helpful hints ("Return the vehicle with a full tank of gas.") and useful phone numbers to call in case of an on-the-road emergency. This list, in the form of a card or fold-out brochure, could be left in each fleet vehicle's glove compartment, along with a proof-of-insurance card.

When it comes to a larger fleet of leased vehicles, a fleet management vendor should help you to:

- Budget accurately for a stable, predictable fleet expense.
- Reduce any incentive for drivers to falsify their vehicle mileage reporting.
- Ensure that vehicles driven by your employees are properly insured with reliable insurance companies, and carry limits approved by your risk manager.
- Provide your drivers with safe, reliable vehicles that also help promote a positive image of your company.

- Provide you with information regarding how each vehicle will depreciate over the course of the lease.
- Minimize maintenance expenses through proper vehicle selection, maintenance program and replacement schedules.

They should also help you:

- Acquire new vehicles with zero or minimal cash outlay.
- Reduce sales tax expense, and take advantage of fleet incentives to reduce acquisition costs.
- Place all orders for new vehicles at the same time, but have them delivered only when needed.
- Process registration renewals without getting you involved.
- Simplify the resale process by taking that function out of your list of duties.
- Ensure that vehicles are regularly serviced by a network of approved, ASE-certified mechanics, and that no unnecessary repairs are made.
- Monitor fuel purchases, mileage reports and maintenance expenses for the fleet as a whole.

If your company chooses to manage its vehicle fleet, your purchasing or finance department should issue company credit cards to employees to use for routine vehicle expenses such as fuel.

So, whether you have a vehicle fleet of a few vehicles or a hundred, using one of the systems recommended above will help you manage the fleet and keep your expenses under control. FMFG

Food Service

W hy is food service included in a facility management book? As David Cotts points out in *The Facility Management Handbook*: "Food and facility services are inextricably intertwined. Capital costs for food service facilities are high. Food products soil carpets and furniture. Food preparation areas have high maintenance costs." We might add that food service is also one of those services that management doesn't quite know whom to make responsible for. When that happens, it tends to land in the lap of the facility manager.

There are several methods of providing food services:

- Full service
- Prepared off-site
- Carry-out and fast food
- Catering (for meetings, after-hours events, other special events)
- Private dining rooms with table service
- Vending service

Full Service – Full service requires a preparation kitchen, food storage (dry, cold, frozen), and serving and dining areas. A full-service operation is typically run by an outside food service. If you lease space in a building and a full-service cafeteria is provided, the landlord most likely has contracted the service with a professional food services firm. If you own the building and you choose to offer a full-service cafeteria, it will be your responsibility to contract with an outside provider. There are both local and national companies that provide these services. A full-service operation will typically offer soups, salads, a cold and hot deli, hot entrees, and full beverage service. It may provide a breakfast menu, as well.

Prepared Off-Site – In this scenario, a food service provider prepares food off-site and delivers it to your building on a daily basis. The type of facilities and equipment (if any) that you need will depend on the type of food being served. For example, if the vendor is providing only packaged meals (box lunches, wrapped salads, fresh fruit, etc.), you may need to provide no more than a small serving area, or the vendor may provide the display cases and check-out station, and you may need to provide only the space and electricity. On the other hand, if the vendor is offering warm entrees, you would need to provide warming tables and/or microwave ovens.

Carry-Out and Fast Food Service – This is a hybrid of the previous two types of operations. It typically consists of a full kitchen with a very limited dining room or none at all. Or it may consist of a limited cooking operation (deep fryer, microwave oven, warming oven, panini maker, soup warmers), refrigerator, a serving counter and check-out station. It could be operated by a fast-food chain franchise or a local deli.

Catering – Regardless of whether you provide any of the services above, there will be situations where the company conducts lunch meetings, special business meetings, or after-hours events that require some type of catered food service. This could range from a continental breakfast to a box lunch or a hot entrée. In some companies, the department sponsoring the meeting or event is responsible for ordering, delivery, set-up, and clean-up. In that case, it would be well to have a policy in place that outlines the responsibilities of the department ordering the catering. As facility manager, you would need to be notified in advance of any special requirements, such as an extra table or extension cords (to accommodate warming plates). Sometimes, catering is the responsibility of the facility manager, who will contract with a local deli or restaurant. Any department that requires catering for a meeting or event must then go through the facilities department, and order from a pre-negotiated menu.

Private Dining – Although no longer as prevalent as it used to be, some companies have private dining rooms with table service for executives, high-level client meetings, employee recognition events, etc. This is typically associated with a full-service food operation.

Vending Machines – The least expensive food service is provided by vending machines. Very little effort is required: typically the only infrastructure needed is a water line, standard electrical outlets, and floor space for the vending machines. Vending machines are usually located in an employee cafeteria or break room.

Whatever you decide to provide your staff by way of food service, you will need to contract with an outside food service vendor. You will need to develop a service level agreement and incorporate it into a Request for Proposal so that you can solicit bids from several vendors. (Please see our chapters, "Service Level Agreements" and "Contracts and Proposals.") Even in the simple case of vending machines, expectations must be set as to: how many machines will be on site, what they will dispense, how often the machines are replenished, response time for service calls, etc. Some of the up-front issues that you will have to deal with in a full-service operation are: who builds out and pays for the space needed to house the operation and the equipment; and who maintains the equipment and the space.

It would be advisable to research the overall costs of the potential types of food service your company is willing to offer, and present those budget costs to management for its feedback. Working with a budget, you can then survey your employees to see what type of service they would be interested in, and willing to support.

You should put service level agreement metrics into place, so that the food service operation can be measured to ensure it is providing the service that was contracted for and that daily customer traffic is what was projected. Your company will have to decide up-front whether to subsidize the food service, or whether the food service vendor will be fully responsible for its own profit and loss. In the latter case, the food service contractor will develop a pro forma based on a mutually-agreed-to number of customers over a given period of time. It is not untypical for the contract to have milestone dates at which times the financials are reviewed, and if the food service vendor is not making the projected profit due to lagging customer traffic, the contract can be modified, re-negotiated, or even terminated. FMFG

Furniture

To say office furniture is a necessity is an understatement. Our offices are full of different types of furniture, serving different needs. The facility manager is usually responsible for a company's furniture. The duties involved often include: selection, purchase, installation, and maintenance of the company's inventory of furniture. Furniture also makes up a considerable amount of the annual facility management operating and capital budgets.

Commercial office furniture can be divided into four categories: case goods, systems furniture, filing/storage, and seating. Case goods are free-standing pieces of furniture such as desks, credenzas, cabinets, bookcases and tables. They are most often used in private offices and conference rooms, training rooms, cafeterias, lobbies, and reception areas. Case goods are either made out of steel or wood. Desks are usually the main working surface in a private office. The credenza is a narrower unit that usually sits behind the occupant and provides additional work surface and file-storage space. Often, there is also a unit that is situated perpendicular to the credenza and desk. This is called a bridge unit. It can be a free-standing cabinet or simply a work surface that connects desk and credenza, and is often used to support the employee's laptop or computer monitor.

Systems furniture is a series of modular components of interconnecting demountable panels, screens, desks, shelves, and other components that fit together in a somewhat flexible but predetermined set of patterns and combinations forming workstations. Systems furniture usually includes provisions for integrating electrical, voice, and data cabling within the panels. Sizes and configurations are seemingly endless. Ever since the cubicle was invented in the 1960s, modern offices have consisted primarily of systems furniture. According to the International Facility Management Association's (IFMA) Benchmark Report #28 of 2007, office spaces are made up of 34% private offices and 66% open office (mostly systems furniture).

The major benefit of cubicles utilizing systems furniture is that they are less expensive than private offices made from studs and drywall. In addition:

- They are flexible and can be disassembled, and then moved or reconfigured.
- The wide array of available components facilitates workstation customization.

The panels that form the workstations are typically fabric-faced. The inside of the panel is made of sound-absorbing materials. The panel edges and raceways are usually metal, but can be trimmed in wood for a more traditional or higher-end look.

The components that constitute the inside of a systems workstation include: horizontal work surfaces typically made of high-density particle board with a plastic laminate surface, and a plastic laminate, rubber, or vinyl edge; overhead bins for storage, that can be opened or closed using a flipper-door; under-counter storage such as a multi-drawer pedestal file or two-drawer lateral files; larger free-standing filing cabinets; and possibly a wardrobe unit.

Filing and storage includes filing cabinets and storage cabinets. The three main types of filing cabinets are lateral files, vertical files, and pedestals. Lateral files are 30 to 48 inches wide, 18 inches deep, and contain from two to five file drawers. They are called lateral files because filing is accomplished from left to right. They can accommodate standard or legal file folders. Vertical files typically come in two widths to accommodate either standard or legal-size filing. They are typically 15 to 28 inches deep and contain two to five file drawers. Vertical files are used when wall space is at a premium. Lateral files can typically accommodate 30% more filing than a vertical file cabinet. Vertical and lateral files are made of steel. Sometimes they include wood drawer fronts. In some cases the entire unit may be made of composite wood with wood veneer facing.

Storage cabinets are upright free-standing units with or without doors. They are most often used in storage rooms, mailrooms, file rooms, and copy rooms. They come in a variety of heights and widths.

Simply put, seating consists of the chairs we use in the office. The chassis of the chair is typically constructed of steel, plastic, or a combination of both. The seating surface and seat backs are typically leather, vinyl, fabric, or plastic. There are many different types of chairs, including: executive chairs, desk chairs, task chairs, side chairs, stacking chairs, training room chairs, conference room chairs, and lounge chairs. Executive and task chairs typically have a five-star pedestal base with castors, as do many conference room and training room chairs. Most of these chairs, at a minimum, have a pneumatic seat-height adjustment. Chairs have many other types of adjustments, as well. (Please see our chapter, "Ergonomics.") Stacking chairs are generally inexpensive plastic or fabric-covered chairs that can stack on top of each other for easy storage. They are typically used in large meeting rooms that are configured theater-style, as well as in cafeterias and break rooms. They may be used as side chairs, as well. Stacking chairs and side chairs are available with a four-leg base or a sled-base design.

Lounge chairs resemble the comfortable furniture used in residential living rooms. They are typically used in lobbies, waiting areas and guest lounges.

In planning a new office, furniture will be one of the first things you will address after the space plan has been completed. Unless you are an experienced space planner, it is best to engage a professional space planner or interior designer to plan the type of furniture that will best suit your office. Most contract furniture dealers (furniture vendors that specialize in commercial furniture) have space planners on staff, and will offer space planning services. Contract furniture dealers do not carry all brands of furniture. They are typically a primary dealer for one of the major systems furniture manufacturers and a few case goods manufacturers.

There are two ways to select and purchase furniture. In the first method, your first step is to prepare a generic furniture plan. If you do not have the experience to do this yourself, you should hire a professional space planner or interior designer. A good designer or space planner will inquire about the specific functions of each of your spaces, then develop a generic space plan that will describe the type of furniture and the configuration for each space. Next, you must prepare a Request for Proposal (RFP). (Please see our chapter, "Contracts and Proposals.") The RFP will be sent to three to five contract furniture dealers. The RFP should ask for specifications of the type of furniture that they are recommending for each space, the price of the furniture in each space, a furniture plan showing how their furniture will fit into your space (it could differ slightly from the generic plan that your space planner developed), the discount (off list price), the total cost for the furniture, and finally the cost of installation and the proposed installation schedule. The lead time on furniture delivery may be anywhere from 4 to 12 weeks. You should also request that the furniture dealer include the standard discount off of the list prices that appear in the furniture catalogues.

TIP: Never pay list price for commercial office furniture. A typical discount is 35% off list price, and can go as high as 70%, depending on the availability of the furniture and the size of the order. What you pay for commercial office furniture is *always* negotiable!

The second method is to prepare a Request for Qualifications or RFQ. (Please see our chapter, "Contracts and Proposals.") Here you are requesting the qualifications, experience, and furniture lines carried by the contract furniture vendor. You should include an electronic floor plan of your space and a written description of the function of each space. (Please see our chapter, "Computer-Aided Design and Drafting (CADD).") If you have furniture standards in place, you should include these, as well. (Please see our chapter, "Space Planning and Programming.") The vendor's response should include: their qualifications, a furniture plan demonstrating how they would outfit your space based on your written specifications, their discount level on the furniture they are specifying, and their installation cost based on a percentage of total furniture cost. This will help you select a vendor. Once you have made this decision, you can finalize the furniture plan and negotiate final pricing. FMFG

Hazardous Materials
and Waste

Whether you realize it or not, hazardous materials may be lurking in your building. A facility may have hazardous materials and waste issues specific to the type of business being conducted in it. According to the U.S. Environmental Protection Agency (EPA), a waste is any solid, liquid, or contained gaseous material discarded by being disposed of, burned or incinerated, or recycled. For example, bio-waste will be found in most healthcare facilities. Compressed gases may be found in a laboratory. The most common types of hazardous materials found in any type of building today are: asbestos, lead paint, and cleaning products.

Asbestos is a naturally occurring fibrous mineral. Because it was fire-resistant, resistant to many chemicals, and an excellent insulator, asbestos was added to a variety of building materials and other products prior to 1981. Although this is by no means an exhaustive list, generally, any of the following materials installed before 1981 may be presumed to contain asbestos:

- Sprayed-on fire proofing and insulation in buildings
- Insulation for pipes and boilers
- Wall and ceiling insulation
- Ceiling tiles
- Floor tiles
- Putties, caulks, and cements (such as in chemical carrying cement pipes)

- Roofing shingles
- Siding shingles on old residential buildings
- Wall and ceiling texture in older buildings and homes
- Joint compound in older buildings and homes
- Plasters
- Brake linings and clutch pads

For example, what we today refer to as vinyl composition tile (VCT), was called vinyl asbestos tile (VAT) prior to the 1980s, because it was composed of vinyl with an asbestos material mixed in.

If the asbestos has not been disturbed or is not located in an area where it could be disturbed, it does not present a health risk. It is when the asbestos fibers are knocked loose and become airborne and ingestible or inhalable that they pose a clear health risk. Over the long term, asbestos can cause asbestosis, lung cancer, and mesothelioma. In the case of the VAT, if it is intact and firmly attached to a floor in a light-to-moderately trafficked area and there is little chance of it being disturbed, there may not be any need to remove it. However, the best approach when asbestos is identified, is to encapsulate or abate it. If asbestos is discovered as a result of a remodeling or renovation project, the work must stop immediately and proper remediation of the asbestos must be implemented.

There are three ways of reacting to the presence of asbestos: Do nothing, encapsulate it, or remove it completely (also referred to as abatement.)

If the asbestos material has not been disturbed to the point of the fibers becoming airborne, and it is located in an area that will likely not be disturbed, it is perfectly acceptable to leave it in place. However, you should note it on your master floor plans so that if the area is ever renovated or in any way disturbed in the future, you will have a record that asbestos is located in the area, and that it will have to be dealt with.

Encapsulating means covering the material with a protective coating. A good example would be installing broadloom carpeting over VAT.

Abatement means getting rid of it. A licensed abatement contractor must be engaged to perform the abatement. The area must be sealed off from adjacent areas, whether they are fully occupied or not. The HVAC system must be shut off so as to prevent any of the asbestos particles from escaping into other areas of the building.

Upon discovery of asbestos, you should document how you found it, its location, its nature (VAT, pipe insulation, fire proofing, etc.) and your reasons for choosing one of the three strategies to mitigate it. You should also notify your property insurance company. If you find asbestos and choose to keep it in place, you should notify your local fire department of its location and nature.

Lead paint is often found in older buildings and poses a health risk when it peels and disintegrates. When it is found in older homes, the risk is that children may ingest it and suffer long-term health problems.

Other hazardous materials often found in office buildings are the **cleaning products** that the janitorial service uses. They can be harmful if spilled, splashed, and ingested, or if fumes from them are inhaled. Some cleaning products available today are environmentally safe. You may want to contact your janitorial service about employing a "green" cleaning program in your building. (Please see our chapter, "Janitorial Services.")

If you store any chemicals in your building, you are required by law to have a Material Safety Data Sheet (MSDS) on file for each chemical. According to IFMA, MSDSs are concise summary documents intended to provide workers and emergency personnel with the critical information necessary for the handling of each chemical, as well as proper treatment of workers who may be exposed to each chemical. MSDSs present standardized information such as physical data (melting point, boiling point, flash point, etc.), toxicity, health effects, first aid, reactivity, storage, disposal, protective equipment, and procedures for handling leaks or spills. You should also make your local fire department aware of the types and locations of all chemicals stored in your building.

When dealing with any type of hazardous material situation, whether a chemical spill or an asbestos abatement project, it is important that you communicate to the occupants of the building the nature of the event and the steps being taken to mitigate it. If you lease space, it is advisable to have language written into your lease regarding notification to you by your landlord or property manager in the case of a hazardous material incident, as well as evidence that a documented hazardous material emergency plan is in place. FMFG

Additional Resources

- For an example of an MSDS, please see our website: www.cormarkpublishing.com/Resources
- www.Epa.gov
- http://web.princeton.edu/sites/ehs/workplacesafety/asbesto sfactsheet.htm
- http://gsishare.com/ifma/FMpedia/index.html

Image and Ambiance

Psychology plays a key role in the design of a workspace. Similar thinking should pervade the design of an entire building. Several factors go into the creation of an image or ambiance. A lot of it may be related to first impressions, which is why creating the right ambiance can be so important. How does your facility's image relate to the image of the product or service your company provides? That is a key decision your management needs to make. (Please see our chapter, "Company Culture.")

Image is the sum total of people's perceptions of the organization. It's a psychological reaction that results from everything that the company does, whether good or bad. It encompasses everything from the look and feel of the product, the customer service, corporate communications in all its forms (corporate logo, letterhead, brochures, website, ads, and commercials) as well as other physical touch points where the company interacts with the public – its buildings, vehicles, personnel, and their uniforms.

Identity as a corporate asset needs to be guarded, maintained, and upgraded (as needed). Internally, a good image enhances staff morale and recruitment. A good corporate image can help improve sales and launch new products as customers associate the cohesiveness with success.

How does a space look and feel when you first step inside it? How do all your senses react, including those of sight, sound, and smell? Does the space look attractive? Is it warm and friendly, or cold and aloof? Is it traditional or contemporary? Is it bustling with noise, or quiet and comfortable? How are visitors and employees greeted when they step in through the front door? These factors can have a major impact on a potential customer's decision to do business with you, or to continue doing business with you. This may be their very first impression of your company. Do the various physical elements presented to a visitor or employee harmonize perfectly into a cohesive ensemble?

The appropriate specification and use of lighting, music, wall coverings and floor coverings can create an effective workplace ambiance. Studies have shown that an effectively and appropriately designed work environment can increase employee productivity, while the knowledge that an employer has cared about the employees' workplace can result in improved employee retention.

Various shapes, sizes, and even colors can influence employees working in an office environment. Square desks and tables convey a formal environment. Round or oval shapes denote a sense of collaboration. Stuffed chairs and couches with low (or no) tables, denote a relaxed, informal atmosphere.

Another trend that has already made its way into the office environment is how color may be used to affect mood and productivity. An effective use of color may tie in brand identification (company logo and letterhead) with the use of the same colors throughout the facility to create a cohesive whole. This sends a subtle signal to customers that the company is well-managed and successful. The brand manifests itself in the physical workplace. FMFG

Additional Resources

- www.smallbusinessnotes.com

Insurance

For most small- to medium-sized businesses, the responsibility of securing insurance coverage may fall to the corporate Risk Manager. It is highly probable that the Risk Manager will in turn be working with an insurance agent. You may be asked to assist the Risk Manager by providing various pieces of information, or updates to values provided a year earlier. Listed below are the typical insurance policies and coverages that a business may seek to purchase.

Commercial General Liability: If you purchase only one form of business insurance, it would most likely be Commercial General Liability. It covers four basic categories of business liability: Bodily injury, property damage, personal injury (including slander and libel) and advertising injury. It includes the cost to defend and settle claims. This insurance covers operations and premises, contractual obligations, leases, etc. You should look for limits of at least $1 million per occurrence and a general aggregate of $2 million.

Building coverage: This coverage is typically written on the replacement cost value on buildings. Factors that are involved are: construction type, occupancy, number of stories, value, fire protection class, and area. If a building is over 30 years old, the insurer may ask for information on updates (if any) to HVAC, electrical, plumbing and roofing. Pay special attention to Flood and Earthquake coverage, as well as Equipment Breakdown coverage.

Contents: This covers the value of business personal property, and equipment and machinery. Property of Others coverage would cover the value of your customers' property that is in your possession on your premises or at a job site, or the accidental damage of customers' equipment in your care.

Computer Equipment: Separate Electronic Data Processing (EDP) coverage is often written to cover computers, servers, media, routers, switches, telephone equipment, and any other technological items. Very often, Mechanical Breakdown coverage is sold with this coverage.

Business Auto Coverage: This would cover any company-owned fleet vehicles (cars, vans, trucks, etc.) used in the business. It reimburses you for stolen or damaged vehicles, or if a driver injures another person or damages other's property. Hired & Non-Owned Vehicle Liability coverage will cover rental vehicles, as well as personal vehicles used by employees on business or for running company errands.

Equipment Floater: This includes coverage for forklifts, golf carts, and mobile machinery that can be taken off premises. Employees' tools can also be covered under this policy.

Workers Compensation: This covers employees' medical and disability expenses caused by work-related illness and on-the-job injuries. Coverage is based on class of business, number of employees, and estimated payroll.

TIP: Make workplace safety a top priority. Initiate safety programs to try to prevent or reduce workplace accidents. This will reduce the number of Workers Compensation claims, and lower your premiums. FMFG

Additional Resources

- www.smallbusiness.findlaw.com
- www.techinsurance.com

International Facility Management Association (IFMA)

The benefits of belonging to a professional association are numerous. In addition to giving you the opportunity to network with your peers, the association serves as:

- An added resource to help you in your profession.
- A source of professional development and continuing education.
- A source to become certified in your profession.

That's why organizations like the International Facility Management Association (IFMA) are so important. IFMA represents, supports, and unites the largest community of facility management practitioners, consultants, educators, students, and product and service providers in the industry.

Through research efforts, educational programs and resources, professional certification, a network of chapters and councils, and global professional development events, IFMA assists facility managers in developing strategies to manage human, facility, and real estate resources.

IFMA's goal is to lead the advancement of facility management by:

- Supporting a community that fosters vitality, momentum, and impact for the facility management professional.
- Anticipating and prioritizing the resources required to enhance effective delivery of products and services.

- Inspiring passion for the facility management profession that compels facility practitioners to want to join the IFMA network, engages volunteer leaders, and attracts/retains top talent to its full-time staff.
- Sustaining IFMA's financial integrity to achieve and fulfill its mission.

Representing more than 19,500 members, IFMA focuses on leading and sustaining the progress of the profession, while also advancing the careers of individual members. IFMA members hail from more than 65 countries and a variety of specialized areas within the facility management profession. The diversity that characterizes the IFMA community enriches members' learning and networking experiences.

IFMA members have a voice in more than 125 chapters and 15 industry and interest-specific councils. Chapters allow you to interact with other workplace professionals locally. Councils provide focused networking with peers in specialized areas of FM. These groups within the IFMA community bring association resources directly to you, making your membership experience more personal.

IFMA offers on-line continuing education, best-practices conferences, and certification processes that lead to the Facility Management Professional (FMP) designation and the Certified Facility Manager (CFM) designation. IFMA also holds the annual World Workplace conference, the largest facility management conference in the world.

Other facility-related organizations are:

- Building Owners and Managers Association (BOMA)
- Association of Facility Engineers (AFE)
- Society of American Military Engineers (SAME) FMFG

Additional Resources

- www.ifma.org

Janitorial Services

Janitorial service is one of the most frequently outsourced facilities services. The common exceptions to this rule are public schools, higher-education facilities, and hospitals, all of which often have in-house cleaning staff. However, these institutions are increasingly turning to outsourcing in order to decrease costs. In most other situations an outside commercial cleaning service is contracted to provide janitorial services.

Owned Space – If you are the facility manager in an owned space, it will be your responsibility to contract with the janitorial service.

Leased Space – If you occupy a leased space, how you negotiated the lease agreement will dictate whether it is your responsibility or the landlord's to contract a janitorial service. For example, in a full gross lease the cleaning service would be included, while in a triple net lease it would not.

It is often less expensive to include janitorial services as a part of your monthly rent. The landlord may have a lower rate with the cleaning contractor based on the volume of space that the contractor is covering. For example, the landlord may contract a janitorial service to perform the cleaning of your entire building, as well as other buildings that he owns, in order to achieve economies of scale.

If you choose to contract with a different janitorial service, your price may be higher because you have less space. You will also need to provide storage space within your suite for the contractor's supplies and equipment. However, if you choose to contract with the janitorial service that cleans the common areas of your building, you may be able to negotiate the same rate that the property manager is paying.

Another situation where you may want to pay directly for janitorial service is if you desire more or less cleaning than the janitorial service is providing through your landlord. Lastly, if your company owns or leases spaces in other buildings, and you have an agreement with a janitorial service to clean all of those other spaces, then adding your space to the mix may result in a more competitive price than what your landlord might offer through your lease.

Janitorial services include routine or regular cleaning, periodic cleaning that occurs at regular but less frequent intervals, and one-off special cleaning.

Routine Cleaning – Routine cleaning is typically performed on a daily or weekly basis. Daily cleaning may include:

- Vacuuming traffic areas (excluding under desks and tables).
- Dusting horizontal surfaces up to 42 inches high.
- Emptying trash bins and recycling bins.
- Cleaning bathroom fixtures (sinks, toilets, and urinals).
- Cleaning horizontal surfaces and sinks in kitchens or break rooms.
- Replenishing paper towel and liquid soap dispensers, toilet paper, and coffee stations.
- Mopping hard-surface floors.
- Cleaning glass at entryways.

Weekly or monthly cleaning activities might include:

- Vacuuming under desks and tables.
- Dusting higher horizontal surfaces (e.g., tops of cubicle panels and overhead storage bins, file cabinets, book shelves, etc.).

- Cleaning interior glass panels.

Periodic Cleaning – Periodic cleaning occurs less frequently, such as quarterly, twice a year or annually. Periodic cleaning may include:

- Stripping and refinishing hard-surface floors.
- Carpet cleaning.
- Window washing.
- Under-floor vacuuming, such as in a computer room.
- Deep cleaning.

Special Cleaning – Special cleaning is most often the result of a specific incident such as a roof leak, or cleaning after a construction project.

Day Porter Services – If your facility is densely occupied, you may want to consider a day porter. This person, provided by your janitorial service, is on-site during normal business hours – as opposed to the regular cleaning crew which typically cleans after hours. The day porter's duties may include:

- Glass-panel cleaning at visible areas like entry lobbies.
- Policing cafeterias, kitchenettes, or break rooms.
- Replenishing consumable supplies such as paper toweling and toilet paper.
- Light cleaning of bathroom fixtures (sinks, toilets, urinals).
- Mopping or vacuuming lobbies and vestibules, especially during the winter in northern climates when people track in snow and ice-melting salt particles, since ice melt can be very damaging to interior floor surfaces.
- Cleaning common touch surfaces, which may help decrease seasonal illness among building occupants.
- Emptying common area trash bins that get heavy use.
- Changing burned-out light bulbs.

- Shoveling snow from entryways.

The day porter may work a regular 8-hour day, or you may choose to have the person work part-time through the lunch hour.

Evening Cleaning – Generally, cleaning is performed after hours Monday through Friday, typically with part-time labor. Using part-time labor is more cost effective because fringe-benefit costs are reduced or eliminated.

If your facility is located in a downtown market, your cleaning service may be required to employ full-time unionized labor. The most common union for janitorial employees in the United States is the Service Employees International Union (SEIU).

Daytime Cleaning – A movement that has gained limited popularity is daytime cleaning with full-time staff. The advantage of daytime cleaning is that your lights are not turned on in the evening to accommodate the cleaning crew, thereby reducing your energy cost. You may also be able to turn off your building's air-handling system sooner. Another advantage is that you can deal with cleaning crew problems as they occur, rather than calling the service upon finding a problem the morning after it happens. Daytime cleaning also helps in that it is visible to the occupants and may reduce complaints of "perceived lapses" in services.

The main disadvantage of daytime cleaning is the disruption, especially the noise of vacuuming, that the services can cause to occupants. To avoid this, many janitorial companies use non-electric carpet sweepers, like those found in restaurants. These carpet sweepers do not effectively remove soil, which may lead to premature carpet wear. Some facility or property managers schedule daytime cleaning so that the cleaning crew vacuums and cleans restrooms either before or after building occupants arrive or leave, but this decreases the benefit of reduced energy costs. Other concerns include chemical sensitivity of building occupants, and fraternization between building employees and the cleaning staff.

Green Cleaning – The effort to 'green' our buildings and conserve our resources is becoming more common today. As noted above, daytime cleaning is considered one pathway to a green or sustainable cleaning program. Other components of green cleaning can include:

- Using cleaning products that are not harmful to human health or the environment. There are a number of certifying bodies for cleaning products, such as Green Seal and EcoLogo/Environmental Choice.
- Training the cleaning staff in the proper dilutions of concentrated cleaning solutions, or using a metered chemical dispensing system.
- Ensuring that the cleaning staff follows the building recycling guidelines.
- Using cleaning equipment that reduces water and chemical consumption (auto-scrubbers) or uses filtration to capture particulate matter (vacuums and buffers).
- Specifying use of recycled content toilet paper and paper toweling.
- Incorporating use of micro-fiber in your cleaning program to decrease use of chemicals.

The U.S. Green Building Council's LEED – EBOM (Leadership in Energy and Environmental Design – Existing Building Operations and Maintenance) certification system is an excellent resource for implementing a green cleaning program.

Materials and Supplies – Typically the janitorial service is responsible for providing all of its own equipment and supplies, with the exception of consumable supplies such as paper toweling, toilet paper, soap, air fresheners, can liners, etc. Most cleaning companies can provide these items to you at an additional charge, which may be less than what you would pay elsewhere because they are purchasing in large volume. Regardless of who provides the equipment and supplies, you will need to provide one or more housekeeping closets for storage.

If cleaning materials are stored in your building, a binder of Material Safety Data Sheets (MSDS) must be kept on file. MSDS contain information as to the make-up of hazardous chemicals, and safety instructions in case of a spill, ingestion of chemicals, eye splash, etc. Your cleaning company will provide this information.

Communication with the Cleaning Staff – Typically, cleaning companies provide a Log Book for communication with the facility manager. This Log Book may be used for different purposes, such as advising the cleaning crew of special events or a recent carpet stain. Likewise, the cleaning crew may want to notify the facility manager if there are maintenance concerns, or if there is an area they were not able to clean due to occupants being present, or if they need disposable supplies provided by you. You can also use the Log Book to track attendance of the contract cleaning staff.

You may want to require that your cleaning contractor have at least one person on site each day who is able to communicate proficiently in English to ensure that you are able to relay your questions and concerns. It is also a good idea to require your contractor to use the U.S. Department of Homeland Security's eVerify system to ensure that the staff in your facility is legally able to work in the United States.

Certifications – One way to ensure that you are working with a reputable, professional cleaning company is to look for one that is certified. The Worldwide Cleaning Industry Association (www.issa.com) has developed the Cleaning Industry Management Standard (CIMS) and CIMS-GB

(Green Building) as a way to help facility managers and others responsible for selecting a cleaning service gain an increased level of confidence in their contractor by using it as a powerful pre-qualification tool.

The CIMS assessment covers five areas of best management practices: Quality Systems, Service Delivery, Human Resources, Health/Safety and Environmental Stewardship, and Management Commitment. The Green Building designation is the optional sixth dimension of CIMS, and it defines the processes, procedures, and supporting documents that are universally recognized as the features of a well-managed, successful cleaning operation with a proven commitment to sustainability.

Franchise-Based Janitorial Services – If you chose to work with a franchise-based cleaning company, be very careful about the termination language in the contract. Since franchise companies resell your account, they tend to make their contracts extremely difficult to terminate. It is highly recommended that you strike their termination verbiage and change it to "Either party may cancel this agreement for any or no reason, with a 60-day written notice."

Hiring a Janitorial Service – The first thing to do when hiring a cleaning service is to write a scope of work to reflect the cleaning services you want done on a regular or periodic basis. For example, you may choose to vacuum only traffic areas every day, and vacuum more thoroughly once a week. The next thing to do is to establish specific service level expectations. For example, you may require the cleaning crew to dust horizontal surfaces, but only if the horizontal surface (such as a desktop) is not covered in papers or personal items.

The result of this exercise is a formal service level agreement (SLA) which will become the basis on which you will measure and evaluate the janitorial service's performance. Measurements must be fully understood and mutually agreed to by both parties. The SLA can become part of the Request for Proposal, as well as the final contract. (Please see our chapter, "Service Level Agreements.")

The request for proposal (RFP) is a document that delineates the SLA and includes other general conditions such as: cause for termination, insurance requirements, contract terms, etc. Ask for references from owners and facility managers where the cleaning service has performed, in a building similar to yours. (Please see our chapter, "Contracts and Proposals.") Also, consider including a pre-qualifier to help you winnow down the field of bidders to a manageable level. When you send out the RFP, include specific information about your facility, including square footages and flooring types.

You may want to engage in a multi-year agreement with the janitorial service and lock in future pricing. It may be less expensive since the janitorial services provider knows that he has a contract with you for a given number of years. However, there should be clear language that spells out when, why, and how the contract can be voided if the contractor's performance consistently fails to meet the mutually agreed-to SLA. At the end of each quarter, meet with your janitorial service representative and review the vendor's performance. The contract should be re-bid every three to five years. FMFG

Additional Resources

- Building Service Contractors Association International: www.bscai.org
- *EcoLogo:* www.ecologo.org
- *Green Seal:* www.greenseal.org
- United States Green Building Council: www.usgbc.org
- Worldwide Cleaning Industry Association: www.issa.com
- Please see our chapter, "Leasing a Facility."

Landscape Maintenance

L andscape maintenance is one of the most frequently out-tasked services. It is rarely performed by in-house staff. K-12 schools, higher-education facilities, and healthcare facilities are examples of the most common types of facilities that have in-house landscape maintenance staffs. In most other situations, the landlord will contract with a commercial landscaper to provide those services. If you lease your space, landscape maintenance will be the responsibility of the landlord and will be factored into your rent.

Landscape maintenance typically includes:

1. Roads, parking lots, and sidewalks:
   * Sealing
   * Crack-filling
   * Striping of parking lots
   * Gates and fences
   * Snow removal
2. Landscaping and grounds:
   * Turf-cutting
   * Routine grounds clean-up
   * Tree-pruning
   * Hedge- and bush-trimming
   * Fertilization
   * Thatching and aerating
   * Annual and perennial flower planting and care
   * Seasonal clean-up
   * Irrigation and irrigation system maintenance

3. The effort to "green" our buildings and conserve our resources is thankfully becoming more common today. Many companies are striving to make their sites more sustainable. There are many ways to do this, such as:

- Limiting dark, paved surfaces that soak up heat.
- Limiting turf areas to reduce fertilization, irrigation, and fuel consumption and pollution (from lawn maintenance equipment).
- Limiting annual flowers and other decorative plantings, and increasing low- or no- maintenance plantings common to your geographical area.

If you want to implement a sustainable site program, visit the U.S. Green Building Council's website (www.USGBC.org) and download the rating guide for LEED-Existing Buildings, Operations and Maintenance (EBOM) certification. You will find information in the section titled "Sustainable Sites."

Hiring a Landscape Service – The first thing to do when hiring a landscape service is to write a service level agreement or SLA. (Please see our chapter, "Service Level Agreements.") You must determine what kind of services you require and with what frequency. For example, you may choose to mow turf areas only when the grass reaches a certain height. And you may require snow to be removed only if it reaches or exceeds 2 inches in depth. Snow of less depth would require only a laying of snowmelt substance. The SLA should clearly spell out your expectations.

The main reason to institute a formal SLA is that it will serve as the basis upon which you will measure and evaluate the landscape contractor's performance. Measurements must be fully understood and mutually agreed to by both parties. The SLA should be part of the Request for Proposal and the final contract. (Please see our chapter, "Contracts and Proposals.")

The request for proposal (RFP) is a document that delineates the SLA and includes other general conditions such as cause for termination, insurance requirements, length of contract, etc. You should ask for references from owners and facility managers from sites similar to yours, where the landscaping service has performed. (Please see our chapter, "Contracts and Proposals.")

You may want to initiate a multi-year agreement with the landscape service and lock in future pricing. It may turn out to be less expensive since the landscape contractor knows that he has a contract with you for a given number of years. However, there should be clear language that spells out when, why, and how the contract can be mutually voided at any time. At the end of each quarter, you should meet with your landscape contractor's representative to conduct a performance review. You should re-bid the contract at least every three years. FMFG

Leasing a Facility

Companies either lease or own their buildings. A lease term can be as short as one year. However, most leases are signed for three, five, ten, or more years. So it is important that you include everything in your lease that you will need to operate and manage your space properly. Before entering into a lease, there are many issues you must first address, such as:

- Determining where the space will be located.
- Identifying what kind of space will be needed to best support the work performed by the people occupying it.
- Deciding how much space you will actually need.

The location of your space will be dictated by your employee base (Where do your employees live now?), your market, and the image you wish to convey. Understanding this will save time later because you will not search in geographical areas that do not meet your business needs no matter how attractive the spaces may look. Your search will also be more focused, and less of a shotgun approach. For example, if you determine that you are currently located in a geographical area appropriate for your business and your employee demographics, you wouldn't want to move so far away as to significantly increase your employees' daily commutes. On the other hand, if you need to be in a better market, with more visibility and a more appropriate image, your company may even choose to relocate to another city or state. This of course raises its own work force and public relations challenges.

Concurrent with determining where the space should be located is the process of identifying what kind of space is needed. This process is called qualitative or functional space programming. It will help you understand what type of space and space plan will best support the work your employees do. For example, if you are an open and collaborative environment, you may want a bigger floor plate that is open, with many different kinds of spaces within it, to allow people to do different kinds of work during the course of the day. (Please see our chapters, "Space Planning and Programming" and "Architectural and Engineering Services.")

Once you know what kind of space you need, you can determine the amount (in square feet). This is referred to as quantitative programming. The quantitative program should tell you the various spaces and rooms that will constitute your space and their net square feet. Once the total net square feet is known, you can apply a grossing factor to ascertain the gross square feet needed. The qualitative and quantitative programming should be done by a facility management consultant, a professional space planner, an interior designer, or an architect. (Please see our chapter, "Architectural and Engineering Services.") A mistake made at this stage could easily turn into a long-term problem.

Once you know how much space you need, the type of space, and its desired location, your company should conduct a lease-versus-own analysis. There are as many advantages and disadvantages to leasing a building as there are in owning one. Some of the main factors that play into a lease-versus-own analysis are:

Financial Impact

For many companies, leasing is an advantage because of the lighter financial impact on their bottom line. If the building is purchased or built (new), the company would carry the amortized cost over the life of the building as a depreciated cost.

Control

If your company owns the building, you have total control over its operation and maintenance. You are in charge of everything from security to cleaning, and you establish the expectations and requirements that you deem to be best for your building and its occupants. When you lease, you have control only over the space you're leasing. Everything else is the landlord's responsibility. He makes the rules and calls the shots. This is where the lease becomes very important because you can negotiate for control over facility-related items that affect you. For example, you might negotiate to have parking spaces reserved for your employees. Or, you might negotiate that the utilities supplying your space are metered separately, so that you are only paying for what you use.

Flexibility

A lease situation allows you more flexibility. If your company grows or shrinks over time, you can negotiate a larger or smaller space when you renew the lease. In an owned building, you're stuck with what you've got, so you either have to build an addition or find supplemental space, should you outgrow your building. If you downsize, you're still paying to manage and operate the empty space within your building. You can negotiate things into your lease that will increase your flexibility, such as a right of first refusal on adjacent space that becomes available. Or you can negotiate the right to sublease any or all of your space should you need to downsize.

The lease-versus-own analysis is a team effort. In addition to the architect whom you may already have on board, you'll need a real estate professional familiar with the local real estate market, someone from your company's finance department to crunch the numbers, and a general contractor to estimate construction costs.

Just as with any professional consultant, you should do your homework when engaging a real estate broker. You should research local and national brokers and talk to others who have recently gone through this process in your geographic area. You should prepare an RFQ for potential brokers to respond to. (Please see our chapter, "Contracts and Proposals.") Real estate brokers typically do not get paid up-front. Once the deal is consummated, a commission is paid, which is usually split between the landlord's broker and your broker.

You should meet with your real estate broker and review the qualitative and quantitative programs so that he or she understands specifically what type of building and what kind of space you need, and what geographic areas in which to conduct their search. If you included the broker in the lease-versus-build analysis, he or she should have a good idea of what you need.

Next, your broker should show you several properties that meet your requirements. So it helps to start the site-search process early.

TIP: When searching for a new building, you should start the process as early as possible. Lease negotiations can drag out over several months. Just building out the space can take six months or more, depending on the size of the space and the extent of the build-out. Start the process at least a year before your current lease expires.

You should develop a list of the very basic criteria that a potential site must meet in order to be considered. Once a short-list has been developed, prepare a more detailed set of selection criteria and prioritize each one based on importance.

Once you short-list your choices, form a team to tour the short-listed buildings. A qualified mechanical engineer should be engaged to assess heating, ventilating, air conditioning, electrical, and plumbing systems. If it's an older building, you might want to employ a structural engineer to look at the roof and the building façade. If they are in need of repair, you may feel the effects both physically and financially during the term of your lease. You may also want to bring along representatives from your IT, Marketing, and Human Resources departments, as well. They may all provide valuable input from their vantage points.

Once a building is selected, the lease negotiations begin. The first thing you and your broker must do is submit a Letter of Intent to the landlord. This document demonstrates that you are serious about leasing the building and want to begin negotiations. The letter of intent should include all of your specific requirements, such as amount of space, type of lease, specific parking requirements, etc. Some of the critical factors to think about in a lease are:

- Square footage lease rate (base rate)
- Common area maintenance (CAM)
- Holdover rights
- Assignment/Sublease rights
- Monthly rent
- Extension options
- Cancellation rights
- Whether you are leasing any other properties from this landlord

TIP: When negotiating a lease it is important to know the core factor of the building. The core factor is the common-area square footage that is not leasable. This includes: elevators, lobbies, fitness center, common circulation, loading dock, etc. The cost to operate these spaces is apportioned to each tenant based on the percentage of the total square feet they occupy in the building. The core factor could be as low at 5% or as high as 20%. It is the difference between usable and rentable square feet. If you find from your programming effort that you need 10,000 square feet and the building's core factor is 10%, you will actually be paying for 11,000 square feet.

The two most common leases are the gross lease and the triple-net lease. In a gross lease your monthly rent includes everything from maintenance and utilities to property taxes. In a triple-net lease, your monthly lease cost includes only your base rent. You will be responsible for all other costs associated with your space.

TIP: When you are quoted a lease rate, it is important to know if it is based on a gross lease or a triple-net lease. The dollar difference between the two can be quite significant. You must know this in order to be able to compare one property with another.

The lease negotiations can be conducted by you, your broker, or your company's attorney. If you have little or no experience in negotiating leases, it is best to rely on a professional. A broker can help you only so far. He can negotiate the terms of the lease on your behalf. But because a lease is a legal and binding document, when it comes to a final review of the lease, your attorney should review it. If your company's attorney is a business lawyer, he may not be as familiar with real estate legalities as a real estate attorney would be. Although attorneys are expensive, this is not the time or place to skimp. A mistake or oversight in a lease can have serious long-term consequences.

Leasing a facility is a major undertaking. Know the steps involved, start the process early, and employ project management techniques like you would for any other project. Develop a schedule and a budget. Understand your company's operational requirements. Conduct the process methodically. And if your broker gets impatient, show him the door. FMFG

Additional Resources

- www.cormarkpublishing.com/Resources

Life Safety

Your basic responsibility as the facility manager is to provide a safe and secure environment, whether you own the building or lease space as one of many tenants within a facility. If you own the building, you will be responsible for the maintenance and operation of life safety systems and occupant life safety planning and training. In a lease situation, you will be responsible for the planning and training portion, while the landlord will be responsible for the maintenance and operations of the life safety systems.

Federal, state, and local building codes stipulate the level of life safety systems you must provide in your building. There are two categories of life safety systems: passive and active.

Passive systems are ones that control ignition and limit the spread of fire. Examples of passive life safety systems are:

- Fire-resistant building materials and assemblies
- Physical barriers
- Compartmentalization (automatic shut-down of heating, ventilating, and air conditioning systems)
- Fire extinguishers
- Emergency egress routes, exit signs, posted evacuation maps

Active systems are those that initiate a direct physical action:

- Fire sprinkler system
- Smoke detection system
- Strobe lights and alarms

The National Fire Protection Agency is the foremost resource on life safety. In addition to having life safety systems in place, you will also be required to test your systems on a regular basis. Check with your local fire marshal for specific requirements.

You should also provide general life safety training for the occupants of your building. Such training includes building evacuation drills and responding to a medical emergency. Your employee manual should indicate the type of emergencies that could occur, and employees' responsibilities in each situation. This manual should be distributed to every employee and should be part of the new employee orientation program. (Please see our chapters, "Emergency Preparedness" and "On-Boarding.") FMFG

Additional Resources

- www.NFPA.org

Lighting

A s part of any new construction or remodeling project, your architect will produce a set of architectural drawings. One of the critical ones in this set is called the reflected ceiling plan. This plan, drawn at the same scale as the floor plan associated with it, with a vantage point somewhere above the ceiling, looks down at the floor through the ceiling. All the light fixtures (including emergency lighting and exit signs), as well as the typical ceiling grid, are shown on this plan.

Lighting can have a significant impact on your facility's ambiance, from the moment one steps into your lobby. (Please see our chapter, "Image and Ambiance.") Just as the need for aesthetics may vary in different areas of your facility, so should the lighting selected for each area. Ambiance is affected by all of the design aspects of the lighting system – fixtures of various sizes and shapes, the color of the light, and the way in which all the elements interact with the interior architecture of your space. By providing lighting in your workplace that is comfortable for, and controllable by, your staff, you help improve the ergonomics and morale. (See: www.lighting.com.)

In general, lighting systems consist of lamps, ballasts, fixtures, and controls. An integrated combination of fixture, lamp and ballast constitutes a luminaire. One way to look at lighting is to consider the effect it has on the surfaces that it illuminates. In an office setting, the work surface is the plane on which light level is measured; in aisles and hallways, it's the floor.

Direct lighting: Here, light comes down from ceiling troffers or pendants, or from furniture-mounted task lights, and reaches the work surface without reflection. On the plus side, direct lighting is efficient (none is lost in reflection), economical, and permits low ceiling heights. However, direct lighting creates problems such as glare, shadows and reflections. Troffers are recessed ceiling-mounted luminaires that shine the light downward. They generally measure 4 feet by 2 feet and feature large-cell parabolic aluminum louvers that keep glare under control without sacrificing efficacy. Prismatic acrylic lenses are a popular low-cost alternative to the parabolic louvers. However, the plastic lenses do not provide the best light dispersion and should be used only in non-work areas such as storage rooms, bathrooms, etc.

Indirect lighting: Here, light bounces off the ceiling, making *it* the brightest object, before it lands on work surfaces. It has the effect of making the space look bright, uniformly lit, and without shadows. Indirect lighting requires a ceiling height of eight feet or more, and the cost of materials and labor to install is generally more than that for direct lighting.

Direct/indirect combination lighting: This is obtained by light shining downward and upward in different proportions. People generally favor such a combination over purely direct or indirect light. With this type of lighting, where shadows are minimal, a ceiling height of at least eight feet is recommended. The cost approaches that of indirect lighting.

Diffuse lighting: The source for this lighting – such as fluorescent lamps – can be either direct or indirect. The result is nearly shadow-free lighting that is well-suited to office environments. Exclusive use of this type of lighting, however, can make the space look monotonous.

Concentrated lighting: This type of lighting works best where bright highlights, crisp shadows and a dramatic impact are sought. Such accent lights are very often track-mounted and adjustable for aiming at specific objects. Wall sconces also provide localized brightness, and are often used in lobbies, reception areas and conference rooms.

Task and ambient lighting: A well-designed lighting plan will incorporate a balanced blend of ambient, task, and accent lighting. Ambient lighting is that which illuminates the general area. Task lighting spreads light on the work area specifically. Accent lighting may be used to highlight areas or objects of interest within the space, such as pieces of framed art on the wall.

Lamps: This term includes both light bulbs and fluorescent tubes. Light output is measured in **lumens** and refers to the quantity of light generated. **Luminous efficacy** is measured in lumens per watt and refers to the efficiency with which the lamp converts electrical energy into light. Higher luminous efficacy translates into lower energy costs. The **average rated life** is that point in time, measured in hours, at which one half of a large group of lamps will eventually fail.

Lamp **color temperature** (the type of white) describes the apparent color of the light generated by a lamp. Warm color temperature is generally lower than 3,000 degrees Kelvin, while cool color temperature is generally greater than 4,000 degrees Kelvin.

Large lamps require correspondingly large fixtures and generate diffuse lighting. Compact lamps, on the other hand, use small fixtures and produce a more concentrated light effect. Incandescent lamps can generally be easily dimmed.

Office lighting is primarily generated by linear fluorescent lamps. They are inexpensive, produce good consistent color, have a long life and produce a diffuse light with high luminous efficacy. The types recommended these days are the T5 and T8 lamps (measuring 5/8 inch and 1 inch in diameter, respectively). These are supplanting the once-common T12 lamps. Compact fluorescent lamps are rapidly gaining in popularity because of their compact size, long life, and energy efficiency. Halogen lamps, generally used in special areas such as conference rooms, reception lobbies and executive offices, produce a whiter light with high efficacy, and are dimmable.

Ballasts are devices required to operate fluorescent lamps. Most ballasts specified and used today are electronic, which are replacing the older electro-magnetic variety. Electronic ballasts are compact, lightweight, use little energy, and produce little noise or flicker. Depending on the model, ballasts can operate from one to four lamps. Dimming ballasts allow for flexibility and control of lighting level, and can reduce energy consumption.

Lighting controls: Traditionally, lighting controls have been used to create the ambiance and mood within a space. Today they are used in conjunction with daylight and electric light sources to create a comfortable, high-quality, energy-efficient system. They are used in a wide variety of spaces, from open offices and private spaces to classrooms, conference rooms, and restrooms.

Benefits of Lighting Controls

Lighting controls can help reduce energy use in several ways:

- They can dim lights or turn them off, depending on the ambient light level.
- They can reduce the number of hours that lighting is left on in the course of a year.
- Cutting down light use reduces heat gain within the space, resulting in lower HVAC costs.

- They give building occupants the flexibility to turn down their individual lights, or turn them off when not needed.

In addition:

- In multi-purpose rooms, lighting can be adjusted to the right level through dimmers, when projectors are in use.
- Occupancy sensors can turn lights on and off when people enter a space or leave it, or when intruders are present.

Types of Lighting Controls

Standard on/off switches: These will turn lights on and off. In conjunction with relays, they can perform these operations on groupings of lights. One variation of this arrangement is to wire alternate lamps in each fixture to go on or off together on one switch, with the remaining lamps on a second switch. In another variation, fixtures close to windows can be wired as one group so that they can be switched off (manually or automatically) when daylight is plentiful.

Occupancy sensors: These may use one or more of several technologies, including ultrasonic, passive infrared, and dual technology. They are used in three general situations:

- To turn lights on automatically (or manually, in one variation) when someone enters a room.
- To keep the lights on as long as the room is occupied.
- To turn the lights off after a preset length of time once a room has become vacant.

A passive infrared sensor, generally installed in the same location as a standard on/off wall-switch, is triggered when a warm body passes in front of its "field of vision." This is ideal for a small private office or conference room.

Ultrasonic sensors emit an inaudible wave pattern that is triggered when a moving object interferes with the pattern. They are used in restrooms. Since they are sensitive to air movements, they should not be located close to HVAC vents, where they might be triggered by air currents.

Dual-technology sensors incorporate more than one technology and make for larger and generally more expensive devices. They help reduce false triggering of the lights (example: turning them off while a room is still occupied.)

Placement and settings of occupancy sensors are very important. Ceiling-mounted sensors can be set for 360-degree coverage or for an elongated hallway coverage; wall-mounted units can be set for a fan-type coverage pattern, as well. The units' sensitivity settings should be adjusted so that they do not pick up people movements from, for example, a room across the hall.

Manual dimming control: This permits occupants to control the light level within a room to meet their specific needs, and potentially save energy as well. A dimmer could be connected to a single luminaire or to a bank of lights, and the light level is then adjusted manually. Alternatively, fixtures can be wired in a pre-determined "scene" setting controlled instantly by a single button or switch. In some retrofit projects, it is possible to use remote infrared or radio frequency devices to control light-dimming, and reduce the cost of re-wiring.

Other controls: Photo-sensors can be used to turn lights (single or bank) on and off or dim them gradually, depending on the ambient light level. Another variation is to turn lights on via a photo-sensor, and turn them off with a clock time-setting. This is a practical solution for a floodlit building exterior. Centralized controls can be used to turn lights on and off as well as dim them, in a large conference room or in an entire building. (See: www.wbdg.org.)

Commissioning: This process involves the final adjustment, tuning, and calibration of the various elements of the facility lighting system after they are all in place and your staff has moved into the space. While this phase is sometimes ignored, or viewed as being too expensive, time-consuming and burdensome to perform, it is a crucial step in the occupancy of the space. When done correctly, it requires the participation of all the key players: the building owner, the lighting designer, manufacturer's rep(s), building maintenance staff, and the electrical engineer. (Please see our chapter, "Commissioning.")

The process may be as simple as burning in all the fluorescent tubes that are on dimmers, to a full-blown tryout of all the planned daily, weekly and holiday lighting schedules. Then, when this has been completed, the building maintenance team should be provided with all necessary documentation in order to maintain the lighting system going forward.

Economic analysis: It is not a simple task to do an economic analysis of a lighting control system: payback periods can vary all over the spectrum. Any analysis would need to take into account both energy savings and reduction in HVAC costs, balanced against the initial cost of installing the lighting control devices.

Energy efficiency: In lighting, energy is the most important life-cycle cost. It has been found that energy-saving technologies generally pay for themselves very quickly.

TIP: The use of compact fluorescents, electronic ballasts, optically efficient fixtures and well-designed lighting controls will all contribute to an energy-efficient lighting system. A combination of these various elements may also result in requiring fewer lamps or luminaires, thereby further reducing costs. Try to standardize on a small number of different lamps and luminaires, thus reducing inventory costs.

And finally, regular maintenance, including group re-lamping at about 70% of average rated lamp life, will further reduce operating costs. This is achieved through the volume purchase of a large quantity of lamps, followed by their installation by a crew working efficiently over a period of a few days. The result is a space that is uniformly lit with freshly-installed lamps. FMFG

Additional Resources

- www.ewweb.com

Mailroom

In a typical facility, the two main functions of a mailroom are to process incoming and outgoing mail. Incoming mail is delivered to the company mailroom, front desk, or building mail facility. It is sorted down to the department or individual level, then delivered to the individual's desk or to a mail slot, one of many in a central location. In a campus setting, the mailroom function will generally include delivering mail to all the buildings within the campus.

Outgoing mail is delivered before the end of the work day to the building mail facility, street mailbox, or post office. As a consideration to employees, personal mail may also be included in the outgoing mail, provided the employee has affixed the appropriate postage. Outgoing mail may include bulk mail sent out occasionally by the company, often at reduced rates.

Within a facility, the mailroom is generally best located close to a building or facility entrance. A windowless interior room will often suffice. Mailroom furniture may consist of free-standing work tables of the appropriate height for sorting incoming and outgoing mail. Mail slot arrangements would sit atop the work tables. The furniture layout should be conducive to the efficient production-line processing of incoming and outgoing mail.

An alternative, albeit less flexible, mailroom layout solution is built-in cabinetry, with counter-tops at the appropriate work height for ease of sorting incoming and outgoing mail.

For incoming mail, your equipment may consist of an electric letter opener, which can very rapidly slit open a large stack of incoming envelopes. For outgoing mail, an electronic postage scale is usually integrated with a postage meter and postage machine. This combination will weigh the mail, determine the appropriate postage, and stamp the postage on each mail piece as it runs through the machine. This machine will also seal the envelopes and stack them, ready to leave the facility in trays or bins.

In high-volume mailroom operations, you can use a folder-inserter. This machine can fold sheets of paper and rapidly insert them into envelopes before they run through the scale and postage machine combination. In addition, where mail needs to be picked up from and delivered to stations spread over a wide area within a building, a mail clerk will work more efficiently while using a mail cart. (Please see our chapter, "Office Services.")

TIP: To reduce the cost of postage on outgoing mail, wherever practical, consider reducing outgoing mail frequency. Instead of mailing every day, simply accumulate your customers' outgoing mail – in labeled mail slots or equivalent compartments – then consolidate the pieces and mail them out one, two, or three times per week in larger envelopes. FMFG

Managing a Facility

In an existing owned or leased facility, you (or the property manager) will have the responsibility of managing the facility. In the latter case, you would be responsible for reporting any facility-related problems to the building's property management company. Management of a facility would last as long as the remaining life of the building, which could span several decades. Ideally, plans for the operational phase of the building's life cycle should be laid out during the design and construction phases.

Facilities come in every size, and vary with each type of business and industry. Managing a facility may include responsibility for some or all of the following: HVAC, utilities, cleaning, vending services, electrical, plumbing, lighting, decoration, grounds care, and security. (Please see our chapter, "Building Operations and Maintenance.") Generally, these functions are not part of your business's core competencies, and may be considered support services.

Depending on the size of your company, lack of in-house expertise, and pressure to lower costs, it is not uncommon to have these services outsourced to an external company or to a number of companies, each specializing in one or more of the various facilities services enumerated above.

Listed below are the general categories of systems that need to be managed within a facility:

- Power systems: They include normal electric power, as well as emergency power systems such as standby generators and uninterruptible power supplies (UPS).

- Mechanical systems: HVAC (temperature control and indoor air quality), refrigeration, elevator maintenance, and systems maintenance (both preventative and predictive).
- Life & Safety systems: The sprinkler system, fire extinguishers (including halon, FM-200, etc. systems), evacuation plans, smoke and fire detectors, and building signage.
- Building systems: Security and locks, building monitoring, and building automation systems. (Please see our chapter, "Building Automation Systems.")
- Space management: Furniture systems, space layout and office equipment.

Managing a facility has been variously described as an exercise in "putting out fires" or moving from Plan A to Plan C between the time you leave your workstation and arrive at the scene of the "event". However, with a good understanding of your facility systems, and a plan for handling routine maintenance and out-of-standard events, it is possible to manage your facility effectively and efficiently.

Practice the art of "managing by walking around." If you do this 15 to 30 minutes before the majority of your staff arrives each morning at the facility, you may be able to "catch" several facility issues – the space is too hot or too cold; a flickering light; a noisy motor; a trash can left un-emptied from the previous night – before anyone else does, and you can initiate fixes before someone else interrupts your day with phone calls or e-mails to report these problems. Problems detected and quickly resolved eliminate bigger, more expensive problems down the road. And in the process, you become invisible within a smoothly functioning facility!

The purpose of preventative maintenance is to maintain equipment and facilities in satisfactory operating condition by conducting systematic (routine) inspections, and the detection and correction of incipient failures before they occur or develop into major defects. Further, it involves performing tests, measurements, adjustments, and parts-replacement so as to prevent faults from occurring. Corrective maintenance or repair is performed to get defective or non-operating equipment working again.

Predictive maintenance techniques help determine the condition of in-service equipment in order to predict when maintenance should be performed. This approach offers cost savings over routine or preventative maintenance, because tasks are performed only when warranted. Condition-based maintenance attempts to evaluate the condition of equipment by performing periodic or continuous (on-line) equipment condition monitoring. The ultimate goal of predictive maintenance is to perform maintenance at a scheduled point in time when the maintenance activity is most cost-effective and before the equipment loses performance within a threshold. This approach differs from routine preventative maintenance, where a piece of equipment gets maintained whether it needs it or not. Most predictive maintenance inspections are performed while equipment is in service, thereby minimizing disruption of normal system operations. Adoption of this type of maintenance can result in substantial cost savings and higher system reliability.

You should provide your facility staff with a list of maintenance vendors and their contact information. Such a list would typically include building maintenance, and telephone and cabling vendors. In addition, each office should be provided a list of numbers to call in case of an emergency.

Each facility should keep an electronic log of building-related problems that have been reported to the property maintenance team. This log will contain the date that the incident or problem was reported, a brief description, and the date it was remedied. Such a log can be very useful in analyzing a problem with the leasing agent following the incident, or to reveal how quickly the maintenance team responded to facility-related problems. For more information, refer to the book, *The Facility Management Handbook* by Cotts, Roper and Payant. FMFG

Master Planning

The master plan is a plan devised to meet specific objectives of the strategic plan. (Please see our chapter, "Strategic Facility Planning.") Master planning may be related to the actual physical facility assets or to the facility management organization that manages the facilities. When it is related to the physical facility assets, master planning may also be referred to as long-range facility planning or long-range capital improvement planning.

A master facility plan will map out the number of facilities, their size in square feet, and the geographical areas where they must be located in order to meet the objectives of the organization's overall strategic business plan projected over a given period of time, typically three to ten years. According to the book *Facility Management* by Edmond Rondeau, Robert Kevin Brown, and Paul Lapides, the typical strategic planning considerations to take into account when developing a master facility plan are:

- Acquisitions
- Expansions
- Curtailments
- New products or programs
- Product phase-outs
- Divestitures
- Plant phase-outs
- Plant relocations
- Consolidations

For example, if a company's business strategy is to grow in a new market, the master plan may stipulate that a new building of a certain size would need to be built or leased in the geographical location of the new market. Since there's a long lead time involved in locating and occupying space, the master plan would show this activity starting many months, if not years, before it needs to be completed. The master plan will also include high-level cost estimates so that funds can be budgeted at the appropriate time. Some of the items to be included in a master facility plan might be:

- Strategic objectives that need to be met
- Assumptions on which the plan is based, such as projected head counts and new market segments
- Real estate market analysis
- Specific requirements related to all facilities regardless of location (e.g., building class, urban vs. suburban, location near a freeway or airport).
- Image and character
- Building performance criteria
- Optimal floor plate configurations
- Amenities required
- Lease versus buy analysis
- Functional space program
- Space allocation standards

The master facility plan should include a standardized implementation procedure as well as site selection criteria. It should also include an overall schedule of major milestone events, and an annual budget. The next step, the tactical plan, is where the activities or tactics required to carry out each milestone event are described in greater detail. (Please see our chapter, "Tactical Planning.")

Business conditions change quickly, and visionary companies understand that they may have to adjust their strategies accordingly. The master facility plan should be reviewed at least annually, if not more frequently, and adjusted as necessary so as to continually support the company's strategic plan.

As is the case with the master facility plan, when the master plan relates to the facility management organization it should be an outgrowth of the strategic plan. Instead of addressing the physical facility assets, however, it would address such things as the organizational structure of the facility management function, the functions it will perform in-house versus outsourcing, and its size. For example, if a growing company that currently leases space for its corporate headquarters is going to double in size and build its own new corporate headquarters, the facility management department will likely be structured much differently than it would be for a leased space. It may be a much larger department that encompasses more non-facility-related responsibilities such as office services and security. (Please see "What Is Facility Management?") On the other hand, if the company's philosophy is to focus only on the core competencies required to run its business, most facility services would be outsourced, and the facility staff may then consist of a more-experienced facility manager, and an administrative assistant who would manage the outside service providers.

Once you understand the type of facility organization you'll need, you can develop the organizational master plan. Some of the other considerations when developing a facility management organizational master plan are:

- Learning and development requirements for staff
- Service level expectations
- Staffing levels and expertise
- Development and implementation of the internal processes needed for the department to function effectively

The master facility management organizational plan should also include an overall schedule of major milestone events, and an annual budget. The next step, the tactical plan, includes more detailed descriptions of the activities or tactics required to carry out each milestone event. (Please see our chapter, "Tactical Planning.")

Just as in the case of the master facility plan, the master facility management organizational plan should be reviewed at least annually, if not more frequently, and adjusted as necessary so as to continually support the company's strategic plan. FMFG

Meeting Spaces

Productive meetings can take place almost anywhere, including at the proverbial water cooler, in a coffee lounge, or on an escalator. Workspace design should include a variety of meeting spaces that encourage the productive generation and exchange of ideas.

Meetings may take place within your facility, or in rented meeting space (e.g., hotel or conference center). Meeting rooms vary in size and layout to support the work styles and the needs of the people using them. Ranging in size from very small to very large, meeting rooms may be classified as follows. (See: www.hq.com/meetingrooms.)

Quiet Room or Enclave: This may be a small (8 foot by 8 foot) room with a round table, small desk, or end table and two chairs, suitable for a one-on-one interview, or for employees to be able to perform heads-down work, or make and/or receive confidential phone calls away from their cubicles.

Medium Meeting Room: This may typically consist of an oval or rectangular 6-foot table, up to six chairs, and a white board or easel, in a 10 foot by 12 foot room.

Board Room: As the name implies, this is generally a larger upscale room (both in finish and furnishings) with a table to seat up to 12, and a wall-mounted conference board or pull-down screen for projected images.

Training or Conference Room: This is generally a larger room with seating for upwards of 20 people in theater-style (no tables) or classroom-style (with tables, permitting attendees to take notes). A variation is a U-shaped arrangement of the tables, which enables attendees to see each other while also permitting eye contact with the speaker.

Team or Project Rooms: These rooms are typically assigned to teams of people at work on a common project. The rooms may be assigned (dedicated) for the duration of a project (which could last days, weeks, or months at a time). Information pinned up on walls or written on whiteboards can stay up as long as the team needs them. The team rooms may be furnished with a combination of moveable tables and small open workstations.

Informal Teaming Spaces: These spaces within a department are in the open or surrounded by low cubicle panels. They are used for impromptu meetings and consist of a table, chairs, a portable whiteboard and easels.

It helps if the meeting space can be flexible so as to meet the diverse needs of the groups that may use the space. Each group can then reconfigure the room to best fit its needs. In addition to the traditional easels and whiteboards, rooms should have jacks that permit voice, data, and internet connectivity. Today's productivity tools include electronic whiteboards, which can be incorporated into the design of meeting spaces. If you require audio-conferencing capability, you will need a conference phone (with extension microphones for a longer table) and an assistant to help make the connections, or use a pay-by-the-minute audio-conference service. For video-conferencing, you will need at each location, in addition to the audio equipment, video equipment, a wall screen and the necessary jacks.

With web conferencing, you can conduct live meetings with people from all over the world, permitting all parties to have a simultaneous view of the same video or slide presentation, which can be recorded for future viewing.

Within a facility, meeting rooms need some kind of identification (naming) system to differentiate them. This could be something as simple as an alpha-numeric system (Conference Room A, B, etc.), or something catchy (Room with a View), humorous (Mushroom), or specific to your company (past company presidents' names).

TIP: Conduct a contest among your employees to generate the best set of meeting-room names.

You need to establish rules and procedures concerning the use of meeting rooms. Scheduling the use of each room might be accomplished through software such as Outlook. If food and drink are allowed within the rooms, you should include rules regarding cleaning up after the meeting is over. Print the rules on a card and post it next to the light switch. If furniture can be rearranged for one group's meeting needs, you need to establish the configuration that the furniture should be returned to when that group's meeting is over. There should be "a place for everything, and everything should be in its place" for the next meeting. (Please see our chapters, "Office Protocols" and "Audio Visual Systems.") FMFG

Additional Resources

- www.effectivemeetings.com/design/workplace

Moving a Facility

For moves of any significant size, it will be necessary to contract for the services of a professional commercial moving company. If a particular moving company has already performed a prior move to your satisfaction, it makes sense to use the same mover on other facility moves. If not, investigate the marketplace to find a mover who can conduct your facility move in an efficient manner and on the scheduled date and time.

Planning for the Move

In move planning, communication is key. Each group of stakeholders needs to know what is happening, when, and in some cases, why. These stakeholders include: company staff, customers, vendors, suppliers, utilities, and delivery services.

At least 10 days prior to the move, the moving company should provide a supply of moving carts that will be used to load items onto, as well as adhesive moving labels. (Moving cartons or boxes are used on a very limited basis in today's moves.) The shelves on moving carts are filled with the contents of offices, cubicles, file cabinets, etc. These can be rolled right into the moving truck and later rolled out into the new space. This saves the time and back-breaking effort of loading individual boxes onto dollies. Once loaded and marked with the appropriate label, carts are shrink-wrapped to prevent items from falling off.

Colored labels can be used for different zones or floors at the destination point. In addition, the moving company's representative should meet with the office staff and go over labeling procedures so as to help facilitate a painless move. The procedures should include the information that is needed on each label, the proper place to apply the label, the proposed start and end times for the move, and any other useful information and helpful hints to facilitate the move. To protect elevator cab interiors and wall corners during a move, make sure your moving company installs protective padding. Lobby and other expensive floors should be protected by sheets of masonite or other similar material so that they do not get marred by moving carts.

You need to recommend when to shut down the office on moving day. This may typically be around 2 p.m. or 3 p.m. on a Friday. After most of the staff has left the office, the moving company arrives, and under your general direction, the move begins. For any size move, it is recommended that one or more staff persons supervise the moving crew at the "origin" building (the space being vacated) and a similar team be located at the "destination" building (the space being moved into) to supervise the moving crew at that end. The two teams may communicate with each other via cell phone, since it is very likely that the phone system will have been taken down early on in the move schedule.

Murphy's Law has been known to apply during facility moves. There are too many things that can go wrong to enumerate here. Two are singled out for consideration. The weather could turn foul during your move. How would you handle that? What can you do to prepare for a snowstorm or a thunderstorm? The other issue is the building elevators, either at the origin or destination. How do you prepare for an elevator failure? One suggestion: Make arrangements prior to a major facility move to have an elevator service technician available on-call should he be needed. Horror stories abound with regard to unforeseen things that could go wrong. You cannot conceivably plan for everything, but you should be as prepared for the unforeseen as possible. As part of your contingency plan, prepare a list containing the contact information of all the key players associated with the move – moving company, cabling contractor, electrician, furniture installer, etc. This list will continue to serve you well after the move has been completed.

In any facility move, a certain portion of the furniture can be relocated and assembled prior to the actual moving day. For example, you could move conference room furniture early, as long as you communicate to your employees that conference space use may have to be curtailed prior to the move. The rest waits for the day of the move. To assist the moving company crew with the layout of the furniture at the destination location, you should post floor plans that show the furniture layout of each work space, as well as room or cubicle number, occupant's name and phone extension number.

In addition, it is helpful to temporarily identify each private office, room and workstation by posting individual (preferably colored, so they are visible from a distance) sheets of letter-size paper showing the workspace number, telephone extension number, employee name and network jack number. This will assist the moving crew, the telephone and cabling vendors, the team responsible for hooking up the PCs and printers, as well as employees (post-move, in locating their workstations).

You will need to decide when employees will be permitted to return to the facility to unpack their moving carts. Typically this can be done over the weekend following a Friday-afternoon move.

During the actual move, keep track of the numbers of workers assigned by the moving company as well their hours worked, so that these figures can be reconciled with the vendor's invoice.

Before the moving crew leaves the new premises, conduct a walk-through to ensure that all items (furniture, equipment, carts, etc.) have been moved into the rooms and spaces as indicated on the floor plan. You should identify an area in the new space to place any carts or other items whose final destination could not be determined. Make notes regarding any damage to walls, doors, furniture, etc. during the course of the move, and provide a copy to the moving company supervisor. In addition, perform a walk-through of the vacated facility to make sure that the space has been cleaned out, all the trash bagged, and that nothing of value has been left behind.

During the days following the move, your office staff should be instructed to communicate to you via e-mail any move-related problems encountered. This is your 'punch list.' If the problems are serious, they should be addressed immediately. Otherwise, you should categorize these items under headings such as: Building Maintenance, Phone, Network, Furniture, etc. These items can then be addressed en masse with each service provider.

About two weeks following the move, conduct a post-move meeting with all involved parties, to make sure that all punch list items have been addressed and resolved. FMFG

Additional Resources

- www.moversdirectory.com

Moving Companies

At some point it may be necessary to relocate a facility. (Please see our chapter, "Moving a Facility.") If you are going to hire a professional moving company to do the job, here are some things you should consider.

When choosing a moving company, draw up a list of candidates from the Yellow Pages, referrals from companies that have completed successful moves, or your landlord. (See: www.moving.move.com.) Inform them about your planned move, the approximate move date, as well as origin and destination addresses.

Here are some questions you should obtain answers to:

- How long have they been in business?
- What types of move-related services do they provide?
- Have any complaints been filed against them? (Check on this with the local Better Business Bureau.)
- How long has the company's salesperson (or estimator) worked in the professional moving industry?
- Will they move your specialty items (computers, copiers, and the like), or turn them over to a third-party mover?
- How many workers will they assign to your move project, and how long do they estimate your move to take?
- What insurance do they carry?

You can gauge the salespersons' abilities and professionalism by their responses to your questions, and by their attention to detail. Ask each bidding company for a written cost estimate, and don't be afraid to ask questions about any items on the estimate that you are unsure about. Obtain cost estimates from at least three moving companies.

You can now carefully evaluate the services provided by each moving company, as well as their corresponding costs, before making your decision. Try to make your decision at least 4 to 8 weeks prior to your move date: this will allow enough time for you and your mover to make detailed plans for the proposed move. It will also ensure that the moving company has adequate lead time to block off the date(s) of your move on its schedule. Movers tend to be very busy on Fridays, whereas Mondays are slow (and moving rates may even be discounted somewhat). Weekend moves are the most expensive because of premium rate charges.

Whether a project is sent out for bids, or a moving company has already been selected, it is necessary to have the mover visit your site so as to take an inventory of everything that has to be moved, as well as to make note of the conditions that prevail at the building site, such as service or passenger elevator availability, the presence or absence of a loading dock, the hours during which it is permissible to move, etc.

It is also advisable for the bidding companies to visit the building being moved into, so as to take stock of the conditions there. Collecting this information will help the moving company provide a more realistic proposal and eliminate the element of surprise on moving day.

During this process, find out what equipment the moving company would propose to use for the move, and determine its suitability. You should specify that the moving company provide protection against damage for the lobby floor as well as door and wall corners during the move. FMFG

Additional Resources

- www.moving-company-guide.com

Moving Tips

Moving day can be crazy, hectic, and stressful. Make it less so by following the steps listed below. Get organized well before the move so that you can manage the actual move without a crisis. (See: www.moving.move.com.)

- Two to six months prior to a planned move, start purging unnecessary files and other materials from your work area or department. The more you discard, the less you will have to move, thus lowering your overall moving expenses.

- Notify your post office, delivery services, suppliers, utility companies, clients, customers, and other significant stakeholders about your planned move. Give them your new contact information and the date the information becomes effective. Have your mail and packages forwarded to your new address.

- To eliminate confusion on moving day, plan to dispose of any items that will *not* be moved to your new location. Having such items off the premises prior to your move will be easier to manage than "Do Not Move" labels or other identifiers.

- *Do* segregate those items that you will need either during or shortly after the move, and move them yourself, so that they do not get intermingled with the items that get loaded onto a moving van or truck. Your employees should take personal items, especially valuables, home with them prior to the move; these items can be brought to the new facility after the move has been completed.

- Get rid of as much trash as possible prior to the move so that the movers do not have to work around it. To facilitate this, have large trash carts or dumpsters situated around the work area, and have employees dump their trash into these large containers days or even weeks prior to the move.

- Everything that gets moved to the new location must be labeled! This simple rule will eliminate a lot of delays when questions are raised as to whether an item gets moved or not because it lacks a label. To simplify matters even more, every moving label should have the employee's or department's name and a location (cubicle number, room number). When moving to a large or multi-storied facility, it further helps to color-code the labels by zone or floor, so that similarly color-coded items can be loaded (and unloaded) at the same time.

- Be available on moving day. Assign at least one employee each at origin and destination buildings, to supervise the move, direct the moving crew, and answer any questions.

- Make things easier for the movers, as well as their trucks, carts, etc., on moving day. This may involve marking off spaces in front of the loading dock with traffic cones, for the moving trucks or vans. Keep hallways clear of cartons or trash so that the movers (and their carts) can move about freely.

- If the moving company is responsible for packing certain special items, they should be set aside so that they do not get mixed up with items that your staff will pack up.

- Take special care of live plants. If you use a service to maintain your workspace greenery, consider having the service move the plants to the new facility.

- Make arrangements to provide bottled water or soda for the moving crew, preferably in your company break room. Show the movers where the restrooms are located at both origin and destination buildings.

- Exchange mobile phone numbers with the moving company supervisor. If a problem develops between origin and destination, either party can communicate with the other. Make sure the truck driver has the correct addresses of the origin and destination locations.

- At the facility being vacated, before the moving truck leaves the property, do a sweep (walk-through) of the facility to make sure that nothing has been inadvertently left behind in closets, in stairwells, etc. Also make note of any damage to walls, doors, etc. caused by moving company dollies or carts. Bring these matters to the attention of the moving crew supervisor.

- At the end of the move, and before the truck leaves, do a walk-through of the destination space to make sure that everything has been delivered to the correct location marked on the label. Make sure you have received a copy of the signed paperwork (bill of lading) before the moving company leaves the destination at the end of the move. Make note of any damage to walls, doors, etc. caused by moving company carts, dollies, etc. Bring these matters to the attention of the moving company supervisor. FMFG

Music in the Workplace

M usic, much like artwork in the workplace, feels very subjective. And yet it has been reported that there are several beneficial effects of playing music in the workplace, including: improved team interaction, better attentiveness, a reduction in workplace accidents, and an increase in productivity.

Companies have to decide whether or not to play music in the workplace. On this issue, there should be general consensus among workers and management. If there is no consensus, drop the idea: it simply is not worth driving some employees away. If you do decide to play music, the first question is: what type? The genre you select to create a sound environment should reflect your type of business and your work environment. All-instrumental selections have been reported to be better suited for workplaces because the tendency for workers to be distracted by lyrics has been eliminated.

In today's workplace, another possible decision you face is whether to permit employees to bring their own music to work, and play it on personal stereos, and better still, with headsets. Research indicates that employees who were allowed to listen to music of their choice were better able to drown out distractions, improve their mood, relieve frayed nerves, and improve their work performance. You may have heard of the Mozart Effect. It has been found that listening to a musical piece such as a Mozart sonata somehow enhances the brain's ability to process abstract information shortly thereafter. For increasing your energy or to help you stay awake, try jazz, pop, or reggae music, with the volume turned up, but not so loud as to distract your neighbors! To heighten your concentration, memory, and imagination, play the adagio movements of a baroque piece. Additional encouraging results obtained were: a positive workplace ambiance, an improved perception by the staff of their employer, and a reduced interest in job-switching. What a winning combination! FMFG

Additional Resources

- www.care2.com/greenliving
- www.externaldesign.com
- www.abtmedia.com

Negotiating

In the course of carrying out your facility management functions, you will, on occasion, be required to conduct negotiations. The main areas where you typically need to employ negotiating skills are:

- Service contracting
- Product purchasing
- Real estate acquisition or leasing
- Employee salaries and benefits

As the facility manager, you will hire a variety of service providers such as landscape contractors, maintenance contractors, and janitorial services. Negotiations usually start after you have solicited several bids and have selected a provisional winning bid or have shortlisted two or three bidders. Negotiations may revolve around one or several issues such as price and service levels.

You will also purchase goods required to operate your facilities, such as office equipment and furniture. Here your negotiations may focus on price, features and quality.

You may also be involved in a real estate transaction such as a building disposition, acquisition, or lease. In these cases you will likely have a real estate broker and possibly a real estate attorney helping you with the negotiations.

Finally, when you hire a new employee, or as part of an employee appraisal, you may need to negotiate matters like salary, benefits, and perks. In these cases it is strongly recommended that you involve your human resources manager.

Whatever the negotiation is, you must first develop a strategy. Some elements of a negotiation strategy might be:

- Setting goals and objectives.
- Understanding the strengths and weaknesses of the other party as well as each other's bargaining positions.
- Setting expectations and rules of engagement.
- Knowing your opponent.
- Understanding the challenges you may face.
- Introduction of alternatives.
- Establishing what constitutes agreement and closure.

No matter what you're negotiating, there are certain skills that you must have in order to be successful. The two most important skills are communication and listening. (Please see our chapter, "Communication and Interpersonal Skills.") Good, clear communication is paramount in understanding each other's side of the negotiation. Listening intently demonstrates a genuine interest in what the other person is saying. Without either of these skills, negotiations will quickly fall apart or never even get off the ground.

Negotiations should always be a win-win proposition. This means that compromises will have to be made along the way. Negotiations seldom succeed without some give-and-take. Without compromise, there will only be one winner. FMFG

Occupational Safety and Health Administration (OSHA)

Occupational health and safety deals with the management issues that affect the health and safety of building occupants. These issues include: indoor air quality, ergonomics, fire egress, and sick building syndrome. The body that oversees occupational health and safety in the United States is the Occupational Safety and Health Administration (OSHA). (See www.osha.gov.) OSHA is the U.S. agency created by federal law in 1970 that sets the safety and health standards in the workplace, and enforces compliance. It is an agency of the U. S. Department of Labor. OSHA is the administrator of the Occupational Safety and Health Act. This federal legislation was enacted to ensure, to the extent possible, that every working man and woman in the nation has safe and healthful working conditions.

Unless your company has a separate Health and Safety department, you as the facility manager are chiefly responsible for ensuring that your facility complies with all OSHA regulations applicable to your situation (e.g., an office versus a manufacturing facility). It is important that you have a general understanding of how OSHA regulations and requirements affect how you operate and manage your buildings. Even if you lease space in a multi-tenant building, you must comply with certain aspects of OSHA regulations that apply to the occupants of your space. FMFG

Office Equipment

There are several categories of office equipment that are essential to the smooth and efficient operation of today's corporate facility. Most, if not all, of the items listed below have become commonplace in today's office.

Multifunction machines: These machines combine, within one unit, the functions of some or all of the following: photocopier, network printer, fax machine and scanner. The advantages are obvious: Several machines are replaced by just one, resulting in less floor space used; one wall outlet for power; you can walk up to a single machine to get many office functions completed. The downside is that if one function within the machine fails, the entire machine might be out of service until the technician arrives. In these situations, having a second machine, either in another department or on another floor within the building, may be your lifeline until the sick machine has been repaired.

In the scanning mode, the machine allows you to scan several documents at a time and send the resulting pdf files to your desktop. When you return to your desk, you may choose to manipulate (highlight, redline, add notes, etc.) the images just created, and save them, or send them on to clients or fellow staff. Multifunction machines can typically handle documents up to 11 inches by 17 inches in size.

Copiers: These machines are essential to every office. (Please see our chapter, "Reprographics.")

Facsimile machines (faxes): These machines are designed to transmit documents as images over phone lines to receiving fax machines, which then typically convert the transmitted signal back to paper document format. Newer machines can convert the original document into a pdf file and send it as an e-mail attachment to the recipient. At the receiving end, the recipient has the option to read the document on a monitor, print it, and eventually save or delete the pdf file. Since the fax is not automatically printed at the receiving end, there is potential for considerable savings in copy paper and toner.

Scanners: An office image scanner (or simply, scanner) is a device that optically scans a document consisting of some combination of text and images, and converts it to a digital image. Standalone scanners are giving way to scanners that are integrated into digital copiers and multifunction machines.

Printers: Dedicated or networked, printers have multiplied like rabbits around the typical office. The trend may, however, be shifting toward fewer large, centrally-located network printers, as well as digital copiers configured as network printers. The trend may result in fewer machines around the facility, potentially reducing space needs, as well as lowering the cost per copy.

Plotter: This is a useful machine if your office has a need for generating large (3 foot by 4 foot and larger) floor plans or drawings. However, if your facility does not have one, you can usually get oversize prints made at a neighborhood blueprint store.

Digital camera: This has become a very useful tool to record images within a facility – space layout, workstation details or notes on a conference white board. It can be used to record progress on a construction project, both within and outside your facility. Images can then be downloaded to a PC and transmitted as e-mail attachments to all interested parties.

Shredders: With the current and growing concern over document security, confidentiality, and identity theft, the use of personal-size shredders has soared. While this solution may be convenient, you would be well advised to analyze your facility needs and research larger document shredders: one or two of these machines may serve your entire company's needs. For larger shredding volumes, consider using an outside shredding service. Some shredding companies will send their trucks to your facility on a regular schedule to pick up the materials you need shredded and haul them back to their facility for shredding. Some will send a mobile shredding unit to your building, and shred documents in your parking lot (while you observe the process). You may also choose to use such a service for an annual mass-shredding project, when you shred or destroy an entire year's worth of documents that have met their destroy date criterion.

Video projectors: These projectors are used to project images from a PC or laptop onto a screen. Their light output is measured in lumens. Select a unit that can handle the actual projector-to-screen distance. If portability is needed, the projector could be placed on a conference table, preferably one equipped with a pop-up electrical power outlet and voice and data jacks. In a large conference room, the unit might be ceiling-mounted, so that power and data cables are out of sight. Since the life of a projector bulb is difficult to predict, it is recommended that you keep a spare bulb in inventory. (Please see our chapter, "Audio Visual Systems.")

Mailroom equipment: (Please see our chapter, "Mailroom.")

Moving equipment (dollies), including 4-wheel furniture dollies: These handy, low-tech devices are invaluable for moving heavy objects, including furniture, paper cartons, and equipment around, into, or out of your facility.

Miscellaneous devices that are occasionally used in facilities include:

Laser pointers: These battery-operated units deliver a red laser dot on a wall screen and can be used by the presenter to point out certain images or words displayed on a screen.

Infrared distance measure: This handy tool measures room dimensions (maximum distance of about 50 feet). You place the unit on one wall, press the button to activate, and read the displayed distance (in feet or meters) on the little screen as the infrared beam bounces off the opposite wall.

Surface-temperature readers: These laser devices, aimed around a room, will give temperature readings of various surfaces around the room. They give an indication of the presence of water (lower temperature), and a signal that there may be moisture on, or just below, the surface.

Many of the items listed above will need miscellaneous supply-type items such as toner, paper, bulbs (for video projectors) and batteries (for some of the smaller digital equipment listed). If you place any of this equipment on service contracts, you will need to stick labels on the front of each, giving the unit's ID number and the phone number to call for service.

Some of the equipment listed above, such as the copiers and printers, may be leased. Include regular maintenance and service calls in the lease agreements. (Please see our chapter, "Office Services.") FMFG

The Office of the Future

Although there have been vast improvements in many aspects of our lives, in some ways the office workplace is much like it was 50 years ago, when the Quickborner team came up with the landscape office plan, and Bob Propst of the Herman Miller furniture company created the cubicle.

The work environment has certainly changed for the better over the years. Furniture systems, lighting, technology, and building materials have all improved and made for more effective workplaces.

The workplace continues to evolve, and much of this evolution is due to the changes in how work is being done, and the recognition that workplaces need multiple kinds of spaces within them for work to be successfully accomplished. We are also recognizing that the workforce is making a significant impact on the way we design our workplaces. Much of the work we do today is knowledge work, defined as: "creating and evaluating knowledge, thinking creatively, analyzing and solving business problems and helping companies innovate and grow." There are more than 40 million knowledge workers in the United States alone.

The latest research tells us that the traditional office, which comprises hard-walled offices, cubicles, and conference rooms, can no longer adequately support this new way of work. Fewer and fewer workers come to the office and do the same work every day. There will always be transactional work like processing insurance applications or paying invoices. But the knowledge worker depends on what

Steelcase calls "Day Customization," which has three components:

- Heads-down work
- Collaborative work
- Socialization

Heads-down work needs little explanation. It is the concentrated work, like thinking and writing, for which a person needs peace and quiet. Collaborative work is done in groups, and is best accomplished in conference rooms, teaming areas, and group spaces. Collaborative work includes activities such as brainstorming, Charette Procedures, and role playing. And finally there's socialization. Many Baby Boomers who have worked their way up the ranks in a hierarchical environment cringe at this term. They consider it too soft, warm, and fuzzy. But socialization in the new workplace is not only necessary but crucial to the productivity and growth of a company's employees.

Socialization is important in many different ways. According to Steelcase:

- It builds trust.
- It gives people access to information.
- It facilitates the transfer of company culture from one generation of worker to the next.
- It provides for an organized transfer of knowledge.
- It creates an environment for generational melding and tacit mentorship.
- It connects people and builds a sense of community

What this means is that a person will do different things and need different environments to do them in. As a result, the employee's home base will be smaller. This means that the same real estate footprint that once housed private offices and cubicles will now also include spaces for collaboration and socialization.

As of 2010, there were approximately 150 million workers in the civilian workforce in the United States, and in the next five to ten years close to 50% of them will retire. Socialization allows for the transmission or sharing of 'tribal knowledge' from experienced workers to the succeeding generations. This will be critical to the success of all companies.

In 2007, Kahler Slater, a multidisciplinary design firm in Milwaukee, WI, published a white paper titled, "What Makes a Great Workplace – Learning from the Best Places to Work," written by Barbara Armstrong and Mark Sekula. In this white paper, the authors listed the attributes most commonly found in a well-designed workplace:

- The ability to perform distraction-free work
- Spaces that support collaboration and impromptu interaction
- Spaces that support undistracted group work
- Flexibility of workspaces to accommodate personal work styles
- Attention to individual thermal comfort
- Direct visual access to daylight and control of glare
- Workspaces designated in size and type by function
- Simple and clear wayfinding
- Appropriate adjacencies to support workflow and productivity
- Ease of accommodations for the changing demands of technology
- Proactive attention to ergonomics
- Inclusion of green plants
- The manifestation of the company's culture

There are other signs that the workplace is changing. The Work Design Collaborative, a research and advisory firm, is taking a close look at the distributed workplace. This workplace isn't located in the corporate headquarters. It's the coffee shop, satellite office, home office, or even a park bench where people can work outside of the traditional office. If you're chuckling or having difficulty taking this seriously, you are in for a rude awakening. The Y Generation is upon us, and it has a different perspective of what work is, and how it is performed. And collectively, the older generation is adapting to the new one's ways. How many Boomers own a Droid phone or an i-Pad?

If you aren't a believer in the new workplace, you had better jump on the bus. If you don't, you'll be left back in 1993 with a bag phone and a pager! FMFG

Office Protocol

Office protocol is the code that governs widely accepted social behavior in the workplace, according to conventional business norms. It covers many aspects that affect facilities directly or indirectly. Protocols can range from decorating personal spaces to conversations in open spaces. Many of them are merely common sense and courtesies. Sometimes they are driven by the organization's culture. Cultural diversity of employees, too, may come into play. So the facility manager cannot assume anything, and documenting office protocols may be the sensible thing to do.

Whether the office protocols are in a separate document or included as part of an employee handbook, here are some of the most common topics covered:

- Speaker phone use
- Food
- Eating at your desk
- Personalizing offices and workstations
- Inter-cubicle conversations
- Meetings (designated meeting rooms, etiquette)

- Dirty dishes
- Kitchen policing

- Privacy
- Conference rooms
- Housekeeping
- Music and radios

- e-mail (may be governed by HR or management)
- Internet use (may be governed by IT, HR, or management)
- Coffee service
- Cell phone use

The above protocols may be documented within an employee handbook or human resources manual. In many cases they are documented in a separate booklet. The protocols document should be distributed to all employees, and to new employees as part of the organization's on-boarding process. (Please see our chapter, "On-Boarding.") They are important to you, as the facility manager, in helping you better manage and "police" your facility. FMFG

Additional Resources

*   www.cormarkpublishing.com/Resources

Office Services

As facility manager, you may be assigned the responsibility for several administrative functions. These functions are often bundled together under the heading of Office Services. Some of the more typical services are:

Reprographics: This function provides the facilities for copying and printing documents. It includes managing copiers, printers, fax machines, scanners, etc. Managing this equipment includes purchasing or leasing the equipment, maintaining it, negotiating service agreements for routine maintenance and repairs, and ordering supplies such as paper, toner cartridges, and fax cover sheets. The office services manager may also be trained to make minor repairs to equipment such as fixing paper jams. If copy machines are located in a central copy room, you may need to provide cabinets for storing supplies, and counter space for sorting, assembling, and binding copy jobs. Depending on the number and size of the copying equipment, the room may also have special electrical and ventilation requirements.

Food Service: Food service can be delivered at a variety of different levels. (Please see our chapter, "Food Service.") Some of them are:

• Coffee and beverage service

This may be as simple as providing a single location with a commercial coffee maker and condiments. It could also include multiple coffee stations at various locations. There are many factors to consider when providing coffee and beverage service. For example, will coffee service be provided through an in-house or an outside service? Typically, an outside vendor, if contracted with, will be responsible for stocking supplies and cleaning, servicing, and maintaining the machines. Will coffee be provided free to employees, or will there be a nominal charge? Will paper cups be provided, or will employees be expected to provide their own coffee mugs? Will other beverages, such as tea, soft drinks, and bottled water be provided to employees, as well? If so, will they be free or will employees be charged for non-coffee beverages?

• Vending services

Vending machines can provide employees everything from beverages and snacks to more substantial food items such as sandwiches, microwavable meals, and fresh fruit. Space must be provided for the vending machines as well as electrical outlets, and possibly plumbing (water lines and drains).

• Catering

Many times food is requested for special meetings or departmental gatherings. In some cases this may be the responsibility of the individual employees. In other cases, it may be part of the office services function. This could entail something as simple as ordering box lunches from the local sandwich shop, or working with a local caterer. If any food is to be prepared on-site, warming or cooking equipment may be required, as well as space for final food preparation. Even china, glassware, and flatware may be required.

• Kitchen and eating facilities

Your company may choose to furnish a kitchen for its employees. This could be as simple as a room with counter space, a refrigerator/freezer, and a microwave. Or it could be more elaborate and include a dishwasher, ice machine, a sink with above- and under-counter cabinets for supplies like utensils, paper plates, paper cups, napkins, and condiments. Your company may want to provide an eating place in addition to the kitchen, such as a lunchroom or break room. This would include tables and chairs in a variety of configurations, a flat-screen TV and a magazine and newspaper rack. Additional factors to consider are: stocking of supplies, equipment purchase and maintenance, and cleaning.

- Full cafeteria service

Some companies choose to provide their employees with a full-service cafeteria. This type of service can come in different shapes and forms. It could be a space where an outside contractor brings in a variety of lunch items every day. In this case you will have to provide the space for the final assembly, warming, and serving of the food. In other cases, a company may choose to have an on-site cafeteria where all food storage, preparation, serving and clean-up is done by the contractor within your office space. Such an operation is essentially a restaurant. The issues surrounding this type of service become more complicated. You will have to decide on the level of food choices offered (e.g., salad bar, deli sandwiches, hot food, desserts). Once you have made these decisions, you will need to write a food service program and develop an RFP (Request for Proposal) based on that program. You will then need to solicit proposals from food service vendors, and negotiate a contract. Space must be provided for the cafeteria operation, and you'll have to decide whether you will furnish the kitchen equipment or if the food service vendor will provide it as part of its contract.

Mail and Package Delivery Service: This service may range from providing space, supplies, and equipment for employees to handle their own incoming and outgoing mail, to employing a full-time employee to run the mailroom. In the case where employees are responsible for their own mail and package handling, the room should be sized for several people to be working in it at the same time. Where a person is assigned the responsibility of managing the mailroom, access to the room itself may be restricted to that person. In either case, the mailroom will typically include things like mailing supplies (various sizes of envelopes, labels, mailing packages, boxes, etc.), a letter-opener, postage metering machine, postage scale, mail boxes or mail slots for individually sorted incoming and outgoing mail, and a layout space to assemble larger mailings. Space for materials such as expedited-shipping packages may be required, as well. The mailroom is the place where general office supplies may also be stored. (Please see our chapters, "Mailroom" and "Office Supplies.")

Other activities that may be included under the office services function are: telecommunications (both land-line system and cell phones), recycling, artwork, records management, and office supplies. FMFG

Office Supplies

Every company needs office supplies in order to function. Office supplies can include everything from pads of paper and pens to three-ring binders. There are several ways to manage the office supplies in your office. One is to centralize office supply management, where you keep a supply of frequently used office supplies readily available for employees to use. Supplies not used on a daily basis can be ordered as needed. In a centralized system, Office Services manages the office supplies and does all of the ordering, distribution, and tracking of supplies. In some operations, the cost of office supplies may be charged back to each department, as opposed to having it under a central Office Services budget. This allows for more control of the amount and cost of the supplies used.

Your company may choose to decentralize office supplies, in which case employees can go to the office supplies storage area and take whatever they need as they need it. Office Services may be tasked with keeping the office supplies cabinet (or room) fully stocked at all times and hold employees to the honor system. In this scenario, inventory and costs are more difficult to control.

A third, and quite common, way to order and manage office supplies is to negotiate a contract with a local or national office supplies vendor that results in a wholesale discount on office supplies. In this case, each department is responsible for ordering its own supplies out of the vendor's catalog. The purchases can typically be made either through the vendor's website, a call-in telephone number, or via fax. Because of the vast array of products typically offered by the vendor, including furniture, office equipment, cell phones, etc., you may wish to limit the types of items that can be ordered under this scenario. Overall costs are better controlled than in a decentralized system because each department is responsible for its own office supplies budget. FMFG

On-Boarding

Most companies have some type of new-employee orientation. It may be an informal process, handled by the employee's manager, or a more formal one, conducted by Human Resources, and involving representatives from various departments. New-employee orientation is also called "on-boarding." Because employees have direct contact with the facility they work in, a representative from facilities management is often part of the process (or, at the very least, a review of specific elements of facility management is included.) Facilities-related issues that the new employee should know about include everything from how to replace a lost security badge to what to do in case of an emergency.

Every company should have some type of facility handbook that outlines policies, procedures, and processes. (Please see our chapter, "Facility Handbook.") It may be a separate booklet, or the information might be included in the HR employee handbook. Either way, the facility information can be used as the agenda for the portion of the new-employee orientation or on-boarding process that relates to facility management. In smaller companies, the on-boarding process may simply be a morning session conducted by an HR specialist who covers everything, including facilities issues. In other companies, you might be called upon to deliver the facilities management portion of the orientation. The latter is the preferred approach. Delivering the information in person enables you to answer any facilities-related questions that the new employee might have. FMFG

Organizational Skills

W e all possess and employ organizational skills, whether to run errands or a business. Organizational skills are important in helping us manage ourselves. Being organized helps us maximize what we can accomplish in a given period of time, thereby reducing our stress level. Here are a few practical ways to get organized:

First of all, create four folders that will sit within arm's reach on your desk. Label them: "To Read–Correspondence," "To Read–Informational," "To File," and "To Do." These four folders can be created for your e-mail files, as well.

Second, set up a spiral notebook as your daily log. Every phone call, significant conversation, or important thought gets jotted down in your log.

Third, you need to inspect and prioritize your mail quickly. Every day, you are inundated with every category of mail imaginable. You absolutely cannot read everything you receive. Many times you can recognize junk without even opening the piece of mail. Throw it away.

If it seems that a piece of mail might be of some use or importance, read the first paragraph to gauge whether to save or pitch the item. If in doubt, file it in the "To File" folder. If you get in the habit of reviewing this on a weekly basis, you'll get to it again at the end of the week and then perhaps decide what to do with it.

If it is truly an important piece of information, either put it in the "To Do" folder, prompting you to act on it, or for future reference in either the "To File" or the "To Read–Correspondence" folder.

Do the same with e-mail. Look at it and assess its value. If you decide it's junk, delete it. If it's important and you need to respond right away, do so. If it's important but not urgent, then put it in the "To Read–Correspondence" e-mail folder.

If it's a trade publication, set it aside. Schedule one hour each week to take your pile of magazines, read their tables of contents and look for articles you are interested in. Cut out the articles and put them in your "To Read–Information" folder. Pitch the rest of the magazine. Set aside a block of time each month and read what's in your "To Read–Information" folder and if you decide to keep it, put it in your "To File" folder. Set aside another block of time each month to go through that file and put each article in an appropriate subject file. Keep a drawer of folders with headings (Management, Organizational, Space Planning, Technology, Sales, Marketing, Maintenance, etc.) and file accordingly.

Read the items in your "To Read" folder any chance you get – on the plane, during your lunch hour, or over a cup of coffee.

Do your reading with highlighter and pen in hand. Make notes in the margins. Then, when you refer to the article later on, you won't have to read the entire article all over again.

At the end of each week go to your "To Do" file and write on the next clean page in your log book what you want to do next week. Review your previous week's log and see if there were any conversations, messages, or thoughts to move into your "To Do" folder. During the course of the week, if something comes up that is a "To Do," write it on that first page of the week. Even if you don't need to do it that week, at the end of the week you can put it in your "To Do" folder. That way you won't lose track of it.

Here are a few more useful techniques:

- Analyze where your time goes. Then prune unproductive time.
- Don't just do those things on your "To Do" list that you like to do. Do those that need to be done. Should you become frustrated that you're not accomplishing anything on the "To Do" list, get started by attacking one simple item. Perhaps that will provide the incentive for doing the next, hopefully more important task, on your list.
- Don't be unrealistic and overload your "To Do" list. You'll just get frustrated. Allow yourself time to get things done. And leave time for the unexpected.
- Always try to leave time on Friday to organize yourself for the next week. Clean off your desk. File stuff away. Make your "To Do" list for the next week. There is nothing more frustrating than going to work on Monday morning with the intention of getting organized for the week and being hit with an unexpected crisis.
- Have the discipline to organize. Being organized will allow you quick access to information so that when you are interrupted from a planned activity you can address the interruption quickly, then return to your work. Being organized lets you know where you are at any given time.
- Finally, always set aside some time for planning, thinking, and other non-reactive, non-crisis, activity. Remember, the best facilities managers have a vision and a plan for their well-run facilities.

For more about organizational skills, Steven Covey's book, *7 Habits of Highly Effective People*, is a must-read. FMFG

Outsourcing and Out-Tasking

Outsourcing in facility management is quite common. Most facility managers have been outsourcing services for years. According the International Facility Management Association (IFMA), the three most common outsourced services are: custodial services, security, and food service. Other services that are typically outsourced are: building maintenance, landscape maintenance, and office services (mail service, reprographics). The term "outsourcing" has changed somewhat, as well. With the advent of large companies that contract with building owners and facility managers to bundle some or all of the typical facility management services under one contract, the outsourcing of individual tasks like cleaning and security has come to be referred to as "out-tasking".

To further clarify: According to IFMA, outsourcing refers to the full transfer of the facility management function to an outside firm. The corporation then manages the outsourcing contract rather than the entire facility management function.

Out-tasking is the providing of individual services by a service provider. These tend to be the kinds of recurring services offered by a full-scale facility management department, such as housekeeping, security, and food service.

If you lease space and have a gross lease, the property manager will provide you with most of the typical facility management services. Make sure you understand what is being provided and at what level of service. Ask to see the service level agreements that the landlord and the individual service providers have agreed to, and make sure those service levels meet your needs.

The primary reason outsourcing or out-tasking is chosen is that the overall cost of these services is typically lower because of the outsourcer's economies of scale – he offers a large volume of these services to numerous customers under contract. However, quite often you may find a jump in costs after the first year. To have better control over your costs, your contract with the outsource contractor should be broken out by services provided, and the overall management fee should be listed separately, as well. Make sure there is a reasonable cost-increase for each consecutive year for the services as well as for the management fee, and try to cap the increases on an annual basis.

Whether you are considering out-tasking specific facility management services or outsourcing the entire facility management function, you must consider the advantages and disadvantages of both options. According to the International Facility Management Association, the most common advantages and disadvantages of outsourcing and out-tasking are:

Pros for In-house Staff	Cons for In-house Staff
• Stability	• Complacency
• Control	• Overhead (benefits)
• Loyalty	• Availability
• Culturally entrenched	• Lack of flexibility
• Ownership	• Difficult to terminate
• Empowerment	• Cost control

Cons for Outsourcing/Out-tasking	Pros for Outsourcing/Out-tasking
• No sense of ownership	• New ideas, best practices
• Personnel turnover	• More efficient
• Lack of control	• More resources
• Dedicated to the outsource provider	• More flexibility

Additional Resources

• Please see our chapters, "Service Level Agreements" and "Contracts and Proposals."

Parking

Parking lots, whether surface, underground, or multi-level covered parking, should be designed to provide adequate parking spaces for the vehicular traffic coming to a building. Surface lots generally occupy more land space than the building(s) they serve, and are the least expensive. Covered parking structures have the advantage of providing shelter to the vehicles from the heat of the sun in summer and from snow and rain in other seasons. They are typically the most expensive types of parking space to build, with prices ranging from $25,000 to $40,000 per parking space.

Parking lots are heat sinks in urban areas, and municipal green-space requirements may dictate how much landscaping at a minimum has to be designed into a parking lot. This may include areas designated for lawn, bushes, and trees. In addition, because parking lots tend to be a source of water pollution from gasoline, motor oil, etc., larger municipalities may require that parking lots have associated retention ponds to capture run-off.

Depending on the city and location, parking lots may provide the service for free, or institute a charge – via parking meters, or monthly or weekly passes.

As a tenant in a building, you are generally assured a certain number of parking spaces per thousand square feet of leased space. You need to determine whether this number is adequate for your staff's needs; if not, you'll need to negotiate for additional parking spaces. Your state's transportation department will determine the ratio of handicap to regular parking spaces in any given parking lot.

Parking lots need to be monitored for damage due to salt and weather conditions, which can lead to potholes and cracks. Such damage needs to be attended to before it becomes worse, and more expensive to fix. In parking structures, winter salt or salt spray in areas near the ocean can cause concrete components to deteriorate to the point of creating unsafe conditions if they are not monitored and repaired. In addition, parking spaces need to be re-striped every three to five years or so, depending on how fast the paint fades due to the weather. The entire lot may need to be re-surfaced every five years. Re-striping would have to be done at that time, as well. (Please see our chapter, "Building Operations and Maintenance.") FMFG

Additional Resources

- www.wbdg.org/design

Plants (Interior)

Few things have the ability to change the appearance and ambiance of an office interior as live plants. In addition to changing the look of an office interior, plants have beneficial effects that relate to stress-reduction. Plants have the ability to put oxygen back into the air and help to eliminate air pollutants present inside the office. Finally, based on the size and shape of the plants selected, they can serve as dividers of an expanse of office space, and provide screening for staff and office equipment. With some planning, you can come up with the right combination of plants for the interior of your facility. (See: www.gardeningknowhow.com.)

Here are some things to consider as you make your decisions:

- How is the lighting level in each of the locations that you have selected to place a plant? Some plants thrive in full sunlight; others can do well in relative shade.
- How much space do you have for each plant? Consider floor space, countertop space, as well as space above cubicles, with planters resting on cubicle panel tops or hanging from the ceiling tile grid.
- Should you take care of the plants yourself (using in-house staff) or outsource the work (watering and pruning) to a plant care vendor? If you do it yourself, remember that the cardinal sin is to over-water plants. Test the soil's dampness before watering.
- What is your budget? After you have done your research and shopped around, you may elect to purchase a number

of plants and containers from a nursery, or rent them from a vendor. If you rent them, make sure that the vendor will provide regular maintenance and will replace (at no charge) any plants that die. (Please see our chapter, "Contracts and Proposals.")

- Be cautious if you permit employees to bring in their own plants. Very often such plants are transporters of fruit flies or other pests.

Several varieties of office plants require little care. Among them are the pothos, philodendrons, and mother-in-law's tongue. Some, like the English ivy, corn plant, and rubber plant, are good at removing indoor air pollutants. The umbrella plant, because of its height, is ideal for providing screening privacy. FMFG

Additional Resources

- www.wikihow.com/Choose-a-good-office-plant

Policies and Procedures

Whether it's your full-time job or just part of your overall job responsibilities, managing the facility is a critical element in the continued success of a company. Administering the facility function employs various processes that need to run efficiently and effectively, and ultimately to provide a safe and healthy workplace.

These processes often require the participation of the occupants. In order to establish expectations and provide an understanding of what actions and behaviors are required of the occupants, you must develop policies and procedures outlining the processes and establishing "rules of engagement" for those affected by the process. For example, a security policy regarding the proper way to deal with bomb threats will help ensure that all occupants act in a consistent manner by outlining the basic steps they should take. In the case of a janitorial policy, communicating the expectations of the cleaning service to the occupants will help them understand the actual duties of the cleaning staff and reduce complaints.

Policies document the "what" and "why," while procedures document the "how" and "when." For example, an emergency evacuation policy will describe what the potential emergencies are (fire, severe weather, security breach, etc.) and why the policy is needed (for the safety of the occupants). The procedure will explain how to evacuate the building (take the stairs; gather outside the building in designated areas) and when (upon hearing the fire alarm). (Please see our chapter, "Emergency Preparedness.")

There are often two procedures associated with a policy – an internal and external procedure. An emergency evacuation policy will have associated with it a very simple step-by-step (external) procedure for occupants of the building. An associated internal procedure should also be written for the facility staff and emergency responders. This will be more detailed, and explain the steps that the staff must take (e.g., check the annunciator panel to see what alarm has been triggered, then proceed to that area to make a visual observation).

The types of processes that may require a policy and procedure are:

- Safety and security
- Parking
- Emergency evacuation
- Conference room set-up / reservation
- Maintenance requests
- Ergonomics
- Moves/adds/changes
- Office protocols
- Coffee/beverage service

- Fitness center use
- Off-hours building access
- Recycling
- Space and furniture allocation
- Office supplies
- Indoor plants
- Visitor access
- Mail services
- Shipping/Receiving

The importance of the process will dictate the breadth of the policy and procedure required. For example, a security policy will describe the various security scenarios that could occur and the expectations of response times. There would be both an external procedure for employees to follow, and an internal procedure for the facility personnel to follow. Because of the breadth and importance of the security policy, it is typically a separate document. On the other hand, a coffee/beverage policy may simply state that the company provides them for free; the procedure may consist of a few simple rules for participants (If you pour the last cup, start a new pot; report spills, etc.). In this case it may be best to include it in a facility handbook. (Please see our chapter, "Facility Handbook.")

Policies and procedures should be readily available to building occupants, typically on the company's intranet and within the employee handbook. In addition, procedures that require urgent action, such as emergency and security procedures, should be located within every occupant's reach (e.g., printed on a card attached to everyone's land-line telephone).

Policies and procedures should be clearly and simply written. The fact that they exist should be communicated to occupants frequently and should be on the agenda for on-boarding new employees. (Please see our chapter, "On-Boarding.") Updates to policies and procedures should be communicated, as well.

The basic structure of a policy typically includes the following:

- Purpose (what it is).
- Why it exists.
- Those it applies to.
- A simply written description of the policy.
- How and when it should be adhered to.
- Who owns it and whom to contact with questions.

The procedure is a succinct set of instructions that occupants must follow should an incident occur where the policy is enacted.

You must always keep in mind that policies and procedures are not developed out of a need to exercise control. Rather, they exist for the benefit of the building's occupants. FMFG

Project Management

O f the many skills required to administer the facility function effectively, the ability to multi-task is near the top of the list. But multi-tasking is not enough. In addition to being able to juggle all of the various activities you will encounter in a typical day or week, you need to have excellent project management skills as well. Whether it's at a macro level, such as managing all of the various annual facility-related projects, or at a micro level, like managing a single reconfiguration project, the same basic skills are required and the same basic steps will be employed.

You may encounter many different types of projects, ranging from the complicated to the mundane. But regardless of their complexity and priority, they must be managed with the same level of focus. Typical projects may include:

- Maintenance projects, e.g., repair of a heating, ventilating, and air conditioning (HVAC) unit.
- Capital improvement projects
  - Installation of a new chiller unit.
  - Construction of a building addition or the build-out of a leased space.
- Space planning projects
  - Moves/adds/changes.
  - Departmental reconfigurations.
  - Building re-stacking.
- Relocation projects

There are two parts to every project, its planning and execution. Planning is extremely important. It can set the stage for a successful project completion, or it can strew the road to success with potholes and barricades. Let's look at the components of an effective project management process:

1. Planning
   A. Define the mission of the project.
      i. Why does it exist?
      ii. What are the drivers?
      iii. What are the objectives?
      iv. What are the measures of success?
   B. Define the scope of the project.
   C. Identify the resources required to complete the project successfully, e.g., human and capital resources.
   D. Develop a Work Breakdown Structure (WBS).
   E. Determine a budget and schedule.
   F. Assemble a team.
   G. Develop a communication plan: Prepare an internal (team) and an external (end users and those affected by the project) communication plan.
2. Implementation
   A. Direct and manage the activities of others.
      i. Create an environment for success.
      ii. In smaller projects you may be performing some of the work yourself, so you'll have to manage yourself just as well as you manage others.
   B. Take control of the schedule and coordinate the team's various efforts closely. Approach each task as being critical to the success of the project.
   C. Evaluate progress constantly, and revise the plan and schedule as needed.

The WBS is used to define and group a project's discrete work elements (or tasks) in a way that helps organize and define the total work scope of the project. It is a chronological list of all of the project milestones and a detailed breakdown of the activities that must be accomplished in order to reach

each milestone. The schedule will reveal what activities are independent from others and which are dependent on each other. You can also attach estimated hours to each activity and create work plans for each team member.

Review the WBS in detail at every progress meeting. Progress meetings should be scheduled on a regular basis. Be disciplined in holding these meetings. Even if there isn't much progress to report, don't cancel a scheduled meeting. Attending these meetings helps give the project continuity. The communication that occurs in these meetings is crucial to the success of the project. And even when you think there isn't much to discuss in a meeting, you'll find that it will run its scheduled length because there are always pertinent issues that tend to come up.

Although it's a bonus if the project manager has expertise in the technical nature of the project, an awareness of the area of expertise in which the project resides is often enough. A good project manager will have team members who will be the experts. The real secret to being a successful project manager is to master the following skills:

- Communication (Please see our chapter, "Communication and Interpersonal Skills.")
- Interpersonal skills (Please see our chapter, "Communication and Interpersonal Skills.")
- Negotiation (Please see our chapter, "Negotiating.")
- Problem solving

Whether you're managing a project with a large team, or you have a small one-person team (yourself), most of the skills referred to in this chapter will apply. FMFG

Property Management

In their book *Property Management,* authors Robert C. Kyle and Floyd M. Baird state that "the primary function of the property manager is to achieve the objectives of the property owners while generating income for the owners, and preserving or increasing the value of an investment company." Although the duties performed by a property manager and a facility manager are very similar, property management is an income-generating function, while facility management is most often considered an overhead cost. As a result, the focus on the end user is different from the perspective of the property manager than it is from that of the facility manager. As a facility manager, you are an employee of your company, so you always have your occupants' best interests in mind when it comes to administering the facility function. The property manager is employed by a property management firm, which in turn is hired by the building owner. In some cases, the property manager works directly for the building owner. That's where his loyalty lies.

In most lease situations you will be your company's liaison with the property manager (PM) and the landlord. Depending on how your lease is structured, the PM will typically be responsible for all building and grounds maintenance, security, cleaning, and life safety. Examples of how you might be required to interface with the landlord are:

- Routine maintenance requests.
- Capital improvement projects.

- Understanding your financial risk in any proposed capital improvements.
- Understanding the impact of capital improvements on your operations.
- Building access and security.
- Life safety testing.
- Disruption to your employees or operation caused by the PM's activities.
- Dissatisfaction with a service provided by the PM.
- Parking.
- Common-area use.

If you lease an entire building, your company may decide it is less expensive to provide its own PM services. Whether you outsource some or all of the services, or perform them in-house, they will ultimately become your responsibility.

Property management ranges in type and scope. If the owner has a single building or a relatively small portfolio of buildings, the property management activities may be provided by his own employees. Or the owner may have a property management subsidiary provide PM services to his portfolio of buildings. If the building owner has a large portfolio of properties in many locations, the property manager may be a third-party entity that provides PM services for the owner nationally, or even globally.

When negotiating a lease, make sure it includes a clause that requires a building maintenance engineer to be on-site during normal working hours, and on call for after-hours problems. (Please see our chapter, "Leasing a Facility.") Understand what the property manager's expectations are in terms of level of service and response times. If they are not satisfactory to you, negotiate more stringent standards, or negotiate a clause in your lease that allows you to use your own contractors if the PM is not available within your time frame. (Understand, however, that you will have to pay for your own contractor.)

Even though the facility manager and the property manager have different goals, their primary objective is the same: To provide a safe and healthy work environment for the building's occupants. The property and facility managers may arrive at that objective from different perspectives, but in the end, there must be a level of trust and mutual respect for each other's needs in order for it to happen. That begins with open and clear communications. FMFG

Additional Resources

- Please see our chapter, "Building Owners and Managers Association (BOMA)."
- www.boma.org

Purchasing

You may be responsible for the procurement of many of the products and services used within your facility. This is a significant responsibility in that every dollar saved or spent is reflected in your company's bottom line. In this light, Facilities may be seen as a profit center.

As part of your job, you will generally have or oversee the following purchasing responsibilities: authority to seek bids from qualified vendors, obtain pricing, negotiate contracts, issue purchase orders, follow up on orders, and develop relationships with vendors.

In some cases, you may need the involvement of another department in the purchasing process. Usually this happens when technical expertise regarding the product or service is outside the Facility Manager's scope. Examples may be information technology, telecommunications, or other technical areas.

What is the right quantity to order? Scientifically, that can be determined by calculating the Economic Order Quantity (EOQ). This balances the need to order a larger quantity of an item in order to obtain a higher quantity discount, against the cost of financing the larger purchase, the additional storage space needed, and the risk of product obsolescence.

Closely tied to ordering the right quantity is getting the product delivered in a timely fashion – right when it is needed, and not too soon (when storage space may not be available), or too late (when it may slow down or halt essential operations).

Service contracts can be obtained for a variety of office equipment – copiers, fax machines, printers, shredders, telecom equipment, etc. (Please see our chapters, "Office Equipment" and "Office Services.") You may negotiate them at the time that the equipment is purchased or leased. A service contract ensures that the equipment will be repaired in a timely manner (within the time range specified in the contract) by a factory-trained or otherwise qualified service technician. If the service contract includes more than the occasional repair, the details of such additional work should be spelled out in the contract. In any case, the service technician should leave a copy of the service ticket with you before leaving the facility, and each machine should include a log sheet showing a brief record of each service call.

It may be ideal to separate responsibilities within the purchasing arena in order to reduce or eliminate the possibility of conflicts of interest. Purchasing, Receiving, and Accounts Payable decisions may best rest with separate individuals within the company so that the same individual is not placing the order, approving the receiving ticket and authorizing payment of the invoice. In small companies, however, this split-up may be impossible.

When selecting vendors it is essential that you are fair with all vendor salespeople. (Please see our chapter, "Contracts and Proposals.") Talking to salespeople from vendor companies that you do *not* currently do business with is a good way to learn about other products, services, and markets. In the process, you may even learn something new about the company that you are currently doing business with. You may become comfortable enough to use an alternate vendor as a back-up in those situations when your regular vendor is occasionally unable to meet a request. You can develop a list of alternative vendors from salespeople or others within your own company, from trade journals, trade associations, and by attending trade shows. The Yellow Pages of your city as well as neighboring communities are additional sources of information about other vendors. Working with local suppliers has several advantages: It is easier to check out nearby suppliers, and you may further benefit by obtaining lower shipping or freight charges, and faster service response times.

Negotiations should result in win-win situations. (Please see our chapter, "Negotiating.") Items that can be negotiated include: price, delivery schedule, shipping costs, installation costs, removal of packaging materials and scrap, payment terms, and credit for items returned. Negotiate on items that have a significant unit cost or high annual volume. Follow the 80-20 Rule: 20% of items purchased comprise 80% of the dollars expended.

Before finalizing the selection of a vendor, request references, and call these individuals to determine how well the vendor has met their needs, and gauge the likelihood that the vendor will meet your company's needs. When you finally make the decision, let the selected vendor know. Also contact the unsuccessful vendors to tell them the result and why they were not selected.

For a high-value purchase, or one that requires a long-term commitment, it may help to visit the vendor's plant (when buying furniture) or distribution facility (when purchasing office or other supplies).

When should you put an item out to bid? When it is a high-unit-cost item, or when annual purchases of any item or category of items exceeds a certain threshold, say $5,000.

When shipping and expected dates are clearly specified and orders are routinely delivered on time, and when service calls are made as promised, little time needs to be spent on expediting orders. When you need to expedite orders, do it sparingly, and preferably on categories of products that represent a large chunk of the company's annual purchasing volume. "Rush" orders should be a rare event. Finally, pay bills on time: It helps in the building of good and lasting relationships with your vendors.

Blanket Purchase Orders (POs) can help to eliminate a lot of repetitive paperwork. They are generally good for a specified period of time, and reference a specific quantity and price. Releases are made against the blanket PO as and when additional product is required.

Companies with multiple locations should try to gain the advantage of negotiating with a single vendor for a particular item or class of items, in order to gain the advantage of mass-buying, assuming that the vendor can make cost-effective deliveries to all of the company's locations.

Avoid creating supply rooms. They tend to fill up with inventory, which is something you should try to minimize. Also, storage space costs as much to operate as finished office space. Many vendors are equipped to make next-day deliveries. This service allows you to let the inventory of a category of items drop to near zero, then place an order with the confidence that you can expect delivery the next day.

Standardization can lead to a significant reduction in the total number of different items being purchased. This, in turn, contributes to the bulk-buying of fewer items, the storing of fewer items, resulting in lower unit costs, and less shelf space needed. Savings go to the bottom line.

Every organization needs to create a purchasing manual. For a small company, it can be a brief document listing policies and procedures. Policies may include the goals of the organization, who may issue POs, and the purchasing authority at different dollar thresholds. Procedures spell out the how-to's.

Purchasing manuals are a great tool for training purposes and for use by the office staff when the regular buyer is away from the facility. The typical purchasing manual will spell out the need for purchasing standardized products and services. It should stress the need to capture data on the descriptions, quantities and costs of the items purchased, and use the data in a way so as to reduce future costs or control expenses.

You should either personally monitor inventory levels of items or be notified by individual departments when the inventory of any item has reached the minimum order point, thereby triggering an order.

Before automatically purchasing a requested item, Purchasing should first check to see if it is in inventory, either in the requestor's facility or at a branch facility. It may sometimes pay to have the item shipped from another location in order to avoid spending for a new purchase, thereby reducing the overall inventory in the process.

Whether a company issues 5 or 50 POs each month, it is a good practice to generate a PO to document every purchase of equipment, furniture, software, supplies, etc.

A Purchase Request (completed by the Requestor) should be used when requesting equipment, furniture, software, etc. (In a "rush" situation, a verbal request may be adequate, but it should be followed up with the electronic or hard-copy version.)

The Purchase Request form will typically include the Requestor's name, quantity and description of the item requested, price (if known), Vendor's name (if known), documentation to justify the purchase of the item listed, and an authorizing signature. The signing authority ascertains that the request is justified, and forwards it to Purchasing.

The Purchase Request may do double-duty as a PO form, once a PO number has been assigned to it. POs should be numbered consecutively. In situations involving purchases from multiple vendors, each vendor should receive a separate PO.

A Purchase Order Log, maintained by the Purchasing Department in hard-copy or electronic format, can be used as a quick reference and should contain the following information: PO numbers listed sequentially, the order date, Requestor's name, Vendor's name, brief description of item, and total price.

The Purchasing Department will transmit the original PO to the vendor, filing a copy in numerical sequence. Sometimes it is permissible to phone in an order, including the PO number. In such cases, it is advisable to follow up by transmitting the PO to the vendor, marking it: "Confirming – Do Not Duplicate."

When goods are received (or service work performed), the Receiving Department will check the items received (or work performed) against its copy of the PO. Any back-orders or other obvious discrepancies should be noted on the PO. The packing slip (or service ticket) and the PO are then routed to Accounts Payable.

Accounts Payable routinely receives invoices for products and services. As they are fulfilled, the invoice is matched up with the corresponding PO and packing slip. If there are no discrepancies, payment is made. If there is a discrepancy in the invoice, it may be returned to Purchasing for resolution.

There are certain situations when payments may be made without the use of POs. Examples: Monthly rent payments, utility bills, monthly copier maintenance invoices.

Consider implementing an automated purchasing system. If selected and executed properly, it will save time and provide you with regular reports.

You may also want to consider allowing some items such as office supplies to be purchased directly by individual departments. You can negotiate a discount with a large office supplies vendor, and then authorize a limited number of employees to order from the vendor's standard catalog.

Some purchasing departments deploy "sustainable" purchasing programs at their companies. This typically involves requiring that certain products, such as copy paper, be recyclable. FMFG

Additional Resources

- William A. Messner, *Profitable Purchasing Management.* 1982. AMACOM, New York, NY 10020.
- http://www.usgbc.org/DisplayPage.aspx?CMSPageID= 221, pages 43-55.

Records Management

Records of all types are generated daily in the course of operating a business. ISO 2001 defines records management as "the field of management responsible for the efficient and systematic control of the creation, receipt, maintenance, use and disposition of records, including the processes for capturing and maintaining evidence of and information about business activities and transactions in the form of records."

Should you also happen to play the role of Records Manager, you may be responsible for some or all of the following:

- Planning the information needs of your company.
- Identifying which information needs to be captured.
- Establishing and enforcing the policies and procedures concerning business records, from creation to disposal.
- A plan for the short- and long-term storage of physical as well as electronic records.
- Coordinating access to records, internally and by the public, while being sensitive to business confidentiality and data privacy.
- Executing a retention policy, including archival storage as well as disposal.

Today, much of this data is stored on company computers. It needs to be backed up regularly for safety and security reasons, and the back-up media taken off the premises for increased protection.

Data is also stored as paper records in (generally) color-coded file folders, which are then systematically stored on shelves, in filing cabinets, or in storage boxes. You may wish to ensure that aisle widths are adequate, and that the shelving area is well lit. In the case of high-density file storage, you may need to seek the services of a qualified civil engineer to determine whether the file room can safely withstand the weight of files as well as the storage cabinets or shelving.

Files and records tend to move from one person to another. It is crucial that the movement or location is tracked. While written procedures may define who may have possession of a given file, and the sequence in which it moves around the facility, current-day technology in the form of bar-code scanners and radio-frequency identification (RFID) integrated with a computerized system can keep track of a file. Commercially available products can manage records through all the processes described above: while it is active, tracking, retention scheduling, and final disposal.

As the need for immediate access to paper records decreases over time, the records may be moved further away from the individuals who generated them or need access to them, and at some point may be transferred into boxes and moved off premises, or converted to another medium (disc, microfilm, etc.) for ease of storage.

A company's records management (RM) program must manage the organization's information so that it is complete, accurate, accessible, useable, timely, and cost-effective. Even though RM may not necessarily be a core competency of your company's business, it makes eminent business sense to establish a good RM system. Here are some specific reasons why:

- To reduce operating costs: A well-designed, well-operating RM system will minimize the volume of essential records being stored, and reduce the cost of storage filing systems and floor space. Reducing the number of lost files holds down the cost of searching for missing files. Moving non-essential files to lower-cost off-site storage significantly reduces storage costs, as well.

- To control the creation and growth of records: The term "paperless office" may have been coined several decades ago; however, the volume of copy paper purchased is at an all-time high! An RM system should control what gets stored in paper format, and should define how long records should be stored in archives before they are destroyed.

- To improve efficiency and productivity: A well-designed RM system, incorporating computer and other technologies as appropriate, will enable the rapid accessibility of files, and reduce the number of lost or misfiled records. In general, a well-managed RM system will result in a professional-looking office with files neatly in place or out of sight, rather than scattered around the office.

- To comply with regulations: A good RM system will assign responsibility for maintaining files as required by current laws and regulations, thereby reducing the likelihood of fines, penalties, and legal consequences. This likewise applies to the systematic destruction of files that have met their destroy date criteria. You should check with your Legal, Human Resources and Risk Management Departments to ensure that you are legally maintaining the correct records for the specified amount of time.

- For improved decision-making: A well-maintained RM system, in conjunction with appropriate indexing, will result in the rapid and timely accessibility of information to enable management to make better-informed decisions, as well as for business planning purposes.

- To keep important records secure: Any company is vulnerable to loss. An RM system needs to include a plan that will help preserve and protect vital records, including confidential records, which are valuable assets of the company.

- To preserve institutional memory: In the day-to-day life of any company, records are created that could someday prove to be valuable for future planning and decision-making. Company records can become part of the organization's institutional memory, and for that reason need to be preserved in an RM system. FMFG

Additional Resources

- www.epa.gov/records/what/quest1

Reprographics

One of the more common services that get assigned to the facility manager is reprographics. Reprographics is the reproduction of text and images by mechanical or electrical means. The images can be reproduced in a number of different ways. Some of the more typical reproduction processes in a business workplace environment are xerography (copying on a copy machine), printing, and scanning. Most of the equipment available today can perform these processes digitally.

Most facilities have an office services area that houses reproduction machines (copiers, printers, and scanners). Horizontal work surfaces, under-counter storage, and overhead cabinets are also co-located in these rooms along with the reproduction machines.

In small offices there may only be one central location for this equipment. In larger offices, there may be a central copy center as well as satellite reproduction rooms or alcoves. The centralized room may be staffed by a person and used for large copying or printing jobs, while the satellite machines may be used for small jobs on an as-needed basis by individual employees. In a multi-floor facility, the satellite stations may be stacked so that occupants know where they are located, no matter what floor they're on.

The mail function is often co-located with reprographics. Office supplies may be stored there, as well. Certain physical characteristics are required for reprographics rooms, whether they're satellite spaces or centralized rooms. The factors that must be closely addressed when planning and designing a reprographics room are:

- Lighting
- Appropriate and adequate work surface area for document assembly
- Ample storage
- Adequate electrical power
- Special electrical outlet configurations (if needed)
- Adequate ventilation
- Ergonomics
- Adequate waste and recycling containers

Office equipment can be purchased or leased. It is much more common today for companies to lease reprographics equipment because of the cost, the fact that the technology changes so often, and the need for maintenance. (Please see our chapters, "Office Equipment" and "Purchasing.")

Select people in the office should be trained to perform simple maintenance tasks such as clearing paper jams, understanding the trouble codes and how to correct them, and knowing when a service technician needs to be called. To avoid unintentional damage to these expensive and complicated machines, it should be your company's policy that only trained individuals are authorized to deal with equipment maintenance issues.

Protocols should be established for reprographics. Some protocols might be:

- Reproduction of draft documents and internal documents should be two-sided. That means you have to have a machine that is capable of doing two-sided copying or printing, and that two-sided printing is set as the default.
- Only copying or printing jobs that are under a certain quantity can be done at satellite locations; larger jobs must be done in the central reprographics room.

- Stipulate the type of paper that can be used for different printing and copying projects: heavy bond versus all-purpose copy paper.
- Institute recycling policies.

Make sure you have an equipment maintenance agreement in place, and verify your vendor's anticipated response time. Reprographics are essential to a company's everyday operations. An extended period of downtime on a critical machine can be very disruptive. FMFG

Security

It is the responsibility of the facility manager to provide a safe, secure, and healthy workplace. One of the key issues to ensuring safety and security is establishing a security program. A security program consists of three major components: policies and procedures, physical deterrent and alarm systems, and communication and education.

First you must understand what you are securing, and then develop an overall security philosophy. Typically a security program should protect people and assets. To assess the extent of your security policy, ask questions like:

- Do certain people (e.g., CEO) or functions (e.g., Research and Development) require more security than others?
- What are the physical assets that need to be protected besides the building and its typical contents?

Once you've identified what needs to be protected, decide on the level of security to provide. One company may want a transparent and passive system that conveys the idea of a more open and welcoming company. Another may want to have a more visible and active system with parking lot gates and visible cameras and security guards to demonstrate to their employees, customers and the community that they are providing a secure environment.

The type of industry your company is in may dictate how you view security. For example, a defense contractor will generally be required to have a much higher level of security.

The type of assets housed in your building may dictate your level of security. If you manufacture sophisticated and expensive electrical devices, you may want camera surveillance in certain areas and metal detectors at exits.

If you are a government agency, located in a government building, or if a government agency occupies part of your building, a high level of security may be a requirement.

The physical location of your building may dictate the level of security. If you are in or near a high crime area, you may want a higher level of security, with an emphasis on its visibility. If you are located in a business park, its covenants may prescribe certain features of your security system, such as a minimum level of exterior lighting, and impose restrictions on fences, parking lot gates, and guard houses.

Your security program will vary depending on whether you own your building, you're a single tenant in a leased building, or you lease space in a multi-tenant building. In the first two cases you will likely be responsible for all security issues, including planning and implementation, and you will deal directly with all security issues. In the latter case you will be responsible for security only within your space, and the property management firm will handle overall security. (Please see our chapter, "Leasing a Facility.") Your responsibility will be limited to making sure that your company's employees understand the building security policies and procedures, the processing of security badges, and reporting security issues.

Once you understand the level of security, develop a set of policies and procedures based on your specific situation. The steps in developing and writing a security policy are:

- Establish a security committee consisting of select employees from a cross-section of the company.
- Assess the current conditions, compare them to the level of security desired, and identify the gaps.
- Develop a plan to close those gaps.

- Write a policy around what you've decided in terms of your company's security philosophy, the level of security required, and what constitutes a security breach.
- Write an external security procedure for employees – easy steps to follow when an employee recognizes what is considered a security breach, and basic behaviors that are expected of each employee, such as: carding in and out, not allowing piggybacking, knowing how to report and replace a lost security badge, etc.
- Write an internal security procedure for your staff that describes the steps to take in case of a security emergency.

The next phase, implementation, is where you will address the physical aspects of the security program with cameras, security badges, card readers, etc.

Finally, the security program must be communicated to all employees. Regular reminders about the importance of the security policy, communicating updates, and communicating security breaches and what was done to correct them, are all part of the ongoing communication process. Including a discussion on the security policies and procedures as part of the new-employee on-boarding process is another way to communicate the company's security policies and procedures, and an opportunity to emphasize the importance of security. (Please see our chapter, "On-Boarding.") FMFG

Additional Resources

- Please see our chapter, "Policies and Procedures."
- For a security policy and procedures template please see our website: www.cormarkpublishing.com/Resources.

Service Level Agreements

A service level agreement (SLA) is an agreement between two parties: the customer and the service provider. Whether a legal contract or an informal agreement, the SLA makes it clear from the outset that expectations are being created that the service provider will be held to.

Before the relationship begins, the SLA establishes expectations of both parties and creates an understanding about services being provided, where they're being provided, how often, and for what price. The SLA may also address:

- Priorities
- Responsibilities
- Guarantees

- Warranties
- Availability
- Performance

An SLA should also describe measurements against which the service or product provider will be evaluated. These measurements should also include target goals.

SLAs serve both parties, providing a fair and equitable process for evaluation, improvement, compensation, and termination. FMFG

Additional Resources

- Please see our chapters, "Contracts and Proposals" and "The Balanced Scorecard."

Signage

Your business sign may play a significant role in your company's visibility and how the public perceives it. Signs may be categorized broadly under three general headings: building-mounted, free-standing, and interior.

The first two categories consist of exterior signs, which may be mounted on a pole or other support, on a building rooftop, or on a building wall-face, so as to be visible from a distance. Alternatively, a sign could be at eye level, in the form of a monument sign near a property entrance, or at the edge of a parking lot. Exterior signs are generally well worth lighting, and the length of time that they are lit may be controlled by a time clock or photo-sensor.

> **TIP:** After you have made plans for a monument sign, be careful when planting decorative landscaping so that is does not grow tall enough to block the sign from view!

Some other signs, located on the outside of the building, may designate locations such as "Service Entrance" or "Shipping & Receiving." Parking lot signage may point to designated areas for "Employee and Visitor Parking." Some signage, such as Handicap Parking, is dictated by law.

If you are leasing space and you desire an exterior sign identifying your company name, be sure to negotiate that with the landlord as part of your lease.

Interior signs may be located in a building lobby, generally in the form of a directory which lists the occupants of the building and their suite numbers. The elevator lobby of each floor could likewise display the names of tenants on that floor. Directional signs could further point the way to ranges of suite numbers on either side of the elevator, and help occupants and visitors alike navigate through the building.

All tenants may have signage to display their company names and logos and/or tag lines inside their own lobbies. Within the suite each tenant may have name plates for employees, attached to their cubicle panels. Occupants of private offices may have name plate signage attached to the walls beside the doors to their offices. Conference and other rooms may also have signage. In many companies, very often driven by company culture, conference rooms are named after U.S. Presidents, trees, rivers, or even company products. It helps if they are in alphabetical order around the office perimeter or aisles, for ease of location.

If you feel that your open office area resembles a maze of cubes where a visitor (or a new employee) might possibly get lost, consider installing department signs at a level above the cubicle tops, and visible from a distance.

TIP: For the benefit of visiting service technicians, you may also wish to install similar higher-level signs identifying the location of equipment such as copiers and fire-extinguishers.

Before installing any exterior sign, check with your local municipality to make sure you are compliant with the sign code, or work with a sign manufacturer who knows the local codes. You may wish to seek a variance if your code-compliant sign would be blocked by other buildings, or if it would disrupt the environment. For identification signage, such as your company name, municipalities typically require you or your sign vendor to obtain a sign permit.

The readability of an exterior sign is a function of its location, overall size, height of the lettering, and the lighting. Signs that are placed parallel to roadways need to be about 70% larger than signs placed perpendicular to the direction of traffic flow. The speed limit of the adjoining roadway also has an impact: the faster the traffic, the larger the sign needs to be. A good rule of thumb in selecting the size of lettering for your sign is one inch in height for every 25 feet in distance between the sign and the passing traffic.

Finally, signs need to be maintained over time. When selecting a sign manufacturer, consider what services you may seek besides design, manufacture, and installation. Find out how long the sign may last, what it will cost annually to maintain, and include that in your facility budget. FMFG

Additional Resources

- www.topics.info.com/Building-Signage

Sound Masking

Sound masking is a privacy-enhancing technique that introduces low-level, barely perceptible, background noise (similar to the sound of a typical office air conditioning system) into an environment, in order to make speech and other sounds less intelligible, and safeguard confidential conversations. A sound-masking system can be used any place where speech privacy is desired – open workspaces, some enclosed spaces, and certain public places. An additional derived benefit is in reducing distractions, thereby making the workspace a more productive area to work in.

An open office layout can sometimes be too quiet or too noisy. In the former case, the slightest noise (voice, music, or equipment) from a neighboring cubicle can be clearly heard in an adjoining cube. Where employees are densely packed on an office floor, conversations from surrounding workspaces can become a major impediment to concentration and productivity.

While it may be assumed that a private office provides speech privacy, in many cases it does not. Thin walls, walls that only go up to ceiling height, and low-quality ceiling tiles will often allow voices to travel into adjoining spaces. In these cases, sound masking in the adjacent areas can provide the necessary speech privacy.

In public spaces such as doctors' waiting areas or reception lobbies, sound masking is desirable so that private conversations cannot be overheard. In these cases, sound privacy is introduced in the common areas, not in the private offices.

In some exterior spaces, sound masking may be provided by a device such as an artificial waterfall to mask the sound of nearby traffic or heavy equipment.

Sound-masking systems fall into several categories:

In-plenum: In a typical office, the plenum is the area between the dropped ceiling and the deck above. In-plenum sound-masking systems use a network of loud speakers, installed in a grid pattern, and facing upward so as to maximize the area covered by the bounced sound waves emitted by the speakers. Because of the various other systems and components located within the plenum – HVAC ductwork, structural beams, ceiling tiles of different materials, and vents – the sound waves reaching the workspaces below may be neither uniform nor totally effective. This can usually be corrected by adjusting the volume and sound spectrum of an individual speaker or group of speakers in the plenum, and by treating vents and open-air returns.

Direct Field: With this type of sound-masking system, the sound travels directly from the speakers to the workspaces below, without bouncing off the deck above or interacting with other components located within the plenum. They can be used, mounted face-down, in spaces with or without ceiling tiles. When a ceiling grid is present, the speakers are integrated into the grid. When the ceiling is open, such as in a converted warehouse, the speakers can be hung from any available structure. The speakers do not need to be tuned or volumes adjusted, and can operate at lower power levels because the sound does not have to travel through intervening materials.

Under Raised Floors: If an office uses raised floors for its cabling system, the sound-masking system can be placed within the space under the raised floor. Depending on the space available, the speakers may be either the normal masking speakers or specially designed to fit into the space. In either case, the coverage is uniform and the system is well accepted by the occupants of the space.

Following are the attributes of an effective sound-masking system:

- Spatial uniformity: The sound-masking system should not call attention to itself. It should produce a background, uniformly dispersed sound, where the individual source cannot be pinpointed. It is often best achieved when there is an intervening material – such as ceiling tiles or a raised floor – between the loud speakers and the workspaces.

- Spectrum contour: The frequency distribution of sound produced by an effective sound-masking system ranges between 160 Hz and 8,000 Hz. Ideally, the contour of the frequency distribution should be a balance between the performance level of the system and its acceptability by the occupants in the area.

- Sound-masking level: For private offices, the masking level may vary between zero to 44 dB(A); for open workspaces, the range is between 43 dB(A) to 48 dB(A).

- Invisibility: Since sound masking is supposed to be in the background, it works best if the speakers are also out of sight (above the ceiling tiles or under a raised floor) and the control equipment is installed in a separate room.

- Sound diffusion: Occupants are less likely to notice a sound-masking system if the sound generated is diffuse – that is, arriving at occupants' ears about equally from all directions. This is more likely to happen when the sound travels through an intervening material (ceiling tiles or a raised floor).

- Portability: You should be able to take the system with you to a new location at minimal cost.
- Applicability: The system you invest in should be flexible enough to work effectively regardless of the environment in which it is installed.
- Phasing: Sometimes a swishing sound may be detected by occupants who happen to be located at a spot mid-way between two masking loud speakers. This sound may sometimes become objectionable. The problem can be resolved by introducing an intervening material between the two speakers, or by a design change.
- Sound masking may not always be successful in achieving speech privacy within a space where there may be underlying noise problems. If these factors cannot be controlled, sound masking may not solve the problem. These other factors are:
- Speech level: If people speak very loudly within a space, a sound-masking system may not be able to cover such volume levels. Occupants will simply have to learn to moderate their voices.
- Background level: The level of a person's voice gradually reduces by the time it reaches the listener. If the final level is less than the background level, the person cannot be heard. Sound-masking system designers try to raise the level of the masking system such that speech is no longer a distraction. (In a well-designed system, it should not be necessary to play music over loud speakers in order to mask the sound of the sound-masking system!)
- Sound attenuation: Three components that help attenuate a sound signal (lower its level) are: blocking (introducing walls between the signal source and the listener); absorption (using sound-absorbing materials like fibrous ceiling tiles and sound-absorbing cubicle panels); and natural spreading (increasing the distance between source and listener).

Sound-masking systems are most conveniently installed when you plan a move to a new facility, when there are no obstructions in the way, such as ceiling tiles, furniture or equipment. If you decide to install a system as a retrofit, the work may need to be done outside normal work hours so that installers can work inside cubicle areas and above the ceiling grid level.

TIP: If you'd like to find out first-hand how effective a well-designed sound-masking system can be, ask your selected vendor(s) to show you around some of their installations. Then ask the host facility managers to turn *off* their sound-masking systems and judge for yourself how effective their systems are by the degree to which voices suddenly become intelligible. FMFG

Additional Resources

- www.speechprivacysystems.com
- www.soundmasking.com

Space Management

According to author David Cotts in *The Facility Management Handbook:* "Facility management will never be successful unless it is clear who controls the space." Departmental space is typically "owned" either by the department that occupies it or by the facility manager. In any case, the facility manager will own the common spaces and the support spaces within the building.

Where the department owns its own space, the company holds the department head responsible for it, and charges the department a pro-rated portion of the overall operational cost of the entire building (if the company owns and occupies the entire building), or a pro-rated portion of the overall operational costs of the entire space that the company occupies (if the company is leasing a portion of the space in a multi-tenant building). This is commonly referred to as a charge back. The disadvantage of this approach to the facility manager is that he or she has little control over the space, and space planning tends to be reactive because department heads rarely think about the space they need when they forecast the growth of their departments.

As a result, space needs become urgent rather than planned. One advantage, however, is that a department head who is responsible for paying for the operational cost of his or her space out of the departmental budget will tend to think twice before requesting more space. If your company's policy states that departments own their individual spaces, you should consider purchasing a computer-aided design and drafting software package. (Please see our chapter, "Computer-Aided Design and Drafting (CADD).") Once your floor plans are loaded into the system, it will enable you to determine the exact square feet that each department occupies and what percentage of the common and support space it should be charged for, as well.

TIP: If the space in your building is controlled by each department, you should consider purchasing a computer-aided design and drafting (CADD) software package to help you manage departmental space needs and charge backs.

A facility manager who "owns" the space is responsible for all of the space occupied by the company, and the associated operational costs are included within the facility management budget. In this approach, the facility manager has control of the space and can proactively plan for the future because he is privy to the overall needs of each department. It should be noted that in order for the facility manager to understand each department's space needs, he has to take a proactive approach and develop an annual forecasting process.

The disadvantage of the facility manager owning the space and paying for its operational cost is that individual departments are tempted to ask for more space than they really need because they aren't paying for it.

When the entire budget for building operations is the responsibility of the facility manager, he is responsible for developing the operational budget, and tracking and managing all costs associated with the operation of the building. In other cases, companies charge each department for their pro-rated share of the building operations budget.

According to the International Facility Management Association (IFMA) Operations and Maintenance Benchmarks," the cost of operations is defined as follows:

"The annual cost of operations includes the total costs associated with the day-to-day operation of a facility. It includes all maintenance and repair costs (both fixed and variable), administrative costs (clerical, timekeeping, general supervision), labor costs, janitorial, housekeeping and other cleaning costs, utility costs, and indirect costs – i.e., all costs associated with roadways and grounds."

The cost of operations may also include real estate taxes, property taxes, and depreciation.

If your company owns the facility, all the costs described above will be borne directly by your company. If you lease space, you will be charged a portion of the landlord's overall cost of operations, including common area maintenance (CAM) costs. You should carefully review your lease to understand clearly what the annual cost of operations is comprised of. If there are any costs of operations not included in your lease but for which you are responsible, be sure to include them in your budget (e.g., moves/adds/changes).

The cost of operations that you are charged for in a lease situation will differ according to the type of lease you have. In a gross lease, the landlord pays for all costs to operate the facility, and you are charged back a pro-rated portion of those costs based on your rentable square feet. Rentable square feet comprises the actual space you occupy plus a pro-rated portion of the common area space such as lobbies, utility closets, stairwells, elevators, etc. On the other hand, if you have a triple net lease, you are directly responsible for some of the costs of operations. For example, you may be responsible for the utilities, as well as the cleaning and maintenance related specifically to your space. In addition, you will also pay a pro-rated portion of the CAM costs.

During the course of any year you may need to rearrange your space plan due to growth of one or more departments. This is commonly referred to as "re-stacking". The term comes from the idea of rearranging the space plan of several floors stacked on top of each other. Generally speaking, it has come to mean the rearrangement of the space plan regardless of whether you occupy one or several floors. The ratio of the number of people you move around in these space plan rearrangements (even if you move the same person several times) to the total number of people who occupy the space is called the "churn rate". For example, if there are 100 people in your building and you move 40 of them in the course of a year, your annual churn rate would be 40%. According to IFMA, that figure turns out to be the average churn rate for most office spaces.

A re-stacking could include one person or hundreds of people. Re-stacking can range from simply moving people from one workstation to another, where the space plan generally does not change, to reconfiguring workstations or even remodeling some or all of the space.

In order to manage your space more effectively, you need to have a moves/adds/changes process in place. This process is commonly referred to as a MAC process. According to Cotts, the MAC process includes:

- Alteration management
- Art program management
- Furniture installation

- Renovation management
- Procurements (to move, alter, or change)
- Preparation of as-built drawings

- Project management
- Provision of furnishings
- Equipping workstations
- Desktop workstation relocation and installation
- Relocations

Whether you set up a workstation for a new employee, or rearrange an entire floor, a MAC policy will help you manage the process. It is a formal request process that requires departments that wish to rearrange their space to justify the request and submit it within a predetermined timeframe. Just like any formal request process, expectations are established early on, a budget created and approved, and all activities are documented. Other departments such as Human Resources and Information Technology (IT) will likely be involved in the MAC process, as well. IT needs to provide or move computers, telephones, and other IT-related equipment affected by the request. Human Resources will need to update its employee information records. It will affect the emergency evacuation planning as well. If you outsource the physical reconfiguration of furniture, you will need to notify your outsource provider. Other entities that may need to be notified of MACs are your security department and your janitorial service.

The MAC process is most often a computer-based system. It may be an internal "home-grown" system of custom forms on your company's internal computer network. Or, if you have a Computer-Aided Facility Management System (CAFM), it will probably include a MAC module (Please see our chapter, "Computer-Aided Facility Management Systems (CAFM).") The CAFM system is a convenient, automated, and accurate way to implement and track MACs. CAFM is tied directly to your space plans and automatically updates the associated database when changes are made. The intricacy of the

CAFM-generated MAC process depends on the complexity of the CAFM package you choose and how much information you want to input initially and then keep updated. FMFG

Additional Resources

- Our website, www.cormarkpublishing.com/Resources, provides a sample MAC request form and MAC process flowchart.

Space Planning and Programming

In the 1950s, a group of management consultants in Germany developed the 'office-landscape' concept. This idea eventually led to today's cubicle furniture system. Since the advent of the cubicle, the modern workplace has been commonly designed as a combination of private offices and cubicles. The ratio of cubicles to private office varies by company, the kind of work being performed, and company culture. For example, the workplaces in technology companies and advertising firms consist largely of cubicles, with private offices allocated to the most senior executives. In law firms, most workstations may be private offices. Most companies lie somewhere in between.

To have a discussion about space planning, it is first necessary to define a few terms:

Workplace: A general term for the entire physical environment for work – the whole floor, whole building, and whole campus. The workplace contains workspaces.

Workspace: The space an employee occupies when in the office. Generally there is one person to a workspace, sometimes two.

Workstation (Cubicle): A workspace whose perimeter boundaries do not go to the ceiling. Workstations are constructed of demountable and relocatable panels, work surfaces, and storage units that are hung from the panels.

Systems Furniture: Systems furniture refers to furniture and panel units whose dimensions, geometries, and connections are pre-engineered for compatibility. Work surfaces and storage units are hung from modular panels, creating both an enclosure and furnishings in one unit. Workstations, as defined above, typically consist of systems furniture.

Hard-Walled Office (private office): A workspace that has four walls (floor to ceiling) and a door, and assigned to a single individual.

Churn: The percentage of the number of employees who relocate from one workstation to another during the course of a year relative to the total number of employees.

A company's headcount changes as it grows or shrinks. The facility manager must plan for this by providing the growth space when the company is expanding, and disposing of surplus space in case of a work force reduction. This planning process consists of four key elements:

- Workspace standards
- Allocation methods
- Programming
- Forecasting

Workspace Standards – Workspace standards refer to the types of workstations and hard-walled offices provided, in terms of size, panel heights (in the case of workstations), configuration of the furniture within the individual space, and the components (such as storage, conference tables, etc.). For example, one company may provide several different-sized hard-walled offices and cubicles with different types of furniture, depending on employees' positions or titles. Another company may have one hard-walled office size and one workstation size, but offer two different panel heights (the higher panels allocated to top managers). Yet another company may provide only one type of hard-walled office

311

allocated to senior management, and one size of cubicle for everyone else from staff to middle management. To make up for the limited variety of workstations, companies may provide other (shared) spaces such as:

- Various sizes of conference rooms for different kinds of meetings.
- Enclaves where an individual can make a private telephone call or perform concentrated heads-down work for short periods of time.
- Teaming spaces (both long-term and short-term).
- Casual meeting spaces.
- Socialization spaces.

Allocation Standards – The allocation of space will affect the way you plan for space. Some companies allocate space by rank, others by function. Some companies have no standards, while others may have one standard. Allocation standards come into play because it relates to the amount of space you will need to provide. In other words, when you forecast space and consider the number of people who will occupy the space, you must look beyond the number of people involved and also consider their titles, grade levels, or work functions. Then, depending on how you allocate space, you can count the various types of workstations that will need to be allocated, add their net square feet to the other non-assigned spaces, and add circulation and grossing factors to get the total square feet required. For example, if the Marketing Department is going to grow by 10 people over the next two years, and you have three types of private offices for different manager levels, you'll need to know the rank or grade level of each marketing employee so you can allocate the right amount of space. Two managers in 100-square-foot offices, and a director in a 150-square-foot office, will require less space than three directors, each in a 150-square-foot office. This may not seem like a lot, but aggregated over your whole company, and over several years, it will add up. To complicate matters, you will need to know not only how much space to provide, but where to provide it. If Marketing is adding three managers but there are no manager-sized offices within or adjacent to the department, you may need to budget capital dollars to build those offices or move the Marketing Department to an area where there are enough offices. That can precipitate a domino effect and result in the reconfiguration of an entire floor or wing.

Forecasting – Knowing your space standards and how you allocate space, you can now begin the forecasting process. Find out how many people each department will add over a prescribed period of time. In today's business world, things change so quickly that it makes little sense to plan out over more than five years. You can obtain headcount projections from each department head and from Human Resources. It would be wise to obtain headcounts from both, and reconcile any variances. The headcount projections or variances may be influenced by a range of factors, such as:

- The department head genuinely believes that growth will occur.
- The department head is overly optimistic.
- The department head wants to increase his budget so that once the money is budgeted he can reallocate some of it to other initiatives.
- The department head is an empire-builder.

Although we include the last two bullets tongue-in-cheek, it has been known to happen.

When you've collected the projected headcount data from the department heads, they should be verified with Human Resources and senior management. Senior management should ultimately approve the final headcount forecast, including full-time and part-time employees, and outside

313

consultants. Counting contractors and consultants is especially important: in some companies they can be hired directly by the departmental manager without having to go through HR. That's why it's also important to compare departmental headcount forecasts against HR's forecasts because the latter may be unaware of the number of consultants and contractors being hired, and may be able to suggest alternate strategies to the departmental managers. It is also helpful to know during which time periods the contractors, consultants, or part-time employees will be working, so that your planning process takes into account shared workstations.

TIP: When requesting departmental headcount forecasts, make sure the department heads include *all* employees who will "need a chair" for part or all of the forecast period, including part-time employees, contractors and consultants.

Programming – There are two types of programming: qualitative and quantitative.

Qualitative programming is the process of determining what kind of space is required. Your space must be designed to best support the work your employees do. For example, if you are an open and collaborative environment, you may want a bigger, open floor plate, with different types of spaces to enable people to perform different kinds of work during the course of the day. Mark Sekula (co-author of this book) and Barbara Armstrong, Principal at Kahler Slater, a multidisciplinary design firm in Milwaukee, WI, conducted research on U.S. companies named by *Forbes* and *HR Magazine* as "The Best Places to Work", to determine whether the physical workplace design had an impact on those companies' rankings as best places at which to work. They found the answer to be a resounding "Yes." The research confirmed that the physical workplace plays a key role in the success of a company, and its design must be carefully addressed from the very beginning.

This information can be collected through high-level interviews with department heads and other key individuals in their departments. These interviews should include questions about the kind of work being done in each department and how it's done. This will begin to shape the physical space. It may be a more open space with various sizes of conference spaces and teaming areas. It may require special workspaces to accommodate special equipment. Specifically, you need to collect information that tells you the amount and type of space for each department for both the short and long term.

- Specify the type and amount of space for each activity.
  - Number of people
  - Productive space
  - Support space, e.g., teaming, casual meeting space
- Identify the equipment and furnishings required in the space.
- Identify work activities that require special accommodations.
- Core functions required to support work areas
  - Reception, visitor areas
  - Utility spaces
  - Service areas
  - Common areas
  - Passage ways
  - Space for building infrastructure

Quantitative programming is the process of adding up the net square footages of the spaces identified in the qualitative programming and the net square feet required to accommodate the headcount forecast in relation to the way that space is allocated.

Once these four elements are addressed and understood, you can calculate your overall space needs. To do this, simply take the total net square footage identified in the programming effort and multiply it by a grossing factor. If you're planning within the walls of an existing building, that grossing factor will take into account things like interior wall thicknesses and secondary circulation. A typical grossing factor would be in the range of 25% to 35% and will depend on how open or closed your office plan is. An open plan (one that has more cubicles than private offices) will require more secondary circulation.

If you were planning a new building from scratch, you would add a building grossing factor as well, to cover exterior wall thicknesses, elevator and mechanical shafts, and vertical building elements. In either case, unless you're familiar with this process, it would be wise to seek the advice of an experienced space planner.

As you determine the overall amount of space you need, you will also have to break it down by department so that you can begin to place blocks of space that represent departments, onto a floor plan. One key question to ask in the programming process is: What other departments or support spaces does each department need to be next to? This is called an adjacency plan. Not every department can be next to every other department, so adjacencies need to be prioritized. The levels of prioritization might be:

- Critical
- Important
- Nice to have
- Not necessary

These adjacencies, and the sizes of the blocks of space that each department needs, will begin to shape the overall space plan. These are called block plans. You may find that adjacencies may need to be compromised because all of the departments that say they need to be next to each other cannot fit on one floor. Adjacencies can be three-dimensional. For example, if two departments are located on different floors, but right above each other with a connecting stairwell nearby, the arrangement may turn out to be more convenient than if they were both on the same floor.

TIP: Meet adjacency requirements by placing two departments on separate floors directly above and below each other, or next to each other on the same floor.

The next step in the space planning process is to locate the various departments and support spaces on the floor plan. Once each area is located on the floor plan based on its square-footage and adjacency requirements, a space plan can be developed for each department. The space plan will show each and every space that makes up the workplace.

TIP: When laying out cubicles on a space plan, be sure to take into account the 2 inches to 3 inches thickness of the cubicle panels. Over a long run of cubicles, these inches can add up, and you might run out of space during cubicle installation. An adjacent aisle may then become too narrow, fail to meet building code requirements, and you may be forced to correct the situation by shrinking the end cubicles. This phenomenon is referred to as "panel creep."

If you have experience in space planning, you can accomplish this work in-house. To make your job easier, you may want to consider purchasing a computer-aided design and drafting (CADD) software package. (Please see our chapter, "Computer-Aided Design and Drafting (CADD).") These types of software packages range from inexpensive and simple to use, to very sophisticated and expensive.

If you do not have space planning experience, you may want to contract with a professional space planning consultant. But even with a professional on board, you should be actively involved in the programming interviews, and review and approve the space plans. Remember, you know your company's business better than an outside consultant. As the facility manager you have an understanding of the entire workplace and how the various spaces fit together. Regardless of whether you draw the plan yourself or oversee a space planning consultant, your input will be invaluable to the process. FMFG

Storage

Businesses have a vast array of storage solutions at their disposal. At the work-station level, you can store paper or files in a drawer, open bookcase unit, pedestal, vertical filing cabinet, lateral file or storage cabinet.

Any of these solutions is applicable for storage of files at the department level. An on-site storage room can become useful for the storage of large volumes of paper, forms, company literature, and office supplies. Within the facility, you may need to set aside some space or a separate secure room for confidential materials (payroll files, personnel files, etc.), as well as for one or more fireproof safes.

Finally, for items that require an even larger storage area or that are not accessed very often, an off-site storage facility can be used for surplus furniture, office and computer equipment, bulk supplies, and archived materials. If you choose to use a facility such as this, company-owned or not, first make sure that it is secure, that you will have ready access to it, and that it is climate-controlled. This may turn out to be an economical solution because storage space is generally available at a significantly lower cost per square foot than office space.

When you need to store a large number of files in a limited amount of space, a high-density filing system is one solution. Here, files may be stored on open shelves mounted on bases that run on tracks. The use of mobile, high-density filing systems minimizes the number of aisles that are accessible at any one time. Instead, rows of files are moved until you reach the row that you wish to access.

Another high-density solution, used when files are not actively accessed, is the records archive. In this case, files can be boxed and stored on metal shelving units in a warehouse environment, going as high as the ceiling and sprinkler system will permit. (Please see our chapters, "Archives" and "Records Management.") FMFG

Additional Resources

* www.ustorage.com/articles

Storm Shelters

Most commercial buildings generally do not have designated storm shelters. They are neither planned for nor designed. So, what does a facility manager do in a violent storm? (Please see our chapter, "Emergency Preparedness.")

Be alert to approaching storm conditions on a National Oceanic and Atmospheric Administration (NOAA) weather radio. It is a good idea to have a radio like this in the vicinity of a receptionist or someone who has access to your facility's paging system. In the absence of such a radio, listen to any radio, or watch a weather report on a TV or computer monitor, especially if a storm is approaching.

If you are under a Tornado Warning (this implies that one has been sighted or has touched down close to your location), make a general announcement over your facility's public address system. Have all employees leave their respective work areas, and proceed quickly and in an orderly manner to the pre-designated area in your building that serves as a storm shelter. This could be a basement, reinforced interior stairwell, interior restroom or hallway, or the lowest building level. Stay away from windows, exterior doors, and outside walls. If your building does not have a basement, go into an interior room, putting as many walls between yourself and the outside of the building. Do not waste valuable time opening windows: Should a tornado strike, it'll blow open the windows for you!

All facility managers at schools, shopping malls, hospitals, nursing homes, skyscrapers, sports arenas and similar venues should have a storm safety plan in place, and visitors and building occupants should be able to get to shelter areas by following easy-to-read posted signs. Do not use elevators: if the power fails, you could get trapped inside them. FMFG

Additional Resources

- www.spc.noaa.gov/faq/tornado
- www.fema.gov/areyouready/tornadoes

Strategic Facility Planning

Strategic facility planning is the process by which you can plan for the future. One definition of strategy is:

A **long term plan of action** designed to achieve a particular goal. Strategy is differentiated from tactics or immediate actions…by its nature of being **extensively premeditated.**

One task of the facility manager is to provide workstations for new employees. You may also need to reconfigure departmental space or entire floors due to growth, a business reorganization, new projects that require people to be grouped into teams, or because a department has changed the way it works. How many such requests can you say were planned? Have you ever received a call on a Friday afternoon from a department head requesting space for a new employee starting on Monday? Has senior management told you that the company is merging with another company, or that it's about to acquire another company, leaving you with twice as much space to manage? Or that your company is downsizing, and you need to quickly restack and reconfigure your space and dispose of the surplus space? How far in advance did you know about those things? Of all the departments in the company that are integral to the success of such business initiatives, facility management is often the last to find out.

Can all these things be planned well in advance? Probably not. We exist in a global marketplace. Things that happen in a tiny corner of the world can affect almost everyone because we are so connected. As *New York Times* columnist Thomas Friedmann writes in his book, *The World is Flat,* the world is so closely interconnected now that businesses must adapt and change very quickly. As we saw in 2008, a U.S. housing market that went bad affected the entire world and the world economy tanked. Maybe we couldn't predict that, and as the facility manager you likely did not plan for the downsizing in space that resulted. But what if you had at least thought about it and had a plan for it in case it did happen? You would have been one step ahead of the game.

This is exactly why strategic facility planning is so important. It forces you to think about the "what-ifs." Maybe you would be doing things differently now if a few years ago you asked yourself: "What if the global economy fell apart six months from now? What if all of a sudden national unemployment teetered near 10%? What if my company's revenues fell off 25% in a matter of months? What would I do?"

You know what your boss would do. He'd tell you to cut costs, cut staff, and cut space. But how would you do that? Where would you start?

Strategic facility planning enables you to create scenarios and develop potential solutions that will help sustain your organization or help it thrive. Nobody can predict the future. But a smart facility manager prepares for it in a way that keeps him or her one step ahead of the game.

The International Facility Management Association's (IFMA) Strategic Facility Planning White Paper Executive Summary states, "The strategic facility plan (SFP) is a two-to-five year plan encompassing the entire portfolio of owned and/or leased space that sets strategic facility goals based on the organization's strategic objectives. SFP helps facility managers do a better job and ensures that all employees are working toward the same goals and objectives. A flexible and implementable SFP based on the specific and unique considerations of your organization needs to be developed through a four-step process. The first step, understanding, requires thorough knowledge of your organization's mission, vision, values, and goals. Second, exploration of the range of possible futures and triggers is needed to analyze your organization's facility needs using analytical techniques— such as systematic layout planning (SLP), SWOT (strengths, weaknesses, opportunities, and threats) analysis, strategic creative analysis (SCAN), or scenario planning. Third, once analysis is completed, plans for potential responses and periodic updates to existing plans in response to changes in the market need to be developed to meet the long-range needs of your specific organization. Fourth, take actions as planned to successfully implement the SFP."

One of the most important things to understand about strategic facility planning is that it is not a static activity, but a dynamic, ongoing process. The world is changing at a faster rate than it ever has before. And it will continue to do so. That's why strategic facility planning is so very important. It makes us think farther out than today or tomorrow. It's thinking strategically. Sure, the chiller is going to break down, the fire alarm is going to go off, and there will always be someone who is too hot or too cold. That stuff will never go away, and we have to deal with it. But facility managers must step back from the details of the daily grind and spend time giving serious thought to what might happen in the future that could affect their company (negatively *and* positively) and what they would do to adjust and adapt to it.

Strategic thinking isn't daydreaming. It is a deliberate, thoughtful, and reflective process intent on understanding the future and how the facility function can best support the overall organization and its most important and expensive asset, its people. If the facility is a hindrance to people getting their jobs done in an effective and innovative way, it's not fulfilling its purpose. And as the facility manager you are not leveraging one of your company's most important and costly assets in order to help ensure the success of your company.

Developing and writing the strategic facility plan should only be the beginning of a continuous strategic planning process. It's like owning a house. You don't go out, buy one, and simply live in it for 50 years without doing anything to it. You think about what it might need to be when your kids are growing up, when they get older, and finally when they leave the house and go out on their own. You put plans in place to accommodate for various scenarios. And then, when the kids live at home longer than you expect, or your mother-in-law moves in, you adapt those plans to the new scenario.

Strategic planning is not about knowing exactly what your facilities will need to be like in ten years. Strategic facility planning is about having a ten-year picture of what they *might* look like based on logical assumptions, good business forecasting, a good sense of history, and then being flexible enough to change direction at any given moment. Just like how the home theater that you added to your house when the kids moved out can be turned into a mother-in-law suite.

One of the keys to planning for the future is to look for those things that will stay the same. They are the non-negotiable intangible things that will exist no matter what happens. In the case of your organization, it's understanding and acquiring a thorough knowledge of its mission, vision, and values. Those are things that steer successful companies. They typically stay constant. However, the activities needed to achieve the mission and vision and carry out the values may change over time. As the facility manager, that's what you have to try and plan to anticipate. In order to do that, you have to stay in touch with your organization's business strategies. According to the IFMA Forecast Report, published in 2007, the number-one trend in facility management identified by a panel of FM experts is to link facility management with business strategy. You need to understand what your organization's business strategy is and what specific business initiatives it must accomplish in order to carry out that strategy successfully. Then you must find ways to leverage your facilities to support those business initiatives. You need to ask questions of senior management. You have to stay connected and in touch. The C-suite doesn't typically reach out to the facility manager until the strategy has already been developed or when the scenario has changed. So it is imperative that the facility manager be proactive and take the initiative to ask first, instead of waiting to find out too late in the game.

That's what strategic facility planning is all about. Create your own strategic facility plan. But don't stop there. Don't file it away after you've finished creating it. Remember, when the plan is done, the planning begins. Keep it on top of your desk as a constant reminder that things change and you must adapt. Talk about it in your staff meetings. Measure everything you do as an FM organization against the basic principles set forth in your strategic facility plan. And then be prepared to change. FMFG

Additional Resources

- The IFMA Strategic Facility Planning White Paper
  http://www.ifma.org/tools/files/SFP_WhitePaper.pdf.
- The IFMA 2007 Forecast Report
- http://www.ifma.org/tools/research/forecast_rpts/2007.pdf

Sustainability

The subject of sustainability has been around for some time. In 1987, the World Commission on Environment and Development defined *Sustainability* as "...our ability to meet the needs of the present without compromising the ability of future generations to meet their own needs." The WCED also defined *Sustainable Facility Management* as the process of integrating the people, place and business of an organization such that it optimizes economic, environmental, and social benefits.

The economic, environmental and social aspects of sustainability are commonly referred to as the "triple bottom line." One side of the triple bottom line triangle is the economic aspect of sustainability or the cost savings one gets from being energy-efficient. The second side of the triangle is the social side or the human benefits resulting from sustainability, such as cleaner air, more daylight, and less exposure to toxic materials. It also refers to the benefits your company might experience, as well. People have shown an increased interest in wanting to work for sustainable companies. Being a sustainable company could help your company attract and retain the best employees. People also have a growing desire to do business only with companies that practice sustainability. The third side of the triangle, the environmental aspect, is related to preserving our planet for future generations by practicing sustainability in our personal and work lives. More and more companies are realizing that practicing sustainability is the socially responsible thing to do. As the facility manager, you can practice sustainability as well. By taking a hard look at your buildings, and establishing your starting point and vision of the possibilities, you can create a sustainability plan that fits your organizational goals and existing funding mechanisms.

According to Christopher Hodges, CEO of Facility Engineering Associates, a recognized leader in sustainability thinking, here are five areas that you should consider if you wish to go forward with a facility sustainability program:

1. How *energy*-efficient is your building?
2. How much *water* do you use?
3. What *goes into* your facility?
4. What *comes out* of your facility?
5. How healthy is your *indoor environment*?

A good starting point in determining the answers to these questions is the United States Green Building Council's LEED point guides. (LEED stands for Leadership in Energy and Environmental Design.) It is through LEED that facility managers and building owners can, if they wish, get their buildings certified as sustainable buildings. There are several different avenues to choose from within the LEED certification process, mostly depending on your company's particular situation:

- Do you own and occupy the building?
- Do you own the building and lease it to others?
- Do you lease space in a multi-tenant building?
- Is it a new building about to be built?
- Is it an existing building?

If you own and occupy an existing building, or lease space in an existing building, you should refer to the LEED-EBOM (Existing Building, Operations, and Maintenance) points guide, or the LEED-CI (Commercial Interiors) points guide.

In either case, the points guide will tell you how to answer those questions.

It is important to note that you do not need to have your building or your space be certified as sustainable. There are many sustainable initiatives that you can undertake that cost little or nothing to do.

Sustainability is not just a facility issue. It is a human resources issue (its impact on employees), a marketing issue (its impact on customers and the world at large), and a financial issue (energy savings). If you are considering developing a sustainability program, it would be wise to first meet with representatives from your company's senior management team, Human Resources, Marketing, and Finance and get their buy-in. Sustainability means many things to many people. Before any company starts to initiate a sustainability program, all of the stakeholders need to be on the same page as to identifying the overall issues that would drive the process for your company. FMFG

Tactical Planning

Tactical planning consists of the detailed steps needed to carry out the milestone events in the strategic facility management plan and strategic facility management organizational plan. The tactical plan cascades from the master plan. The core competency required by the facility manager to develop and implement a tactical plan is Planning and Project Management. (Please see "What is Facility Management" and our chapter, "Project Management.")

Some of the typical tactical activities that will cascade from the strategic facility plan are:

- Site searches.
- Acquisition/relocation/disposition of facilities.
- Renovation, remodeling, and expansion projects.
- New construction.
- Project budgets.
- Space reconfigurations and major re-stacking projects.
- Scheduling.

Some of the typical tactical activities that will cascade from the strategic facility management organizational plan are:

- Policies and procedures.
- Contracting with service providers.
- Writing staff job descriptions.
- Hiring employees.
- Capital improvement planning and budgeting.
- Operational planning and budgeting.

- Implementing preventive maintenance programs.
- Researching and selecting appropriate facility management technology systems.

You will need to schedule and budget for the implementation of the various tactical plans that cascade from your strategic plans. FMFG

Additional Resources

- Please see our chapters, "Budgeting", "Master Planning", "Space Planning and Programming" and "Strategic Facility Planning."

Telephone and Voice-Mail Systems

The selection of a *phone system* is an important decision for any business. The system allows you to communicate easily with customers, employees and the outside world. The choice of a phone system is generally based on the size of the organization projected over the next three to five years. (See: www.buyerzone.com/telecom-equipment.)

Now for some telecommunications terminology. For a very small office, with under ten phones, a KSU-less system will suffice. (KSU stands for Key System Unit.) With no central "control box", the phones themselves contain the features needed, such as Hold, Forward and supporting multiple lines. If you need to relocate, the system can be unplugged and moved.

For a growing business, with between 10 and 40 phones, you can move up to a Key System which uses a control unit, the KSU, and provides most of the functions needed in a business environment. One typical key system will handle 12 phone lines and 36 extensions.

For an even larger business (over 40 phones) a PBX (Private Branch Exchange) is recommended. This system has features that are more numerous and advanced than the Key System's. This option provides enormous growth capacity. A PBX's capacity is defined by the number of "ports", which are the total number of connections (phone lines, extensions, etc.)

that can be made to the system. Both the KSU and PBX will require professional installers.

Try to standardize your telecom equipment across all your company sites. Check to determine whether you will be able to make basic system modifications, such as adds, moves and changes, yourself. Where there are multiple vendors handling the same system, it may be possible to obtain competitive bids. Make sure that the vendor you select will provide training to your office staff, and is also capable of providing ongoing support (servicing and additional equipment) for your phone system.

If you are planning to move to a new space and are considering buying a new phone system, plan far enough ahead to ensure that the system will be in place prior to the move date. The phone system vendor should be given a floor plan showing the names of all employees and the work spaces they will occupy. Extension numbers (and sometimes customized feature-sets) are assigned to each phone.

The phone system vendor may sometimes serve as your liaison with the local phone company, or you may choose to work directly with the local phone company. You will need to establish the office's main phone number and the number of phone lines required. Down the road, you will need to contact your phone vendor whenever telephone system changes need to be made as your office expands, contracts, or relocates.

Larger phone systems come loaded with hundreds of features. Most companies, however, generally use no more than 10 percent of them. The most popular and useful functions include: auto-attendant (if you don't have an operator, this will direct inbound phone calls), Hold, Transfer, Forward, Conference, Caller ID and Direct Inward Dial (DID).

A practical accessory to the desk-phone is a wireless headset. This device gives the user the flexibility to walk away from one's desk and still be able to have, or continue, a conversation in a hallway, conference room or team area.

Most phone switches will permit the addition of a music-on-hold feature. For this you will need a CD player and appropriate CDs. In addition, if you have a large conference room, you may wish to install a conference speaker-phone.

A *voice-mail system* will generally go hand in hand with the phone system. This may be either a standalone system compatible with the phone switch, a centrally located shared system, or it may simply consist of a card plugged into the phone switch. Voice mail messages can be listened to when you return to your phone, or may be accessed from another phone when you are away from your desk. Voice-mail messages may also be forwarded, saved, or deleted.

Training on both the phone and voice-mail systems is generally scheduled during the week prior to the installation of the new systems.

TIP: To avoid missed calls when you are away from your workstation, consider setting your desk phone to Forward to your mobile phone (assuming you carry the latter device on your person). Another useful feature is Voice Message Notification, which can be set to ring your mobile phone to alert you to a voice-mail message received at your desk phone. FMFG

335

Voice over Internet Protocol (VoIP)

Voice over Internet Protocol (VoIP) is a fairly new, and rapidly expanding, technology that enables you to make and receive telephone calls over the Internet using a broadband Internet connection instead of a familiar phone line. It achieves this by using the Internet's packet-switching capabilities to provide phone service.

Depending on the service you subscribe to, the types of call that you can make will vary widely, all the way from being limited to calling parties on the same service as you are, to calling anyone anywhere with a phone number that might be local, long-distance, international, or mobile.

Some VoIP services may require you to use a special VoIP phone, which plugs directly into your broadband connection (via an RJ-45 ethernet jack), and is used just like a standard phone. Some will work only over your computer in conjunction with a microphone, speakers, a sound card, and VoIP software. Still others will permit you to use a standard phone in conjunction with an analog telephone adaptor (ATA), and dial just like you are used to. Wireless "hot spots" located in coffee shops, airports, and parks enable you to connect to the Internet, and may enable you to use VoIP wirelessly. Bottom line: You can make a VoIP call from wherever you have a broadband connection.

VoIP works by first converting your analog voice signal into a digital data signal, which is then compressed and translated into IP packets and then transmitted over the Internet. If you are calling a regular phone number, the digital signal will be converted back to a regular analog phone signal before it reaches its destination. In most cases, you can use your computer and talk on the phone at the same time. You do not necessarily have to have your computer turned on, unless required by your VoIP service. However, all VoIP services require that your broadband internet connection be active.

Some benefits of VoIP over standard phone-line service:

- You can avoid paying for a regular phone line.
- Packet-switching permits several calls to be made simultaneously in the amount of space occupied by a single call in a traditional circuit-switched network.
- VoIP service providers offer a host of features and services not generally available with regular phone service (except as extra-charge add-ons). These include: Caller ID, call waiting, three-way calling, repeat dialing, and call transfer. Additional features allow you to handle incoming calls in a variety of ways, including forwarding calls to a specific number or sending an incoming call directly to voice-mail.

Some disadvantages of VoIP service:

- VoIP services need wall-outlet power, and do not work during power outages.
- VoIP service is dependent on the underlying broadband connection. If that service goes down, so will your VoIP. In addition, hiccups in your Internet service can result in degradation of call quality in your VoIP service.
- VoIP service providers may not provide White and Yellow Pages listings.

- Not all VoIP services offer emergency 911 service. VoIP uses IP-addressed phone numbers, unrelated to geographic (street) addresses. So, a 911 operator would have no way of knowing what street address an emergency call originated from. FMFG

Additional Resources

- www.communication.howstuffworks.com/ip-telephony
- www.fcc.gov/voip

What Makes My Facility
So Special

The authors asked facility managers from around the country to contribute their perspectives to this chapter. We asked them to respond to the question: What makes your facility so special? These seasoned managers chose to comment on the big picture – the visual, emotional, symbolic, and even historical impact of their facility in total. Their responses transcend, yet also pay tribute to, those innumerable details and concerns that define their daily professional lives.

*****

"Our Gateway West Sustainable facility is a living, breathing example of who we are and what we do. Built to achieve LEED certification, the building employs practical applications of cutting-edge building management systems and design that provide an unparalleled work environment for our employees and a wonderful resource that serves the community."

Ernie Allen, Environmental Systems, Inc.

*****

"It is a wonderful feeling to drive into the site every day. You are first impressed by the landscape, featuring a stream and several ponds and mature plantings. The park-like atmosphere gives way to a stately granite facade. As you enter the building, the large granite stairway, bright brass, and rich mahogany take your breath away. It is truly a pleasure each day to work at a site that impresses everyone so much."

Anonymous

*****

"Our space was once the manufacturing facility for the Allis Chalmers Tractor Company. It has since been remodeled, while still retaining the integrity of that former use. We kept the exterior perimeter masonry, original structural beams and supports, some of the cranes that were used on the production lines, as well as the glass skylights and clerestory windows. This provides for a very open feel and a positive work environment. The color palette was selected to match the natural colors in the exterior masonry – making it a very pleasant space."

Lorna Anschuetz, WellPoint, Inc.

*****

"It is our goal to provide facilities that support our corporate mission, to provide peace of mind to our customers through sound insurance and exceptional service. To achieve this, our facilities and our staff must play a key role in attracting and retaining the very best professionals in the insurance industry."

Randy Stark, West Bend Mutual Insurance Company

*****

"My favorite place at the National Gallery of Art is standing on the east side steps near sunset time, looking to the east across the plaza at the East Building. In front of me are the cascading fountains and reflective glass pyramidal prisms. The glow of the building's Tennessee pink marble and the sun's shadows provide contrasting angular lines and geometrical shapes in the pale blue sky, while the fountain water pounds the pavement and the crystal prisms reflect the setting sun, all of which cause me to pause in awe."

David W. Samec, P.E., CFM, National Gallery of Art

*****

"Our company prides itself on our solid, dependable and longstanding reputation and our buildings reflect that – especially our oldest building, which was built in the early 1900s. From its granite columns outside to its marble lobby and brass fixtures inside, the building reinforces our message to our clients that our company will always be standing strong and our services will always be there when they need us."

Anonymous

*****

"Our beautiful facilities are laboratories and offices housing some of the greatest minds in their fields, bringing the miracles of medicine to market sooner for our clients. Our clients and other visitors are greeted by 'story walls' of the over 60 years of our history and scientific contributions. Where there is not room for a wall we provide electronic kiosks for visitors to find that information and more."

Gary P. Broersma, CFM, Covance

*****

"Beneath the elegance of the glass and brick façade, and invisible to those casually passing by, lies the foundation of the Johnson Building. Like the associates of the Johnson enterprises that work above it, this unassuming foundation is consistently supportive, and content to quietly perform as part of a larger whole. It is appropriate that one of these foundation walls should commemorate the pride felt by all Johnson associates. In many ways, this is their building. So, in March, 2002, just weeks before the building's Grand Opening, each of the over 1,000 associates of the building's three Johnson companies was permanently recognized with a signature brick in the "Wall of Pride." It is a symbolic acknowledgement of their steadfast support and unwavering commitment to our customers, our community, and our enduring legacy." FMFG

Sue Bunker, Johnson Financial Group

Valued Sponsors

We would like to thank the following individuals and companies whose generous contributions helped make this book a reality. Thank you!!!

AVI Systems
262-207-1300
www.avisystems.com

J+J/Invision-Robert Schuler
414-975-5487
www.jj-invision.com

Building Services Inc.
800-353-3600
www.buildingservice.com

Stratagem, Inc.
262-532-2700
www.stratagemconsulting.com

CleanPower
1-800-388-1608
www.cleanpower1.com

Judy Vandervest
262-492-9581
jvandervest@wi.rr.com

Faith Technologies
920-225-6500
www.faithtechnologies.com

About the Authors

Cornel Rosario, CFM, obtained his MBA at Marquette University in Milwaukee. Since 1977, he has managed facilities at medium-sized companies. He currently operates

Facilities Consulting Partners, assisting companies in the areas of: site selection, space planning and layout, construction management, facilities operation, purchasing and office administration.

In 1991, Mr. Rosario was elected President of the Southeastern Wisconsin Chapter of IFMA, and in 1992 helped create the IFMA-Wisconsin Tri-Chapter Symposium, an all-day FM Event that has been running annually ever since.

As a writer and photographer, Mr. Rosario has produced two books on The Basilica of Holy Hill, including *Inside Holy Hill*. He is Vice President of the Town of Erin, WI School Board and serves on the Town's Newsletter Editorial Committee.

Mark Sekula, CFM, LEED-AP, IFMA Fellow, is President of Facility Futures, Inc., a facility management consulting  firm that provides strategic facility planning, real estate planning, programming, workplace design, facility management organizational planning, owner's representation, occupancy management and sustainability consulting. With 34 years of facility management experience, he has served as a facilities management practitioner in the manufacturing, healthcare, and technology industries.

Mr. Sekula has served as President of the Southeastern Wisconsin Chapter of IFMA, and on the IFMA International Board of Directors. He was also Co-Chair of the IFMA Strategic Planning Task Group which in 2009 published the nationally recognized Strategic Facility Planning White Paper. He is certified by IFMA as an instructor of the facility management industry's nine competencies.

Among his accomplishments, Mr. Sekula has published more than 20 articles and speaks nationally on facilities management and business issues. He holds a Bachelor of Science degree in Architectural Studies from the University of Wisconsin-Milwaukee School of Architecture and Urban Planning and a certificate from the Kellogg Management Institute-Management Certificate Program at Northwestern University. FMFG